WHAT YOUR COLLEAGUES

"In *Text Structures From Nonfiction Picture Books*, Kayla Briseño and Gretchen Bernabei unlock one of the secrets to teaching students to write well: make text structures visible and invite students to try them. This practical book is jam-packed with lively, high-engagement lessons that use beautiful and powerful picture books as a launchpad for excellent, well-crafted writing."

—**Carl Anderson**, writing consultant K–12, and author of
Teaching Fantasy Writing: Lessons That Inspire Student Engagement and Creativity K–6 and
How to Become a Better Writing Teacher, Brooklyn, NY

"Finally!! Teachers finally have more tools at their fingertips to tackle nonfiction. *Text Structures From Nonfiction Picture Books* is a must-have resource for teachers. The book's approach seamlessly integrates reading and writing instruction into a cohesive framework and should be a staple in teachers' lessons."

—**Lesley Sallee**, 5th-grade ELA, San Antonio Academy

"My ninth-graders had so much fun working with these texts. Bringing picture books into my secondary classroom allows us to examine craft moves and the organization of less complex texts as a way to prepare students to do more complex tasks. Using these lessons allows me to see who gets it and who needs more support before we move on. The Craft Moves prompted them to write insightfully and the Kernel Essays guided them to write structured yet personal pieces. What a powerful tool for high schoolers!"

—**Amy Watkins**, English teacher, Novi, Michigan

"Briseño and Bernabei eschew the sage-on-the-page approach and invite educators of all grade levels to choose our own adventure in this compendium of non-fiction picture books and strategies. They provide structure and then encourage us to change their lessons to meet classroom needs. By empowering educators to take ownership of lessons, Briseño and Bernabei remind us to empower students to take ownership of their writing."

—**Kathrine Sullivan**, English teacher, Essex High School, Essex Jct., VT

"A good professional book should feel fresh and inspiring—this one is both! I learned about an array of nonfiction picture books, snappy approaches to jump starting essays, and clear, organized lessons to help students grow. Right from the first page the book gave me a good check-in with the principles of excellent literacy instruction at any level."

—**Brett Vogelsinger**, English teacher and author of *Poetry Pauses:
Teaching With Poems to Elevate Student Writing in All Genres*, Sellersville, PA

"Not only does this book introduce its readers to powerful nonfiction picture books, but it also offers practical and engaging strategies to help our students better understand the abundant craft opportunities available in the world of nonfiction. This book invites us all to engage more deeply and intentionally with nonfiction picture books so that we can better understand our world and add our own stories to the rich tapestry of experience that nonfiction helps us weave."

—**Erin Vogler**, English teacher and literacy coach, Keshequa Central School, NY

"Teach nonfiction like never before! Kayla Briseño and Gretchen Bernabei have packed *Text Structures From Nonfiction Picture Books* with innovative techniques that transform picture books into springboards for quick writes, kernel essays, and theme exploration—all while uncovering the craft and structure of informational texts. With this resource in hand, your students will be inspired to write alongside talented creators while deepening their understanding and sparking curiosity about the world around them."

—**Maria Walther**, traveling teacher, literacy consultant,
and author of More *Ramped-Up Read Alouds:
Building Knowledge and Boosting Comprehension*, Aurora IL

TEXT
STRUCTURES FROM
NONFICTION
PICTURE
BOOKS

Dedications

For the loves of my life, Stephen and Zinnia. You are my treasures, and I love you a bushel and a peck. And for Gran—ana behebik khollis, and I miss you terribly.

—Kayla

For the Pumphrey girls, especially Mary Lois.

—Gretchen

TEXT STRUCTURES FROM NONFICTION PICTURE BOOKS

Lessons to Ease Students Into Text Analysis, Reading Response, and Writing With Craft

KAYLA BRISEÑO = and = GRETCHEN BERNABEI

Foreword by Kate Messner

CORWIN Literacy

FOR INFORMATION:

Corwin

A SAGE Company

2455 Teller Road

Thousand Oaks, California 91320

(800) 233–9936

www.corwin.com

SAGE Publications Ltd.

1 Oliver's Yard

55 City Road

London EC1Y 1SP

United Kingdom

SAGE Publications India Pvt. Ltd.

Unit No 323–333, Third Floor, F-Block

International Trade Tower Nehru Place

New Delhi 110 019

India

SAGE Publications Asia-Pacific Pte. Ltd.

18 Cross Street #10–10/11/12

China Square Central

Singapore 048423

Vice President and
  Editorial Director: Monica Eckman

Senior Director and Publisher,
  Content and Product: Lisa Luedeke

Content Development Editor: Sarah Ross

Product Associate: Zachary Vann

Production Editor: Tori Mirsadjadi

Copy Editor: Melinda Masson

Typesetter: C&M Digitals (P) Ltd.

Proofreader: Barbara Coster

Indexer: Integra

Cover Designer: Gail Buschman

Marketing Manager: Megan Naidl

Printed in the United States of America

LCCN 2024057312

This book is printed on acid-free paper.

25 26 27 28 29 10 9 8 7 6 5 4 3 2 1

Contents

LESSONS

BOOKS ABOUT PEOPLE

BOOKS ABOUT PLACES

BOOKS ABOUT THINGS

BOOKS ABOUT ANIMALS

APPENDIX

Visit the companion website at
https://companion.corwin.com/courses/TS-nonfictionpicturebooks
for downloadable resources.

Note From the Publisher: The authors have provided video and web content throughout the book that is available to you through QR (quick response) codes. To read a QR code, you must have a smartphone or tablet with a camera. We recommend that you download a QR code reader app that is made specifically for your phone or tablet brand.
Videos may also be accessed at
https://companion.corwin.com/courses/TS-nonfictionpicturebooks.

Reference Chart

For a visual list of the books, visit https://bookshop.org/lists/coming-soon-text-structures-from-nonfiction-picture-books.

			BOOKS ABOUT PEOPLE			
	TITLE	**AUTHOR**	**TEXT STRUCTURE**	**TOPICS**	**BIG IDEAS**	**CRAFT CHALLENGE**
1	*Building an Orchestra of Hope*	Carmen Oliver, with illustrations by Luisa Uribe	**A Problem Solver's Journey**	trash, landfills, Paraguay, South America, the environment, recycling, music, orchestras, musical instruments, music programs, people working in landfills, village life, subsistence living	hope, determination, problem solving, dreaming for a better life, resourcefulness, caring for others, trash to treasure, teaching others, the power of music, lifting others, poverty, hope for the future, the power of performance	**Noun + Verb Pitchfork** **Catalog** **Anaphork (Anaphora + Pitchfork)**
2	*Emmanuel's Dream: The True Story of Emmanuel Ofosu Yeboah*	Laurie Ann Thompson, with illustrations by Sean Qualls	**Outpowering a Challenge**	Ghana, West Africa, cyclists, bicycles, bike riding, Challenged Athletes Foundation, people with health conditions or impairments	perseverance, resilience, tough love, supporting your family, working hard, overcoming obstacles, poverty, journey, raising awareness, breaking stereotypes, ability, strength, hope	**Anaphork (Anaphora + Pitchfork)** **Anaphork With an Antithetwist**

	TITLE	AUTHOR	TEXT STRUCTURE	TOPICS	BIG IDEAS	CRAFT CHALLENGE
BOOKS ABOUT PEOPLE						
3	*Finding My Dance*	Ria Thundercloud, with illustrations by Kalila J. Fuller	**Doing What You Love**	memoirs, Ria Thundercloud, Indigenous dancers, Indigenous women, jingle dance, jingle dress, Native Americans, "powwow trail," dance, powwow circle, travel, dance teams, professional dancers	finding your place, identity, language, culture, tribes, ceremony, cultural inheritance, using art for expression, overcoming difficulties, following your passion, passing down traditions, commitment to celebration of heritage, becoming who you were meant to be, freedom through the arts	**Isn't/Is Simile** **Ba-Da-Bing** **Antithesis** **Translanguaging**
4	*Fish for Jimmy*	Katie Yamasaki	**Coping With a Bad Time**	World War II, Japanese Americans, Japanese internment, bombing of Pearl Harbor, imprisonment, internment camps, family separation, war, fish, food, American citizenship	doing for others, survival, taking a risk, broken spirit, protecting your family	**Polysyndeton** **Ba-Da-Bing**
5	*Free as a Bird: The Story of Malala*	Lina Maslo	**A Hero's Journey**	Malala Yousafzai, Pakistan, girls' education, Middle East, heroes, role models, parent–child relationships, education, terrorism, authoritarianism, propaganda, human rights	courage, struggle, violence, persistence, oppression, suppression, human rights, gender inequality, equality, speaking up, standing for what is right	**Anaphork (Anaphora + Pitchfork)** **Personified Reasons**

(Continued)

(Continued)

			BOOKS ABOUT PEOPLE			
	TITLE	**AUTHOR**	**TEXT STRUCTURE**	**TOPICS**	**BIG IDEAS**	**CRAFT CHALLENGE**
6	*Hidden Hope: How a Toy and a Hero Saved Lives During the Holocaust*	Elisa Boxer, with illustrations by Amy June Bates	**Risky Solution**	World War II, the Holocaust, Nazis, German occupation of France, Jews, Jews in hiding, false papers, the French Resistance, anti-Semitism, young heroes	hidden identity, fear, resistance, bravery, risking one's life for others, saving lives, caring for others, taking risks, overthrowing evil, heroism, resilience, freedom	**Exclamations + Absolutes + Fragments** **Onomatopoeia + Simple Sentence + Participial Phrases**
7	*Joan Procter, Dragon Doctor*	Patricia Valdez, with illustrations by Felicita Sala	**A Curiosity That Changed the World**	reptiles, Komodo dragons, science, scientists, female scientists, zoos, national history museum, observation, animal study, lifelong passion, habitats, war, wartime conditions, how war changes the world	lifelong passion, following your interests/passions, being different, being yourself, pursuing your passion, sharing knowledge, world-changing	**Alliterative Pitchfork** **Antithesis** **Myth Explosion**
8	*José Feeds the World: How a Famous Chef Feeds Millions of People in Need Around the World*	David Unger, with illustrations by Marta Álvarez Miguéns	**A Hero's Journey**	food, chefs, cooking, food activists, humanitarianism, disaster relief, natural disasters, Haiti earthquake, Hurricane Maria (Puerto Rico), Hurricane Dorian (Bahamas), Fire Volcano (Guatemala), Navajo Nation, COVID-19 pandemic, war in Ukraine, World Central Kitchen	community, caring for others, volunteering, finding a need and meeting it, feeding people, acts of service, the power of food to nourish and heal, relief, humanitarian aid, persistence, problem solving, sharing your passion, people in crisis, not hesitating to help	**Anaphork (Anaphora + Pitchfork)** **Translanguaging** **Antithesis**

		BOOKS ABOUT PEOPLE				
	TITLE	**AUTHOR**	**TEXT STRUCTURE**	**TOPICS**	**BIG IDEAS**	**CRAFT CHALLENGE**
9	*Magic Ramen: The Story of Momofuku Ando*	Andrea Wang, with illustrations by Kana Urbanowicz	**Cooking Up a New Idea**	ramen, inventions, inventors, Japan, poverty, post–World War II, Japanese food, experiments, nutrition, cooking, processes	innovation, feeding the hungry, meeting the needs of others, observation, experimentation, trial and error, perseverance, serving others, helping, balance, food insecurity	**Translanguaging** **Anaphork (Anaphora + Pitchfork)** **When–What Pattern**
10	*Martin & Anne: The Kindred Spirits of Dr. Martin Luther King, Jr. and Anne Frank*	Nancy Churnin, with illustrations by Yevgenia Nayberg	**A Powerful Life**	Dr. Martin Luther King Jr., Anne Frank, World War II, Holocaust, Hitler, Jews, Jews in hiding, civil rights movement, racism, history, historical figures, segregation, Rosa Parks, the "I Have a Dream" speech, Gandhi, nonviolent protest, historically Black colleges and universities (HBCUs)	kindness, equality, the power of words, the power of writing, inequality, prejudice, anti-Semitism, mistreatment, hate (the effects of), human rights, inspiring others, speaking out against hate, racism, genocide, using one's voice in the face of injustice, character	**Different– Different–Alike Pattern**
11	*Mr. Crum's Potato Predicament*	Anne Renaud, with illustrations by Felicita Sala	**Cooking Up a New Idea**	food, potatoes, potato chips, cooking, restaurants, inventions, inventors, African American inventors, Native American inventors, George "Crum" Speck	trial and error, creating something new, persistence, creativity, unexpected discoveries, pushing through setbacks, failure leads to success	**Alliterative Pitchfork** **Polysyndeton** **Anaphork (Anaphora + Pitchfork)**

(Continued)

(Continued)

				BOOKS ABOUT PEOPLE		
	TITLE	**AUTHOR**	**TEXT STRUCTURE**	**TOPICS**	**BIG IDEAS**	**CRAFT CHALLENGE**
12	*One Plastic Bag: Isatou Ceesay and the Recycling Women of the Gambia*	Miranda Paul, with illustrations by Elizabeth Zunon	**A Growing Problem and a Solution**	Gambia, West Africa, women creators, women entrepreneurs, plastic, trash, recycling, reusing, plastic bags, litter, harm to animals, the dangers of litter	seeing a need and meeting it, caring for one's community, ingenuity, community, creativity, working together, resourcefulness, entrepreneurship, taking action as a group	**Personification** **Translanguaging** **Beg-to-Differ Sentence Pattern** **Personification** **Translanguaging** **Beg-to-Differ Sentence Pattern**
13	*Queen of Leaves: The Story of Botanist Ynes Mexia*	Stephen Briseño, with illustrations by Isabel Muñoz	**Discovering a Life Purpose**	women in STEM, female scientists, the environment, science, botany, plants, plant specimens, specimen collecting, wax palm, endangered plants, nature, Mexican Americans, travel, California, Texas, Mexico, Ecuador, Alaska, Brazil, Colombia	curiosity, exploration, nature's beauty, appreciating nature, adventure, blooming later in life, finding your passion, forging a new path, preservation, study, risk-taking	**Personification** **Extended Simile + a Pitchforked Description** **Metaphor** **Antithesis**
14	*Sweet Justice: Georgia Gilmore and the Montgomery Bus Boycott*	Mara Rockliff, with illustrations by R. Gregory Christie	**Making a Change**	Georgia Gilmore, Montgomery bus boycott, Rosa Parks, Dr. Martin Luther King Jr., incarceration, civil rights movement, segregation, protests, Montgomery, Alabama	racial inequality, justice, equality, racism, taking a stand, oppression, working together, change, persistence, teamwork, courage, nonviolent protest	**Pitchforked Metaphor**

	TITLE	AUTHOR	TEXT STRUCTURE	TOPICS	BIG IDEAS	CRAFT CHALLENGE
				BOOKS ABOUT PEOPLE		
15	*Swimming With Sharks: The Daring Discoveries of Eugenie Clark*	Heather Lang, with illustrations by Jordi Solano	**A Curiosity That Changed the World**	sharks, marine life, scientists, zoology, oceanography, ichthyology, ocean fish, women in science	passion, discovery, exploration, curiosity, study, misunderstood creatures, misconceptions, advocacy	**Antithesis** **Catalog** **Refrain** **Anaphork (anaphora + pitchfork)**
16	*Tamales for Christmas*	Stephen Briseño, with illustrations by Sonia Sánchez	**Accomplishing a Big Task**	tamales, Christmas, cooking, Mexican Americans, grandparents, homemade food	family/*familia*, Hispanic culture, serving others, helping others, making sacrifices, hard work, working together, generosity, resourcefulness, tenacity	**Metaphor With a Pitchforked Description** **Varied Refrain** **AAAWWUBBIS Opener**
17	*The Boo-Boos That Changed the World: A True Story About an Accidental Invention (Really!)*	Barry Wittenstein, with illustrations by Chris Hsu	**An Inventor and the Invention**	Band-Aids, inventions, inventors, accidents, problem and solution, first aid, Boy Scouts, injuries, World War II	trial and error, problem solving, ideas becoming popular, meeting a need	**Hyphenated Adjectives** **Geographic Pitchfork**
18	*The Boy Who Harnessed the Wind*	William Kamkwamba and Bryan Mealer, with illustrations by Elizabeth Zunon	**An Inventor and the Invention**	William Kamkwamba, wind power, electricity, Malawi, Africa, farming, drought, famine, village life, science, engineering, inventions, inventors, windmills, water, water scarcity, food scarcity	resourcefulness, seeing a need and meeting it, serving your community, poverty, helping others, creativity, determination, hard work, challenge, problem solving, wonder, hunger, perseverance, impact, self-teaching	**Ba-Da-Boom** **More-Than Metaphor** **Beg-to-Differ Sentence Pattern**

(Continued)

BOOKS ABOUT PEOPLE					
	TITLE	**AUTHOR**	**TEXT STRUCTURE**	**TOPICS**	**BIG IDEAS**	**CRAFT CHALLENGE**

	TITLE	**AUTHOR**	**TEXT STRUCTURE**	**TOPICS**	**BIG IDEAS**	**CRAFT CHALLENGE**
19	*The Crayon Man: The True Story of the Invention of Crayola Crayons*	Natascha Biebow, with illustrations by Steven Salerno	**An Inventor and the Invention**	crayons, Crayola, color, inventors, inventions, experiments	history, discovery, invention, ingenuity, curiosity, creativity, seeing a need and meeting it, listening to others, problem solving, seeing beyond	**Microscope Sentence** **Hypophora** **Hyphenated Adjectives**
20	*Whoosh!: Lonnie Johnson's Super-Soaking Stream of Inventions*	Chris Barton, with illustrations by Don Tate	**Doing What You Love**	inventions, inventors, African American inventors, failed inventions, accidental inventions, scientists, science fairs, engineers, NASA, Super Soaker, toy companies, building things, STEM, technology	failure, success, grit, ingenuity, tenacity, curiosity, trial and error, problem solving, facing challenges, setbacks, creating, perseverance, overcoming obstacles, pursuing passion	**Shaka-Laka-Boom** **Pitchforked Verbs** **Wasn't–Wasn't–Was Pattern**

BOOKS ABOUT PLACES					
	TITLE	**AUTHOR**	**TEXT STRUCTURE**	**TOPICS**	**BIG IDEAS**	**CRAFT LESSON**

	TITLE	**AUTHOR**	**TEXT STRUCTURE**	**TOPICS**	**BIG IDEAS**	**CRAFT LESSON**
21	*Caves*	Nell Cross Beckerman, with illustrations by Kalen Chock	**All About a Place**	caves, ecosystems, speleology, spelunkers, limestone, rock formations, stalactites, stalagmites, crystals, fossils, underwater cave systems, bats, cave paintings, bioluminescence, lava, volcanic rock	exploration, curiosity, wonders of the earth, discovery	**Noun + Verb Pitchfork**
22	*I Am Made of Mountains: An Ode to National Parks—the Landscapes of Us*	Alexandra S. D. Hinrichs, with illustrations by Vivian Mineker	**A Place Personified**	national parks, geography, the United States, nature, landforms, landscapes, weather, wildlife, plants, animals, forests, oceans	exploration, nature's beauty, appreciating nature, travel	**Personification Rhyming Couplets**

		BOOKS ABOUT PLACES				
	TITLE	**AUTHOR**	**TEXT STRUCTURE**	**TOPICS**	**BIG IDEAS**	**CRAFT LESSON**
23	*Over and Under the Rainforest*	Kate Messner, with illustrations by Christopher Silas Neal	**Birdwalk**	rainforests, rainforest canopy, hiking, trees, rivers, flora and fauna, ecosystem, wildlife, Costa Rica	exploration, exploring nature, discovery, the wonder of nature, being in the wild, appreciating nature, outdoor adventure, the natural world	**Alliteration** **Strong Verbs** **Hyphenated Adjectives Directional Echoes**
24	*The Brilliant Deep: Rebuilding the World's Coral Reefs*	Kate Messner, with illustrations by Matthew Forsythe	**Saving Something You Love**	coral reefs, conservation, environmental science, scientists, coral reef restoration, Ken Nedimyer, Coral Restoration Foundation, pioneers, oceans, sea life, Florida Keys, scuba, diving, rock farms, coral colonies, experiments, climate change	wonder of nature, human ingenuity, caring for the earth, problem solving, observation, regrowth, hope, volunteering, making a difference, reversing climate change	**Anaphork (Anaphora + Pitchfork)** **Metaphor** **Echo Ending**
25	*The Floating Field: How a Group of Thai Boys Built Their Own Soccer Field*	Scott Riley, with illustrations by Nguyen Quang and Kim Lien	**An Inventor and the Invention**	Thailand, Koh Panyee, village life, island life, high tide, low tide, full moon, sandbar, buildings on stilts, soccer, sports, 1986 World Cup, soccer teams, engineering, STEM, history	overcoming obstacles, overcoming the odds, working together, resourcefulness, ingenuity, solving a problem, creative solutions, determination, grit, passion, teamwork, community, going after your dreams, forging new ground, blazing a new path	**Two-Word Sentences** **Pitchforked Participial Phrases Directional Echoes**

(Continued)

(Continued)

BOOKS ABOUT PLACES					
TITLE	**AUTHOR**	**TEXT STRUCTURE**	**TOPICS**	**BIG IDEAS**	**CRAFT LESSON**
26 *The Secret Kingdom: Nek Chand, a Changing India, and a Hidden World of Art*	Barb Rosenstock, with illustrations by Claire A. Nivola	**A Problem Solver's Journey**	Nek Chand, India, the partition of India and Pakistan, art, folk art, recycling, nature, secret gardens, art gardens, sculptures, mosaics, the Rock Garden of Chandigarh, reusing trash, governments, gardens, village life, city life, reconstruction, building	creativity, imagination, ingenuity, beautifying your environment, trash to treasure, perseverance, working hard, grit, overcoming obstacles, change, progress, going against the grain, breaking the rules, activism, speaking up for others, sharing your gift with others	**Microscope Sentence** **Anaphora + Participles**

BOOKS ABOUT THINGS					
TITLE	**AUTHOR**	**TEXT STRUCTURE**	**TOPICS**	**BIG IDEAS**	**CRAFT LESSON**
27 *A Garden in Your Belly: Meet the Microbes in Your Gut*	Masha D'yans	**Zooming In on a System**	gut health, human body, stomach, intestines, microbiome, microorganisms, microbes, taking care of one's body, healthy food, junk food, digestion, mood	health, your incredible body, taking care of yourself, going outside, nourishment, cause and effect	**Prepositional Phrase Catalog** **Metaphor**
28 *Blue: A History of the Color as Deep as the Sea and as Wide as the Sky*	Nana Ekua Brew-Hammond, with illustrations by Daniel Minter	**Origin Story**	colors, blue, the history of color, slavery, myths, farming, textiles, royalty, idioms	history, deception, difficult past, journey, suffering, discovery, invention	**Parallel Paradox**

			BOOKS ABOUT THINGS			
	TITLE	**AUTHOR**	**TEXT STRUCTURE**	**TOPICS**	**BIG IDEAS**	**CRAFT LESSON**
29	*Branches of Hope: The 9/11 Survivor Tree*	Ann Magee, with illustrations by Nicole Wong	**A Memory**	9/11, trees, 9/11 Survivor Tree, 9/11 memorial, New York, terrorist attacks, Ground Zero, Twin Towers, first responders, seasons	survival, memorials, hope, life after destruction, resilience, the healing power of nature, devastation, rebuilding, hope amidst hardship, recovery, how nature depends on people, community, coming together through tragedy, working together	**Personification** **Sensory Details**
30	*Fire Shapes the World*	Joanna Cooke, with illustrations by Cornelia Li and Diāna Renžina	**The Whole Story of Something**	fire, wildfires, adaptation, plants, animals, campfires, earth's history, the environment	destruction, creation, change, effects on our planet, survival, power, rebirth	**Participles and Participial Phrases** **Fragmented Metaphor**
31	*Fry Bread: A Native American Family Story*	Kevin Noble Maillard, with illustrations by Juana Martinez-Neal	**Extended Metaphors**	fry bread, Native American culture, Native American history, food, cooking, North American tribes, Indigenous peoples	culture, community, family, friends, heritage, bringing people together, tradition, legacy, Native identity, passing down traditions, the cultural importance of food	**Similes** **Metaphors**
32	*Fungi Grow*	Maria Gianferrari, with illustrations by Diana Sudyka	**How Something Grows**	plants, mushrooms, fungi, spores, the growing process, mycelium, roots, trees, forests, life cycles, mycology, nature, ecosystems	growth, new life, appreciating nature, symbiosis in nature	**Two-Word Sentences** **Onomatopoeia** **Pitchforked Verbs**

(Continued)

(Continued)

	TITLE	AUTHOR	TEXT STRUCTURE	TOPICS	BIG IDEAS	CRAFT LESSON
	BOOKS ABOUT THINGS					
33	*The Only Way to Make Bread*	Cristina Quintero, with illustrations by Sarah Gonzales	**Steps for Doing Something: A How-To Structure (Plus a Truism)**	bread, making bread, how-tos (procedures), baking, ingredients, baking tools, food preparation, food literacy, recipes	making things your way, making things together, diversity, culture building, traditions, different ways to do things, community, togetherness, spending time together	**Anaphork (Anaphora + Pitchfork)** **Similes** **Pitchforked Contrasts**
34	*The Secret Code Inside You: All About Your DNA*	Rajani LaRocca, MD, with illustrations by Steven Salerno	**All About Something (With Infoshots)**	DNA, genetics, genes, the human body, cells, family traits, proteins, chromosomes, biology, double helix, STEM	identity, uniqueness, personal choice, being one of a kind, parts of a whole, science	**Anaphork of Questions** **Rhyming Pattern** **Polysyndeton + Catalog**
35	*Your One and Only Heart*	Rajani LaRocca, MD, with illustrations by Lauren Paige Conrad	**Extended Adjectives**	the heart, the human body, the circulatory system, vital organs, anatomy, physiology, blood, the body's functions, muscles, arteries, STEM	our wonderful bodies, uniqueness, contrasts, resilience, strength, parts of a whole, science	**Parallel Paradox** **Personification** **Catalog of Gerunds**
36	*Zap! Clap! Boom! The Story of a Thunderstorm*	Laura Purdie Salas, with illustrations by Elly MacKay	**A Weather Event**	weather, thunderstorms, clouds, rain, lighting, thunder, forces of nature, atmospheric elements, atmospheric change	change, universal experiences, cycles	**Rhyming Pattern** **Onomatopoeia** **Refrain** **Personification**

	TITLE	AUTHOR	TEXT STRUCTURE	TOPICS	BIG IDEAS	CRAFT LESSON
				BOOKS ABOUT ANIMALS		
37	*Bee Dance*	Rick Chrustowski	**Steps for Doing Something: A How-To Structure**	bees, honeybees, forager bees, honeybee behavior, beehives, hive behavior, pollination, honey, nature, insects	communication, working together, teamwork, listening to others, following directions	**AAAWWUBBIS Opener** **Imperative Pitchfork**
38	*Ivan: The Remarkable True Story of the Shopping Mall Gorilla*	Katherine Applegate, with illustrations by Brian Karas	**A Memory Reflection**	gorillas, *The One and Only Ivan*, animal trapping, poaching, zoos, animal care, wild animals, Africa, nature, the mistreatment of animals, animal advocacy, habitats, treatment of animals in the wild	loneliness, animal cruelty, caring for nature, activism, fighting for others, speaking up, taking action, respect for life	**Anadiplosis** **Simile Pair**
39	*Sergeant Reckless: The True Story of the Little Horse Who Became a Hero*	Patricia McCormick, with illustrations by Iacopo Bruno	**A Memory (Plus a Truism)**	horses, racehorses, pack horses, warhorses, military, military ranks, Marine Corps, soldiers, training animals, Korean War, history, combat, war, ammunition, Purple Heart	serving your country, unlikely hero, underdog, taking a chance, bravery, wartime camaraderie, heroism, earning respect	**Renaming** **Catalog of Fragments** **AAAWWUBBIS Sandwich**
40	*Whale Fall: Exploring an Ocean-Floor Ecosystem*	Melissa Stewart, with illustrations by Rob Dunlavey	**An Ending That Causes a Cycle**	whales, ocean life, life cycles, variety of species, symbiotic relationships, food chain	new beginnings, end of life, community, interconnectedness, interdependence, hidden worlds	**Antithesis**

(Continued)

(Continued)

			BOOKS ABOUT ANIMALS			
	TITLE	**AUTHOR**	**TEXT STRUCTURE**	**TOPICS**	**BIG IDEAS**	**CRAFT LESSON**
41	*Winged Wonders: Solving the Monarch Migration Mystery*	Meeg Pincus, with illustrations by Yas Imamura	**Solving a Mystery**	monarch butterflies, migration, North America, Mexico, Canada, scientists, research, endangered animals	curiosity, exploration, discovery, nature's beauty, appreciating nature, working together, teamwork, long-term study, finding answers, scientific discovery, helping nature, experimenting in the field	**Anaphork of Questions** **Character Anaphork**

Foreword

Beverly Cleary taught me how to write.

She wasn't a mentor in the formal sense of the word—we never met for lunch or talked over tea—but growing up, I borrowed her books from my hometown library almost every week. Embedded in the pages were master classes in everything from character development to pacing to dialogue, and I soaked up every word.

But I never left the library with just one book. I had two great loves—Ramona and nonfiction, especially if the cover featured natural disasters or dangerous animals. Bring on the tornadoes! The earthquakes, sharks, and venomous snakes! These titles were my teachers, too, offering lessons in research, organization, and text structure.

I still love Ramona and rattlesnakes, and now, as an author who visits schools and libraries all over the world, I'm often asked what advice I have for young writers. My answer to that question is always the same.

Read.

Read everything you can get your hands on. And especially, read in the genres in which you'd like to write. A teetering pile of books from the library or bookstore offers a treasure trove of mini lessons.

In this user-friendly volume, Kayla Briseño and Gretchen Bernabei have taken the guesswork out of choosing mentor texts and shining a light on the diverse strategies authors use in crafting nonfiction. When students read widely—and read like writers, analyzing the choices authors make and the tools they use in their work—they're empowered to take risks with their own writing as well, experimenting with out-of-the-box text structures and storytelling techniques that make their informational writing shine.

One of our most important jobs as teachers of young writers is to help them realize they can always find resources to learn more, and that mentors abound. They're always waiting on the library shelves.

Yours in curiosity,
Kate Messner
Author of the *Over and Under* nature books, *The Next Scientist*, and *The Brilliant Deep*

Acknowledgments

Thank you to the *many* people who have supported us along the way:

Everyone who used, passed along, promoted, shared, and loved our first book, *Text Structures From Picture Books*. Your heart and enthusiasm touched us so deeply, and we are honored to be a part of your classrooms!

Our Trail of Breadcrumbs team: Judi Reimer, Stacy Lewis, Dottie Hall, Heather Fletes, Maureen Ucles, Shona Rose, Jenny Martin, Alana Morris, Marie Cleary, Selina Jimenez, P. Tim Martindell, and Stephen Briseño.

Lisa Luedeke and all of our Corwin team: Monica Eckman, Sarah Ross, Zachary Vann, Tori Mirsadjadi, Melinda Masson, Barbara Coster, Gail Buschman, Megan Naidl, Tori Bachman, and Sharon Wu.

Elizabeth Snow: Thank you for always being ready to talk about picture books and for providing me with stacks of good titles, many of which ended up in this book! —Kayla

The fabulous faculty, staff, and families at San Antonio Academy: Your support is priceless, and I am honored. —Kayla

Holden Dewar: Thank you for thinking of a name for the "Beg-to-Differ" sentence pattern we first discovered in the *One Plastic Bag* lesson!

The Notebook Nerds (Erin Vogler, Kathrine Sullivan, Amy Watkins, and Sarah Krajewski): It's such an honor to be a part of this group. I have grown tremendously from our meetings and NCTE presentations. Thank you for your support and encouragement! —Kayla

Kate Messner: Thank you for writing a beautiful foreword for this book! We greatly appreciate your support!

Rene Tutt Jackson: Thank you for sharing your diligent list of prompts.

We're indebted to the following people who helped us pilot the lessons and gather student examples:

Lesley Sallee: for being such a great cheerleader and teammate, and always being ready to try out things I throw at you! —Kayla

Troy Wilson: for being such a fantastic teammate over many years. I've learned so much from you! —Kayla

Siomha Garcia: for being my go-to book-checker and letting me bounce ideas off of you constantly. —Kayla

Terry Collier: for letting me bring my students to work with your students and for always supporting the writing of my books! —Kayla

Amy Mulvihill: for always being willing to get samples from your students all the way across the world!

Amy Watkins: for all the extra work and enthusiasm you put into using these lessons with your high schoolers!

Cori Spellane: We appreciate your continued support over the years!

P. Tim Martindell (and his students at the Village Middle School!): Thank you for the popping kernels lesson!

Tara Temprano: for pulling family and friends in to gather samples (Nicolas Ricart, Samantha Ricart, RJ Drexler, Sara Drexler, Maggie Zagatta, and Abigail Alberta).

Tina Stimpson: Cheers to our connection over X! Thanks for reaching out! —Kayla

Allison Dunsmore: I'm so glad we met at Nowhere Books and grateful for all that came from that quick meet! —Kayla

Melissa Kleschult: Thank you for spreading the love throughout Minnesota and getting your teammates on board! —Kayla

Cathy Flaig and Jordan Sandoval: Thank you for letting me come to your classrooms again this year and for being such great educators to Zinnia! —Kayla

Melissa Dean (and her fellow teachers)

Mary McCatherine

Jennifer Stevens

Denise Besch

Tami Blythe

Vanessa Sanchez

Sarah Ledwig

Shannon Miller

Mo Shipp and family

Caitlyn Kirkpatrick and family

Debbie Oblitas and family

Samantha Foster and family

About the Authors

Kayla Briseño has taught English all over the world and to nearly every age, from elementary through adults. She has conducted professional development workshops with Gretchen Bernabei for over a decade, sharing and generating impactful writing instruction while being a longtime contributor to Trail of Breadcrumbs publications. *Text Structures From Picture Books* was her debut book. She and her husband, Stephen, are both self-declared book nerds, coffee aficionados, and national park fanatics. When she's not teaching or helping teachers, you can find her creating art with her daughter, Zinnia, reading a good book, or enjoying a stroll along the San Antonio River Walk, where she lives with her family. Follow her on Instagram @brisenos_teach.

Gretchen Bernabei was a teacher for over thirty years and a workshop presenter for over twenty-five years. She has written many books and articles with innovative instructional strategies for teaching reading and writing.

Introduction

According to *The New York Times*,[1] James Holzhauer "dominated 'Jeopardy!' like no one else." In 2019, he played a perfect game and had $2.4 million sitting coolly in his bank account. Surely someone of this caliber must have multiple degrees, speak several languages, or spend his free time reading college textbooks for fun. But to what does he accredit his immense knowledge? Children's books. He calls them his "secret weapon" and spent many hours in his local public library where he could "get books tailored to make things interesting for uninterested readers."

We have a confession to make. We have been unfair to nonfiction. Nonfiction, like poetry, has a bad reputation among many teachers. It seems boring. It seems like the dark corner of the library with dusty shelves where nobody browses for fun. It's a part of the library with the reputation that you only go there when you need to research something. Otherwise, why bother? After all, who makes movies about potatoes, a quick way to make soup, or the water cycle?

But we've discovered, like James Holzhauer (and many reluctant readers), how lively, animated, and compelling nonfiction has become in the hands of picture book authors and illustrators, completely reshaping our view. And even more wonderful is that these compelling stories about people, places, and things are actually true, so they fill us with even more wonder and hope about our own world.

The calling card of good nonfiction is how it awakens our wonder, driving us to know more about something. And there is something magical and deep and real and true about thumbing through a picture book to learn something that starts that itch of curiosity.

Our world has evolved since the days of dry and boring film strips or public television delivered in monotones. Nonfiction has become a spectator sport with people inspiring new inventors, innovators, and problem solvers from among our own very young people.

We hope the pages of these picture books inspire you and your students as they have us, moving us all to know that we can overcome hardships. Problems can be solved. People are basically good.

And by the way, Ron Howard *has* made a movie about one of the nonfiction stories in this book.

---

[1]Mather, V. (2019, April 24). How did James Holzhauer turn "Jeopardy!" into his own A.T.M.? We asked him. *The New York Times*. https://www.nytimes.com/2019/04/24/arts/jeopardy-james-holzhauer-interview.html

HOW TO USE THIS BOOK

For any grade level, you can start with reading a story or with writing. Either way is fine, as one leads to the other.

Let's say you want to begin with writing:

Begin with a quick write. Show students the quick write prompt and let them write for about 3 minutes. Or use it as a discussion starter or a topic for your morning meeting. Put aside the quick writes and launch into reading and discussing the story.

OR

Begin with a kernel essay. Show students the quick write prompt and the text structure and have them write a kernel essay (demonstrated on the next pages). Put aside the kernel essay and launch into reading and discussing the story. Bonus—they can even look for the parts of the structure as you read.

OR

Begin with the big idea. Show the students a few of the big ideas listed in the lesson and ask them to write what they know about each big idea or a memory that they associate with it. Put aside the writing and launch into reading and discussing the story.

Let's say you want to begin with reading:

Read the story aloud as a whole group, stopping to discuss noticings, make predictions and inferences, and highlight skills or a craft you've taught in class.

To move to writing, read the quick write prompt on the lesson page. Invite students to use the text structure to write kernel essays (either to retell the story or to craft their own stories). Move on to some of the lessons for going deeper in order to highlight the author's craft, analysis (using big ideas and truisms), and even reading response (using the reading response question stems and text structures in the appendix).

Rules you are invited to break:

1. Use every aspect of the lesson.
   No way! These lessons are full of great things for you to try, so pick and choose what works for you. Make it yours!

2. Stick to the quick writes and text structure offered on the page.
   You don't have to. Choice is essential for good writing. Some situations require freewriting, without a structure at all.

3. Use all the picture books or read them all in order.
   Who cares? Use the ones you want, when you want!

4. Don't change the words in the text structure boxes.
   Keep it real. Change anything about them you need to (verb tense, point of view, their order, anything).

Ideas to embrace (our soap box moments):

1. Writing should be social, and sharing is the main course, not the dessert, in the process.
   Don't skip the sharing.

2. Good teachers write with their students. It is incredibly powerful, as it acts as a model, a community builder, a heart-stitcher. It builds empathy. As teacher and author Rebekah O'Dell tweeted, "Modeling and writing alongside our kids keeps us engaged and curious."
   Write with your students.

3. Students want to learn and improve, not just repeat exercises. Give them the gift of great stories and wonderful craft. The lessons for going deeper ("Want to Go Deeper?") and the appendix are full of tools to help with this.
   Variety is both refreshing and necessary.

4. Writers should have as much choice as we can figure out how to give them: to choose their topics, their beliefs, their structures, their craft. If all of the essays seem alike, we need to reexamine what we're asking.
   Let writers make choices.

5. Picture books can be paired with any other genre. Feel free to pair any of these books with nonfiction texts, class novels, articles, poems, student writing, or even other picture books.
   Don't put yourself in a box.

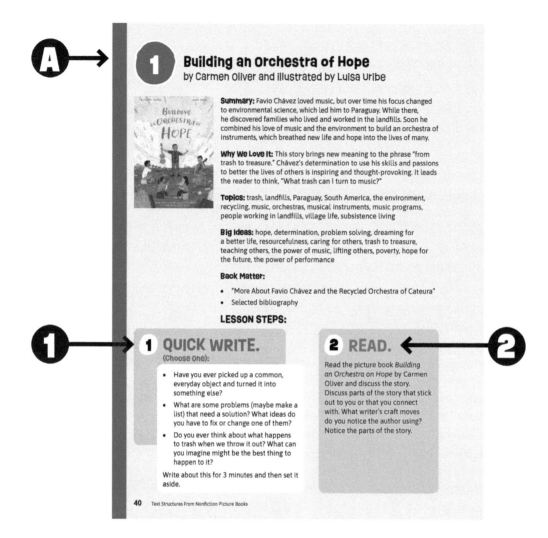

A

1 **Building an Orchestra of Hope**
by Carmen Oliver and illustrated by Luisa Uribe

Summary: Favio Chávez loved music, but over time his focus changed to environmental science, which led him to Paraguay. While there, he discovered families who lived and worked in the landfills. Soon he combined his love of music and the environment to build an orchestra of instruments, which breathed new life and hope into the lives of many.

Why We Love It: This story brings new meaning to the phrase "from trash to treasure." Chávez's determination to use his skills and passions to better the lives of others is inspiring and thought-provoking. It leads the reader to think, "What trash can I turn to music?"

Topics: trash, landfills, Paraguay, South America, the environment, recycling, music, orchestras, musical instruments, music programs, people working in landfills, village life, subsistence living

Big Ideas: hope, determination, problem solving, dreaming for a better life, resourcefulness, caring for others, trash to treasure, teaching others, the power of music, lifting others, poverty, hope for the future, the power of performance

Back Matter:

- "More About Favio Chávez and the Recycled Orchestra of Cateura"
- Selected bibliography

LESSON STEPS:

1 **QUICK WRITE.**
(Choose one):

- Have you ever picked up a common, everyday object and turned it into something else?
- What are some problems (maybe make a list) that need a solution? What ideas do you have to fix or change one of them?
- Do you ever think about what happens to trash when we throw it out? What can you imagine might be the best thing to happen to it?

Write about this for 3 minutes and then set it aside.

2 **READ.** **2**

Read the picture book *Building an Orchestra on Hope* by Carmen Oliver and discuss the story. Discuss parts of the story that stick out to you or that you connect with. What writer's craft moves do you notice the author using? Notice the parts of the story.

40   Text Structures From Nonfiction Picture Books

AN OVERVIEW OF THE LESSONS

What follows is a snapshot of a lesson—at least one way to do it. Keep in mind all the options detailed previously.

A **Choose your book.** Browse the reference chart in the front of this book for a text structure you'd like to use, a big idea, a craft move, or even a title or author you love. (See page x.)

1 **Do a quick write.** Use the quick write prompt to get students writing or talking about a topic and/or big idea found in the book. Write for 3 minutes. If the prompt we have provided doesn't quite work for your students, feel free to change it to suit your needs.

2 **Read** and discuss the story using the questions provided. After you read, point out the craft moves the author used. These can be explored and utilized in students' writing later in the "Want to Go Deeper?" section.

3 **Share with students the text structure (harvested from the nonfiction book).** Use the text structure to have students retell the story (orally or in writing), or have them use it to create their own written pieces. They can use it to write a kernel essay or to guide their longer writing.

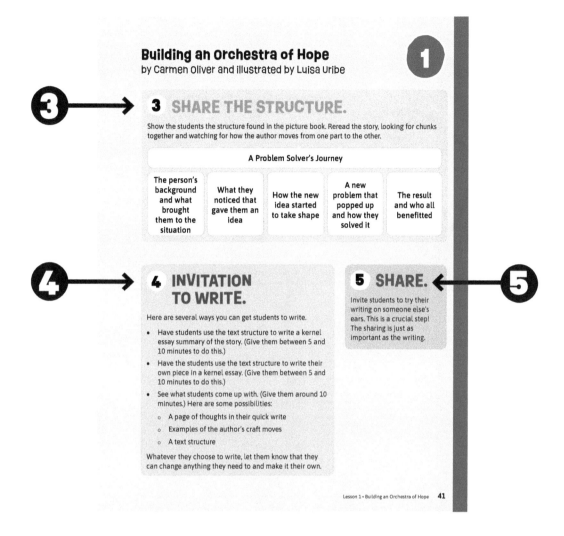

Building an Orchestra of Hope
by Carmen Oliver and illustrated by Luisa Uribe

3 SHARE THE STRUCTURE.

Show the students the structure found in the picture book. Reread the story, looking for chunks together and watching for how the author moves from one part to the other.

A Problem Solver's Journey				
The person's background and what brought them to the situation	What they noticed that gave them an idea	How the new idea started to take shape	A new problem that popped up and how they solved it	The result and who all benefitted

4 INVITATION TO WRITE.

Here are several ways you can get students to write.

- Have students use the text structure to write a kernel essay summary of the story. (Give them between 5 and 10 minutes to do this.)
- Have the students use the text structure to write their own piece in a kernel essay. (Give them between 5 and 10 minutes to do this.)
- See what students come up with. (Give them around 10 minutes.) Here are some possibilities:
  - A page of thoughts in their quick write
  - Examples of the author's craft moves
  - A text structure

Whatever they choose to write, let them know that they can change anything they need to and make it their own.

5 SHARE.

Invite students to try their writing on someone else's ears. This is a crucial step! The sharing is just as important as the writing.

Lesson 1 • Building an Orchestra of Hope   **41**

 Give students time to write. There are several ways you can get students to write. Let students choose one of these:

Summary: Have your students use the text structure to write a kernel essay summarizing the story. (Give them between 5 and 10 minutes to do this.)

OR

Kernel essay: Have your students use the text structure to write their own piece in a kernel essay. (Give them between 5 and 10 minutes to do this.)

OR

Free choice: See what students come up with. (Give them around 10 minutes.) Here are some possibilities:

- A page of thoughts in their quick write
- Examples of the author's craft moves
- A text structure

Whatever they choose to write, let students know that they can change anything they need to and make it their own.

 Let students share what they wrote. *Remember, don't skip this step!*

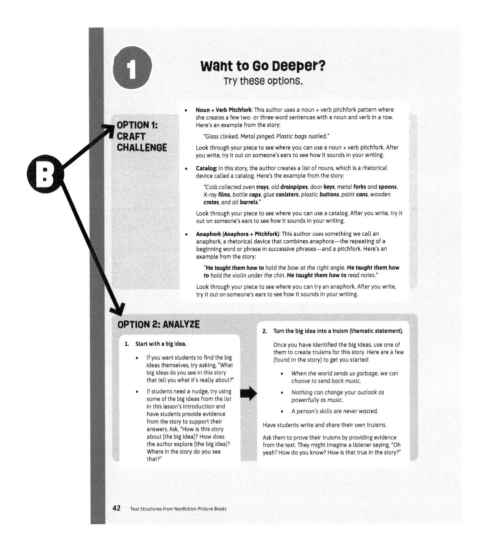

1

Want to Go Deeper?
Try these options.

OPTION 1: CRAFT CHALLENGE

B

- **Noun + Verb Pitchfork:** This author uses a noun + verb pitchfork pattern where she creates a few two- or three-word sentences with a noun and verb in a row. Here's an example from the story:

  "Glass clinked. Metal pinged. Plastic bags rustled."

  Look through your piece to see where you can use a noun + verb pitchfork. After you write, try it out on someone's ears to see how it sounds in your writing.

- **Catalog:** In this story, the author creates a list of nouns, which is a rhetorical device called a catalog. Here's the example from the story:

  *"Cold collected oven **trays**, old **drainpipes**, door **keys**, metal **forks** and **spoons**, X-ray **films**, bottle **caps**, glue **canisters**, plastic **buttons**, paint **cans**, wooden **crates**, and oil **barrels**."*

  Look through your piece to see where you can use a catalog. After you write, try it out on someone's ears to see how it sounds in your writing.

- **Anaphork (Anaphora + Pitchfork):** This author uses something we call an anaphork, a rhetorical device that combines anaphora—the repeating of a beginning word or phrase in successive phrases—and a pitchfork. Here's an example from the story:

  *"**He taught them how to** hold the bow at the right angle. **He taught them how to** hold the violin under the chin. **He taught them how to** read notes."*

  Look through your piece to see where you can try an anaphork. After you write, try it out on someone's ears to see how it sounds in your writing.

OPTION 2: ANALYZE

1. **Start with a big idea.**

   - If you want students to find the big ideas themselves, try asking, "What big ideas do you see in this story that tell you what it's really about?"

   - If students need a nudge, try using some of the big ideas from the list in this lesson's introduction and have students provide evidence from the story to support their answers. Ask, "How is this story about [the big idea]? How does the author explore [the big idea]? Where in the story do you see that?"

2. **Turn the big idea into a truism (thematic statement).**

   Once you have identified the big ideas, use one of them to create truisms for this story. Here are a few (found in the story) to get you started:

   - *When the world sends us garbage, we can choose to send back music.*

   - *Nothing can change your outlook as powerfully as music.*

   - *A person's skills are never wasted.*

   Have students write and share their own truisms.

   Ask them to prove their truisms by providing evidence from the text. They might imagine a listener saying, "Oh yeah? How do you know? How is that true in the story?"

BUT WAIT! THERE'S MORE!

 Try one or all of the options labeled "Want to Go Deeper?"

These lessons will help students to take the writing further. Choose from a writer's craft lesson or an analysis lesson, using big ideas and truisms.

Check out the online companion for even *more* ideas about analyzing using truisms.

Students can also choose to compose short or extended responses to demonstrate understanding by answering any of the questions for reading response. Other options are included in the extension ideas to take the subject further.

WHAT IF YOU WANT TO SHAKE UP THE LESSON ORDER?

While this sequence provides a solid experience weaving writing and reading together, there are plenty of variations that could also prove useful. Here are some things you might try:

1. Do a quick write.

2. Look at the text structure.

3. Create an original piece of writing using the text structure.

4. Share the picture book.

5. Identify some writer's craft (using one of the options for going deeper) and try that same craft in writing.

OR

Use the text structure to write a poem, a letter, a skit, an essay, or a speech.

OR

Use the text structure to write a response to the book.

OR

Read the picture book and write a one-sentence summary of each box in the text structure, as a way to summarize or kernelize the story.

OR

Use the question stems and text structures in the appendix to do some reading responses, writing, discussing, and even preparing for a standardized test.

Questions and Text Structures for Constructed Reading Responses

Questions and Answers About Understanding the Reading

GENERIC QUESTION STEMS	TEXT STRUCTURES TO ANSWER THE QUESTIONS
1. What happens in the story? (Retell the story.)	**QA12345**
2. What is the story mostly about right now?	
3. How do you think ____ feels at the beginning and/or end of the story?	
4. What is the conflict or problem of the story so far?	
5. Who is more ____ (helpful, nicer), ____ (a character) or ____ (another character)?	
6. How does ____ change during the story?	
7. Why does ____ do/think/say/believe/ want?	
8. What's one word you would use to describe ____ (character)?	
9. What lesson does ____ learn in the story?	
10. What is the moral of the story?	
11. In sentence ____, what does the word or phrase ____ suggest?	
12. How are ____ and ____ alike/different?	
13. Why does ____ become ____ (upset, happy) when ____?	
14. What does ____ (character) mean when he/she says ____?	
15. What can the reader tell (conclude) from the action in sentence(s) ____?	
16. What is ____'s reaction when she/he learns ____ show about her/his character?	
17. How do the actions of ____ and/or ____ support the theme or moral?	
18. What causes ____ to realize ____?	
19. Why does ____ agree to ____?	
20. What is ____'s attitude about ____?	
21. What argument does ____ (a character) make to support ____'s (that character's) behavior/opinion?	
22. What challenge(s) does ____ face?	
23. What does ____ represent in the story?	

QA12345

Question	Answer	How do you know?	What does that mean?	How else do you know?	So . . . your answer is . . . what?

RACE

Restate the question	Answer	Cite evidence from the text	Explain what the evidence means

BA-DA-BINGING THE EVIDENCE

Answer to the question	What the character does, says, and/or thinks that proves my answer	What that shows

FIGURING OUT THE READING

I read the words "____."	Which told me	Then I read	Which told me	And then I knew

EXPLAINING A CHANGE

How ____ changes in the story	At the beginning, . . . (with evidence)	At the end, . . . (with evidence)	Another way to describe the change

Source: Briseño, S., Briseño, K. & Bernabei, G. (2023).

See p. 322 for the full-sized versions of these templates.

Questions About Author's Choices

GENERIC QUESTION STEMS	TEXT STRUCTURES TO ANSWER THE QUESTIONS
1. Why is ____ (an event or character) important?	**RACE**
2. Why does the author ____?	
3. How does the author show that ____ (character) is ____ (characteristic)?	
4. Why did the author write this story?	
5. What does the author show us by including a description of ____?	
6. How did the author help visualize ____?	
7. What is the main reason the author included the sentence(s) ____?	
8. Why does the author choose this setting for the story?	
9. In sentence ____, the author uses the word(s)/phrase(s) ____ to suggest what?	
10. What does the sensory language in the sentence ____ illustrate?	
11. How does the description in the sentence(s) ____ affect the reader's understanding of the setting/character?	
12. The author includes the information in the sentence(s) ____ to help the reader do what?	
13. What is the author's purpose in writing this story?	
14. How does the author's description of ____ help the reader understand ____?	
15. What effect does the word/phrase ____ have in the sentence ____?	
16. How does ____ contribute to the development of the author's ideas?	
17. ____ is important in the story because it shows what?	
18. How does the setting influence the plot of the story?	
19. What is the effect of the author's use of ____?	

RACE

Restate the question	Answer	Cite evidence from the text	Explain what the evidence means

NOTICING THE AUTHOR'S MOVES

I read the words "____."	Which told me	Then I read "____."	Which told me	And then I knew the author did ____ to create ____

THE EFFECT ON A READER

When I read "____."	It made me feel/picture/think ____	Which created ____	If the author had used a different word/phrase, such as ____	It would have had this effect	So I think the author was trying to create ____.

THE EFFECT OF AN AUTHOR'S CHOICE

The author uses (pick one) ☐ Vocabulary ☐ Sensory images ☐ Figurative language ☐ Device: ____ ☐ Something else	An example	Another example	This creates (pick one) ☐ A mood of ____ ☐ A feeling of ____ ☐ A ____ tone ☐ A character who ____ ☐ Interest in ____ ☐ Understanding in ____ ☐ Something else

Source: Bernabei & Hover (2022).

Basic Reading Response Text Structures

STORY OF MY THINKING

I used to think . . .	But this happened	So now I know . . .

CHARACTER FEELINGS

____ felt ____	I know because they did ____	I also know because they said ____	What this shows

MAKING A CONNECTION

When I read ____	I made a connection to (self, text, world)	Because ____

SUMMARY

Somebody wanted ____	But ____	So ____	Then ____

THE EFFECT OF AN AUTHOR'S CHOICE

The author uses (pick one) ☐ Vocabulary ☐ Sensory images ☐ Figurative language ☐ Device: ____ ☐ Something else	An example	Another example	This creates (pick one) ☐ A mood of ____ ☐ A feeling of ____ ☐ A ____ tone ☐ A character who ____ ☐ Interest in ____ ☐ Understanding of ____ ☐ Something else

Source: Bernabei & Hover (2022).

Timing the Lesson

With students we've worked with, the whole lesson (steps 1–5) takes 40–55 minutes.*

- 3–5 minutes to introduce the prompt and allow students to quick write
- 5–10 minutes to read the story
- 5 minutes to talk about the story
- 5–10 minutes to model the writing
- 10–15 minutes to "go deeper" (truisms, writer's craft, reading response)
- 5–10 minutes to share (in partners and whole class) and wrap up

* The timing depends on the length of the nonfiction book, the age (and needs) of the students, and what activities you choose to do.

Revisions can take one or more sessions or can go on indefinitely.

The "Want to Go Deeper?" options can be done on a separate day or even as the main lesson. The craft lesson can take 15 to 20 minutes, and the analysis lesson can take 40 to 55 minutes, depending on how far you take it.

What Can You Do With All That Great Writing?

Have students share their work out loud! Cover your walls and bulletin boards with kernel essays, stories, poems, and truisms that students have written. Share them with the author of the picture book, and us, of course!

Every lesson includes

- A quick write topic
- Craft moves to notice
- A text structure to use for retelling a story and/or generating new writing
- A craft challenge to try
- Big ideas and truisms for analysis
- Questions for reading response

At a time when the strain and pressures of the world are as intense as ever, everyone needs moments to heal. We hope that you find that these lessons offer hope and spread joy—and inspire every writer in your classroom.

WHAT IS A KERNEL ESSAY?

A writer can write about a topic by using a text structure as a guide, creating one sentence per box. These sentences make a kernel essay. Here's an example using the text structure we call "The Story of My Thinking."

> **The Story of My Thinking**
>
> | **I used to think . . .** | **But this happened** | **So now I know . . .** * |
>
> ***This is a good place for a truism!**

QR Code 0.1
Stephen explains what kernel essays are and how to use them
qrs.ly/cyg7dv9

To read a QR code, you must have a smartphone or tablet with a camera. We recommend that you download a QR code reader app that is made specifically for your phone or tablet brand.

If I (Kayla) wanted to write about a time that my thinking changed, I might write a kernel essay like this:

1. **I used to think** that brussels sprouts were pretty gross.
2. **But then** my husband cooked them with bacon, onions, tomatoes, and a little bit of butter.
3. **So now I know** that brussels sprouts can be absolutely delicious!

After the kernel essay is written, the next step is for the writer to read the kernel essay aloud to several listeners to see how the structure worked.

A kernel essay is like a kernel of corn: a small thing packed with possibility. What can you do with a corn kernel? You can *leave* it. You can *pop* it. You can *toss* it. You can *plant* it.

KAYLA
BRISEÑO

MY TOPIC: BRUSSELS SPROUTS

THE STORY OF MY THINKING

| I used to think... | But this happened... | So now I know... |

MY KERNEL ESSAY

1. I used to think that brussels sprouts were pretty gross.

2. But then my husband cooked them with bacon, onions, tomatoes, and a little bit of butter.

3. So now I know that brussels sprouts can be pretty delicious!

I HEARD THIS!
1. _Stephen_
2. _Zinnia B._
3. _____

What can you do with a kernel essay? Writers can treat it just like a kernel of corn. They can leave their essay just like it is; they can "pop" it (i.e., develop it into a full essay by adding details and craft); they can toss it out (if they don't like the way it sounds); or they can "plant" it to let it grow into something even bigger, like a research project or a book.

The great thing about a kernel essay is that it offers writers a quick way to get thoughts on paper and see if they have something worth developing or if they need to try something else. A student doesn't have to slog through writing a page or two before knowing whether this writing is on the right track.

QR Code 0.2
Gretchen walks us through how to write a kernel essay
qrs.ly/3ag7dvm

WHAT ARE TEXT STRUCTURES?

A text structure is the plan, or path, that a writer uses in order to "track movement of the mind." In other words, the structure will allow a reader to glimpse what the writer knows and how they know it. It can be created intentionally by a writer or gleaned from reading. For simplicity, we place these steps into sequenced, horizontal boxes, resembling stepping stones.

Text structures can be revised to make them work for the writing situation. Writers are free to use the text structure as it is provided, or they may wish to add, delete, change, or rearrange it in some way. A writer may even want to create a new and unique text structure—and that is absolutely OK! In fact, it's great! The structures are tools that are meant to be manipulated for each writer and task.

OK, So What Does All This Have to Do With Nonfiction Picture Books?

All nonfiction picture books use different text structures, offering writers a chance to

- use the text structure as a pre- or post-writing exercise, as an entry or reentry into the text;

- use the text structure to retell the story they have read in the picture book; and

- use the text structure to create their own piece of writing.

Other text structures serve as handy reading response templates. Some of our favorites are in the appendix. Using these reading response structures, writers can demonstrate what they know by

- responding to something they have read (without a question or prompt),

- writing answers to questions provided for each picture book,

- constructing a short answer response,

- constructing an extended response, and

- composing a full essay (a theme, literary analysis, or other form).

QR Code 0.3
Gretchen teaches how to use text structures to respond to reading (Part 1)
qrs.ly/bog7dvo

QR Code 0.4
Gretchen teaches how to use text structures to respond to short answer questions (Part 2)
qrs.ly/aig7dvq

QR Code 0.5
Gretchen teaches how to use text structures to compose literary essays (Part 3)
qrs.ly/2gg7dvt

INTRODUCING YOUR STUDENTS TO KERNEL ESSAYS

What's the Classroom Problem?

It's time to compose a piece of writing. You announce to the class, "OK, today we are going to write about how our thinking changed about something. Here is your paper. Get started writing your five-paragraph essay on this topic."

The response comes in the form of blank stares.

Students stare into the endless abyss of the blank page, and one raises their hand to announce, "Uh, Miss, I don't know what to write about."

After writing two "sentences," a second student raises their hand to declare, "I'm done!"

Another student gets started right away, to which you breathe a sigh of relief. However, while dutifully observing the writers, you discover that this student is writing in a stream of consciousness, and only about three lines might be viable for the assignment.

Let's face it: When it comes to writing an essay, a response, a story, or even a poem, it is often hard to know where to start. That blank page can be daunting to even the most experienced writer. And then, once they get started, it is sometimes even more difficult to know where to go from there!

So, What's the Solution?

Enter kernel essays and text structures.

We have found that using a text structure to get our students to write, and asking them to write "just one sentence per box," has helped to jump-start their thinking and provides them with a road map of how to track their thinking.

The following is an introductory lesson for writing a kernel essay that you can teach tomorrow.

> "I believe the beginning of my realization that this class would not be average was when we learned about kernel essays. I remember thinking to myself, 'How on earth can writing a four-sentence story help me write an essay?' I, of course, ended up astonished at the fact that it did help me. It helped me write more than any brainstorming or chart I had ever done before. I told my mother about how natural writing an essay felt after that lesson, [and] she told me 'Cherish that class, it'll help you more than any grammar or lit classes you'll ever take.' I chose to listen."
>
> —Lucia Sears, 11th Grade

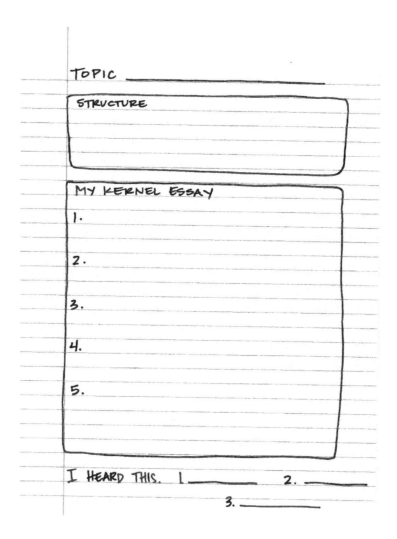

Basic Steps:

1. Choose a topic (from a quick list,* a quick write, a prompt, anywhere).
2. Choose a text structure.
3. Have students use the text structure to write about their topic by writing one sentence per box.
4. Have students share their kernel essays with other writers.
5. Repeat often to give them practice with a variety of other structures.
6. After writing several, have students choose one to "pop" by adding details.

Tools/Supplies:

- A quick list,* quick write idea, or topic
- Student journals
- A text structure

*A quick list is a list you can have students make of things and experiences that are personal to them. These lists are meant to be created quickly and to be kept in a writer's notebook for later use. They can be made about anything. Find some examples in many of Gretchen Bernabei's other books.

Step 1: Choosing a Topic

Depending on what you want your students to write, you may need to create a quick list, use a quick write topic (there is at least one provided for each lesson in this book), or choose a topic.

Say: *Look at your quick list and choose a topic* [or] *Think about this topic on the board. We are going to write about this topic in a kernel essay.*

Step 2: Choosing a Text Structure

Whether you are writing a reading response, a story, a piece about your life, a literary analysis, or an argumentative essay, there are text structures for every kind of writing. Choose a text structure that fits the writing needs of the moment in your classroom, and project it on the board, write it on chart paper, or display it under a document camera.

When you are first starting out with kernel essays, we recommend using one text structure with the whole class. Practice the same structure a few times, over a couple of days, so students have a chance to internalize it and get the hang of using a structure to guide their thinking and writing.

Step 3: Writing a Kernel Essay, One Box at a Time

Have students create a page in their journals that looks like this.

Say: *Now to write our kernel essay, we are going to need a text structure. Today we are going to write about a time our thinking changed by using "The Story of My Thinking," which has three boxes. A kernel essay is small—you will only need to write one sentence per box, so how many sentences are we going to write?* [Hopefully your students will tell you three sentences.] *That's right, three. Remember that sentences start with a capital letter and end with some sort of punctuation. Now let's get started.*

We always recommend writing with your students, so you may wish to write your own kernel essay (on the board, chart paper, or the document projected by the document camera) as you walk them through the steps.

Say: *OK, I'm going to write about a time when my thinking changed about a food—brussels sprouts. The first box says, "I used to think . . ." So I'm going to write,* **"I used to think** *that brussels sprouts were pretty gross." Go ahead and write your first sentence. If you need to change the words from the box in some way, go ahead.*

Give students time to write their sentences.

Say: *Now let's write our second sentence. The second box says, "But this happened . . ." I need to tell what happened to change my thinking. So I'm going to write,* **"But then** *my husband cooked them with bacon, onions, tomatoes, and a little bit of butter." I don't need to use the words "But this happened." I'm just going to say what happened. Go ahead and write your next sentence.*

Give students time to write their sentences.

Say: *Now let's write our last sentence. The third box says, "So now I know . . ." I need to tell how my thinking changed. So I'm going to write, "**So now I know** that brussels sprouts can be absolutely delicious!" Go ahead and write your last sentence. If you need to change the words from the box in some way, go ahead.*

Give students time to write their sentences.

Step 4: Sharing the Kernel Essays (Don't Skip This Step!)

Writing should be social, and sharing is the main course, not the dessert, in the process, so *don't skip the sharing.* There will be students who think they didn't do it correctly or who didn't understand it at all, so their page might be blank. Sharing will help with that. They will have a chance to hear what other writers did with the structure.

Say: *OK, now that we have written our kernel essays, it's time to share what you wrote. Before I tell you how to move around, here are some ways not to do it.*

1.   **Say:** *Here's my kernel essay. Read it.* [This is your chance to poke fun at—I mean, imitate—the lethargic behavior of your students when they just toss their journals at someone else when it's time to share. Ham it up. Have fun with this.] *What am I doing or not doing?*

     Students: *You're not sharing with your voice! You're just trading papers.*

     Say: *Exactly. We need to read our own writing, with our own voices.*

2.   **Say:** *Here's another wrong way to do it. "I used to think that brussels sprouts were pretty gross. My parents didn't really like them, so they never made them. In fact, whenever we'd see them at a restaurant or something, they would turn up their noses and talk about how gross they were. . . ."* [It helps to do this part quickly, imitating that one student who always adds on a bunch of extra details. You know the type.] *What am I doing?*

     Students: *You're adding a whole bunch of details you didn't write. You're going on and on.*

     Say: *Yep. And while it is great to add details to your story (that's what we'll do when we pop and revise our kernel essays later), that's not the job for right now. Just read what you wrote and then listen to your partner's essay.*

Say: *OK, so now that you know how to do it wrong, here's how to do it correctly. Write "I heard this" at the bottom of your page. Then draw three lines next to it. When I say "go," I want you to stand up, find a partner, and take turns reading your kernel essays. Once someone has listened to your kernel essay, have that person sign on one of the lines. Your job is to have three people listen to your kernel essay, get three signatures, listen to at least three kernel essays, and then sit down when you have finished. I'll know we are finished sharing when we have all returned to our seats.*

Allow students to move around the room and share their kernel essays. Once they have had a chance to get their signatures, gather them back together again and ask for volunteers to share with the class.

Say: *Now that you've had a chance to try out your writing on a few people's ears, who would like to share theirs with the whole class? Did anyone hear a good one that we all need to hear?* [Watch as hands fly up after that question.]

Allow as many students to share as time allows. As students share their essays out loud, point to each step of the text structure to reinforce the structure.

If a student has changed the structure in some way, celebrate it by writing it on the board or chart paper. **You might say**: *"Oh, I noticed how Clementine has used the words 'Now I believe...' instead of 'Now I know...' and Cuate has added an extra 'But this happened...' because he just couldn't keep it to one sentence. If you'd like to use Clementine's 'Story of My Thinking' or Cuate's 'Story of My Thinking' next time we use this text structure, go ahead."*

Allowing students to make these structures their own has powerful results. Not only will students start tweaking the structures to make them work for their writing, but before long, many will start finding and/or inventing their own. If you keep the text structures you use and discover on the wall, it will be filled in no time with student-created additions. They will quickly see themselves as writers who make choices.

> "Kernel essays have helped me really make my paragraphs better. They have helped me with my structure of writing. Writing is way more fun and easier with this type of writing. It's also quick and efficient, and it doesn't waste time."
>
> —Zayd Ehab Samir Zabaneh, 6th Grade

Step 5: Repeating the Process (Often)

Once students have practiced writing and sharing a kernel essay, repeat this process often to give them practice with a variety of other structures.

If you really want them to internalize a certain structure, consider having them practice it three or more times in a week. You may choose to type the structure for them to glue to the top of the page of their journals or have them write it themselves (this helps with internalizing the structure).

If you would like them to use a variety of structures, once you have practiced a few together, consider giving them a few to choose from and having them share what they come up with.

Step 6: Popping a Kernel Essay (Adding Details)

Once students have had some practice with writing kernel essays and have a few to choose from, ask students to choose one they think they could pop (by adding the rest of the story with plenty of details—perhaps turning each sentence into at least one paragraph). If they are having trouble choosing, consider inviting them to choose two or three and try them out on some listeners to see which one others find most interesting.

To develop a kernel essay, start by turning each sentence of the kernel essay into a paragraph. Here are some ideas for how to do that.

- Use the "like what" button. (After a statement, imagine a reader asking, "Like what?" The student will know what details to add.)

- Use jerk talk. (After a statement, imagine a real or imaginary listener who says, "No, it's not!" Prove it!")

- Add some ba-da-bings. (These are sentences that traditionally tell what someone was doing [*ba*], what someone saw [*da*], and what someone felt [*bing*]: where your feet were, what you saw, and what you thought.)

- Add some pitchforks. (A pitchfork sentence or series of sentences will take one thing and branch it off into three or more.)

- Hunt for vague writing and change it into something specific.

- Add dialogue.

- Add text evidence.

- Add a truism and explain it.

- Add descriptions.

- Add metaphors, similes, or other writer's craft tools.

- Use the "three questions" technique: Listeners write three questions, things they want to know about the writing.

- Use the "Writer's Tools Chart" (found on the companion website) as a handy tool for revision.

TEACHER DEBRIEF

This intro lesson offers a pattern of writing that, with repeated practice, becomes routine and can be used for any sort of writing. In this book, lessons are built around the text structures found in nonfiction picture books. However, if you want to get your students used to writing kernel essays that follow a text structure, you may want to try having them write a few kernel essays using these simple structures:

THE STORY OF MY THINKING		
I used to think . . .	But this happened	So now I know . . .

THE MEMORY STRUCTURE				
Where I was and what I was doing	What happened first	What happened next	What happened last	What I learned or realized

HOW ONE EVENT CHANGED A CHARACTER		
How a character was before	What happened	How the character changed

11-MINUTE ESSAY				
Truism (something I believe is true)	One way I know it's true (an example from a book, a movie, history, or my life)	Another way I know it's true (an example from a book, a movie, history, or my life)	Another way I know it's true (an example from a book, a movie, history, or my life)	Truism (said differently) or I wonder . . .

Once students have the hang of it, jump into some of the lessons in this book to see how real authors use text structures in their writing.

We write kernel essays regularly to do all kinds of things: write about our lives, respond to something we've read or watched, reflect, or compose a persuasive or informative essay. As we have said, text structures can be found everywhere and can be created for just about any writing purpose. In their kernel form, they act as an outline for where the writing should go, and they provide an entry point for even the most reluctant writers.

GOING FURTHER

Here are several ways to use the text structures in this book.

- Use a text structure to write a kernel essay summary of a story.

- Use a text structure to write an original piece in a kernel essay.

- Use a text structure to write a piece of longer writing.

- Use the list of question stems and reading response text **structures (see** "Questions and Answers About Understanding the Reading" and "Questions About Author's Choices" on page 8) to do some reading responses, writing, discussing, and even preparing for a standardized test.

- Use the text structure to launch a discussion or compose a poem, a letter, a skit, an essay, or a speech.

Consider providing a permanent home for text structures in your classroom (bulletin board, wall, back of door, the side of a filing cabinet). Have students collect text structures in their journals for easy access.

INTRODUCING YOUR STUDENTS TO TRUISMS

What's the Classroom Problem?

You give your students a piece ("All Summer in a Day" by Ray Bradbury, for example), and after they read it, you ask them, "What's the theme?"

They don't hesitate.

"It's about my grandmother!"

"My kindergarten teacher!"

"It's about rain."

"Turtles."

Like people playing darts with their eyes closed, they just hope something sticks to the board and you get off their backs. Teachers all over agree: *Theme* is one of the most difficult concepts to teach. However, it is a vital skill for students to be able to read between the lines, to pick up on subtleties and nuances, and to explain their thinking accurately and succinctly. And if we can get them to do it with some style and eloquence, all the better.

So, What's the Solution?

The solution to get your students to analyze for the theme accurately is to teach them how to write truisms. A truism is simply a life lesson—what an author or creator might want us to take away from a work.

The following is an introductory lesson you can teach tomorrow.

Basic Steps:

1. Project a compelling photo or piece of art.

2. Practice point-it-out observations.

3. Practice noticing "big ideas."

4. Practice composing truism statements.

Tools/Supplies:

- Two or three photographs (We like to use photos from many sources, including "Photos of the Week" from *The Atlantic*, "Best Photographs of the Day" from *The Guardian*, the *National Geographic* "Photo of the Day," images from the website Unsplash, and others.)

- Student journals

Step 1: Project a Compelling Photo or Piece of Art

You want something that will grab your students' attention—something that will get them talking as soon as it's up on the projector and the lesson hasn't even begun. This photo is a great one to get them talking.

Source: iStock.com/PeopleImages

Say: *Go ahead and look at the photograph of children playing tug-of-war on the screen. Take a good long look. Pay attention to every detail.*

Today, we're going to break apart this photo. But before we do that, we're going to need to define an important word.

Who knows what the word inference *means?*

That's right; it means an educated guess based on clues or evidence. Keep that definition in your mind today.

Step 2: Practicing Point-It-Out Observations

Say: *Now that you've looked at it closely, imagine you could step into this photo. What are some things that you would be able to touch? Look for things that you can point out. For example, a detail I see is the rope. If you can place your finger on it, then that's a detail. So, what do you see?*

Allow students to share what they see. If they jump to an inference, like "The boy looks happy," redirect them by saying, "I like that inferencing, but let's focus just on the details. Instead, we could say, 'The boy is smiling.'"

Step 3: Practicing Noticing "Big Ideas"

Say: *Next, we're going to look at the photo and identify what I call "big idea words." These are words of things that you can't really touch. For example:* love, friendship, heartache. *Those are big idea words. What are some other big idea words that come to mind?*

Allow students to share some big idea words. Correct them as necessary.

Say: *Great work! Let's look at this picture again, but this time, instead of looking for details we can touch, let's look for details that we can't touch—big idea words. What do you see? Whatever you come up with, you're going to have to have point-it-out evidence to back it up.*

Allow time for students to think about and then share what big ideas they see. As they share, write their ideas down on the board.

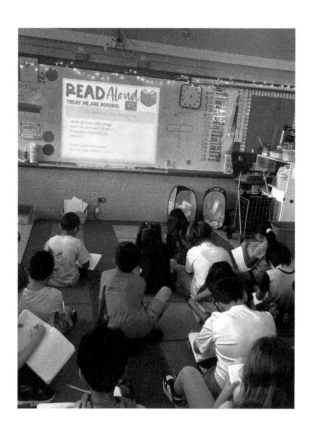

A list of big idea words is provided on the companion website. Big idea words our students have seen in this photo include *teamwork, childhood, competition, excitement, joy, enthusiasm,* and *struggle.*

TRUISMS

WHAT I SEE	BIG IDEAS	TRUISMS
– Kids pulling a rope	teamwork	We accomplish more when we work together.
– Boy smiling	hard work	
– grass	competition	A strong team can be made up of all kinds of people.
– glasses	working together	
– Hands	struggle	There can be joy in struggle.
– Jacket	joy	
– Someone in the back (not pulling)	team	

Say: *All artists or authors usually have something they want the audience or reader or viewer to think about or understand—a message they hope their audience learns. In your journal, on a blank page, write the word "Truisms" and the following definition [write the definition on the board, too].*

> A truism is a message or a truth about life that applies to nearly everyone.

> Truisms do not describe, and they do not command.

Say: *At this point, we've (1) broken down this photograph and (2) identified a huge list of big ideas. Look through our list of big ideas. Choose the one big idea that you think this photograph is mainly about. Write a truism for this photograph using the big idea word you chose. For example, let's say you think that teamwork is the most important big idea in this photo. Ask yourself, "What is the photographer trying to get me to understand about teamwork?" Your answer is your truism.*

I have three requirements for your truism.

1. *You must be able to provide point-it-out evidence for your truism. Don't just pull something out of your hat! It should connect with the picture in some way.*

2. *Your truism should be written as a complete sentence.*

3. *Your truism should not be a command—don't tell me what to do.*

If you're stuck, start with the word sometimes. *Let's see what you come up with!*

Give students a few minutes to write. Purposefully don't give them an example. See what they come up with on their own. Give them a chance to share with a small group or partner before sharing with the whole class. Some example truisms could be

- We accomplish more when we work together.

- A strong team can be made up of all kinds of people.

- There can be joy in struggle.

Say: *Let's hear a few. Who heard a truism that is powerful or the whole class should hear? That's a great truism! What point-it-out evidence do you have that supports your truism? Good!*

TEACHER DEBRIEF

This intro lesson demonstrates a pattern of analysis that, with repeated practice, becomes shorthand in your class and can be used for any sort of media. We'll be analyzing nonfiction picture books, but we recommend starting with a photograph to make the analytical process concrete and as simple as possible for your students. We try to do this at least weekly, with poems, pictures, videos, stories, announcements—you name it. ("Oh, what would a truism be for this?") Remember, you are laying the groundwork for analysis skills that students will use all year long—and hopefully the rest of their lives!

GOING FURTHER

For scaffolding purposes, it is best to start with a picture. As students get more practice and gain confidence, consider using short videos, short texts, poetry, picture books, and eventually novels.

- *Photographs* (the more thought-provoking, the better). Historical photographs and *National Geographic* "Photo of the Day" images work well.

- *Artwork.* Pieces by these artists often work well: Norman Rockwell, Paweł Kuczyński, Banksy.

- *Short, wordless videos.* "Alma," "The Invention of Love," and "Wire Cutters" are a few favorites for middle schoolers. Pixar shorts are great for elementary students.

- *Short stories or excerpts of mentor texts.* "Love" by William Maxwell, "All Summer in a Day" by Ray Bradbury, and "Thank You, Ma'am" by Langston Hughes are a few staples for fifth grade and up.

- *Poems.* A few of our favorites for middle and secondary grades are "Gate A4" and "Kindness," both by Naomi Shihab Nye; "Teenagers" by Pat Mora; "A Rainy Morning" by Ted Kooser; "Allowables" by Nikki Giovanni; "First Love" by Carl Linder; "What Love Is Not" by Yrsa Daley-Ward; and "Death Barged In" by Kathleen Sheeder Bonanno.

- And, of course, we recommend nonfiction picture books! We'll provide starting points in this book, but any favorite picture nonfiction picture book will do.

We recommend doing a group practice after this lesson. Project a new picture, review the process, and have students discuss with those around them at each step.

Consider providing a permanent home for truisms in your classroom, such as a bulletin board, a wall, the side of a filing cabinet, or the back of a window shade. This will be a place for students to post their own truisms, ones they've found in the real world, as well as the "keepers" from their independent reading.

QR Code 0.6
Stephen and Kayla explain the power of truisms
qrs.ly/w1g7dvu

QR Code 0.7
A Prezi we created to teach this to our seventh graders
qrs.ly/7jg7dvv

OK, so what do I do with all these truisms? Visit https://companion.corwin.com/courses/TS-nonfictionpicturebooks to download the following resources that will help you teach truisms.

- Big idea word list
- Truism tree
- Truism sentence frame (see "Truism Reteach Lessons")
- Theme chart
- Truism braid (with video)
- 11-minute essay (with video)

A growing wall of truisms in Kayla's classroom.

INTRODUCING YOUR STUDENTS TO READING RESPONSE

What's the Classroom Problem?

You've just read something together as a class, and now it's time to see if anyone understood it. You ask the class, "Can anyone tell me how our character changed from the beginning of the story to the end?"

"Her hair got shorter!"

"She fell asleep."

"She got older."

"Uh. . . ."

"She got nicer?"

Encouraged with that last response, you say, "OK! How do you know that?" No response.

The facts are these: Getting students to *talk* about what they have read, what they think, and why they think that (beyond the surface level) can be nearly impossible—let alone asking them to *write* about these things. And even if you *do* get them started, they tend to go in circles and never really form the answer. Nor do they provide that ever-elusive text evidence to back it up.

Some states require this form of writing on their state assessments, so there is a real urgency for our students to do this well.

So, What's the Solution?

Once again, we turn to text structures and kernel essays.

Just as we have seen kernel essays and text structures work wonders in other genres of writing, we have found that providing students with a structure to follow is like leading them along a path with a trail of breadcrumbs.

Without being forceful or formulaic, we can naturally show them how to provide a solid answer supported by evidence from the text. Students can easily learn a concrete way to say, "This is what I think" and "This is how I know that."

The following are a few introductory lessons for writing a reading response that you can teach tomorrow.

Basic Steps:

Basic Reading Response Text Structures

STORY OF MY THINKING		
I used to think . . .	But this happened	So now I know . . .

CHARACTER FEELINGS			
____felt ____	I know because they did ____	I also know because they said ____	What this shows

MAKING A CONNECTION		
When I read ____	I made a connection to (self, text, world)	Because ____

SUMMARY			
Somebody wanted ____	But ____	So ____	Then ____

THE EFFECT OF AN AUTHOR'S CHOICE			
The author uses (pick one) ☐ Vocabulary ☐ Sensory images ☐ Figurative language ☐ Device: ____ ☐ Something else	An example	Another example	This creates (pick one) ☐ A mood of ____ ☐ A feeling of ____ ☐ A ____tone ☐ A character who ____ ☐ Interest in ____ ☐ Understanding of ____ ☐ Something else

Source: Bernabei & Hover (2022).

See p. 325 for the full-sized version of this template.

If you want students simply to respond to reading (no prompt)

1. Read something together.

2. Show students the reading response text structures.

3. Let them choose a text structure.

4. Have students use the text structure to write about the text by writing one sentence per box.

5. Have students read their kernel essays to other writers.

6. Repeat often to give them practice with a variety of other structures.

7. After students have written several, have them choose one to "pop" by adding details to turn it into a full essay.

Questions and Text Structures for Constructed Reading Responses

Questions and Answers About Understanding the Reading

GENERIC QUESTION STEMS	TEXT STRUCTURES TO ANSWER THE QUESTIONS
1. What happens in the story? (Retell the story.) 2. What is the story mostly about right now? 3. How do you think ____ feels at the beginning and/or end of the story? 4. What is the conflict or problem of the story so far? 5. Who is more ____ (helpful, nicer), ____ (a character) or ____ (another character)? 6. How does ____ change during the story? 7. Why does ____ do/think/say/believe/ want? 8. What's one word you would use to describe ____ (character)? 9. What lesson does ____ learn in the story? 10. What is the moral of the story? 11. In sentence ____, what does the word or phrase ____ suggest? 12. How are ____ and ____ alike/different? 13. Why does ____ become ____ (upset, happy) when ____? 14. What does ____ (character) mean when he/she says ____? 15. What can the reader tell (conclude) from the action in sentence(s) ____? 16. What is ____'s reaction when she/he learns ____ show about her/his character?	**QA12345** | Question	Answer	How do you know?	What does that mean?	How else do you know?	So . . . your answer is . . . what? | **RACE** | Restate the question	Answer	Cite evidence from the text	Explain what the evidence means | **BA-DA-BINGING THE EVIDENCE** | Answer to the question	What the character does, says, and/or thinks that proves my answer	What that shows | **FIGURING OUT THE READING** | I read the words " ____ "	Which told me ____	Then I read " ____ "	Which told me ____	And then I knew ____ | **EXPLAINING A CHANGE** | How ____ changes in the story	At the beginning, . . . (with evidence)	At the end, . . . (with evidence)	Another way to describe the change

GENERIC QUESTION STEMS	TEXT STRUCTURES TO ANSWER THE QUESTIONS
17. How do the actions of ____ and/or ____ support the theme or moral? 18. What causes ____ to realize ____? 19. Why does ____ agree to ____? 20. What is ____'s attitude about ____? 21. What argument does ____ (a character) make to support ____'s (that character's) behavior/opinion? 22. What challenge(s) does ____ face? 23. What does ____ represent in the story?	

Source: Briseño, S., Briseño, K. & Bernabei, G. (2023).

Questions About Author's Choices

GENERIC QUESTION STEMS	TEXT STRUCTURES TO ANSWER THE QUESTIONS
1. Why is ____ (an event or character) important? 2. Why does the author ____? 3. How does the author show that ____ (character) is ____ (characteristic)? 4. Why did the author write this story? 5. What does the author show us by including a description of ____? 6. How did the author help visualize ____? 7. What is the main reason the author included the sentence(s) ____? 8. Why does the author choose this setting for the story? 9. In sentence ____, the author uses the word(s)/phrase(s) ____ to suggest what? 10. What does the sensory language in the sentence ____ illustrate? 11. How does the description in the sentence(s) ____ affect the reader's understanding of the setting/character? 12. The author includes the information in the sentence(s) ____ to help the reader do what? 13. What is the author's purpose in writing this story? 14. How does the author's description of ____ help the reader understand ____? 15. What effect does the word/phrase ____ have in the sentence ____? 16. How does ____ contribute to the development of the author's ideas? 17. ____ is important in the story because it shows what? 18. How does the setting influence the plot of the story? 19. What is the effect of the author's use of ____?	**RACE** | Restate the question	Answer	Cite evidence from the text	Explain what the evidence means | **NOTICING THE AUTHOR'S MOVES** | I read the words " ____ "	Which told me ____	Then I read " ____ "	Which told me ____	And then I knew the author did ____ to create ____ | **THE EFFECT ON A READER** | When I read " ____ "	It made me feel/picture/think ____	Which created ____	If the author had used a different word/phrase, such as ____	It would have had this effect ____	So I think the author was trying to create ____ | **THE EFFECT OF AN AUTHOR'S CHOICE** | The author uses (pick one) ☐ Vocabulary ☐ Sensory images ☐ Figurative language ☐ Device: ☐ Something else	An example	Another example	This creates (pick one) ☐ A mood of ____ ☐ A feeling of ____ ☐ A ____ tone ☐ A character who ____ ☐ Interest in ____ ☐ Understanding in ____ ☐ Something else

Source: Bernabei & Hover (2022).

See p. 322 for the full-sized versions of these templates.

If you want them to respond to reading with a student-written prompt

1. Read something together.
2. Show students the question stems and write some questions together.
3. Ask them to choose one of the questions to answer.
4. Show students the reading response text structures.
5. Let them choose a text structure.
6. Have students use the text structure to answer the question about the text by writing one sentence per box.
7. Have students read their kernel essays to other writers.
8. Repeat often to give them practice with a variety of other structures.
9. After they have written several kernel essays, have students choose one to "pop" by adding details to turn it into a full essay.

Common Extended Constructed Response Prompts and Text Structures

Informational	TWO VOICES, ONE MESSAGE				
How do the two pieces have the same message (or theme, life lesson, purpose, point . . .)?	The message	How one voice says it	How another voice says it	What does that mean?	Why the message is important to both
Informational	SOMETHING CHANGED				
How does _____ (a character, a situation, a place, an idea) change?	A noticeable change	In the beginning, . . .	Later . . .	Finally . . .	How to explain the change
Informational	WAYS WE ARE ALIKE				
How are _____ and _____ alike (or different)?	We both basically are _____	Another (surprising) similarity	A moment we reacted similarly	How our reactions were similar	Overall, how we are alike
Informational	A SYMBIOTIC RELATIONSHIP				
How do _____ and _____ benefit each other?	Who A and B are	How A helps B	How B helps A	What would happen if A and B didn't have each other	So that's why . . .
Argument	THIS IS BETTER THAN THAT				
What's better? _____ or _____ ? (or more important, more beneficial, more valuable, more beautiful, more impactful)	_____ is better than _____	One way I know	Another way I know	Even though some people _____	. . . overall, _____ is better

Source: Briseño, S., Briseño, K. & Bernabei, G. (2023).

See p. 321 for the full-sized version of this template.

If you want students to respond to reading with a teacher-provided prompt

1. Read something together.

2. Show students the question they will answer.

3. Show students the reading response text structures.

4. Let them choose a text structure.

5. Have students use the text structure to answer the question about the text by writing one sentence per box.

6. Have students read their kernel essays to other writers.

7. Repeat often to give them practice with a variety of other structures.

8. After they have written several, have students choose one to "pop" by adding details to turn it into a full essay.

- A common text

- Student journals

- A text structure (or a collection of reading response structures)

- A prompt or question (or the list of question stems)

Step 1: Reading a Common Text

Read one of the books together (or any selection). You may wish to start with the quick write provided, but you don't have to. Stop to discuss the story.

You can ask about any aspect of the story. Here are a few questions to get you started:

- What happened in the story?

- What did you notice?

- What confused you?

- What did you connect with? Why?

- What was the main character like?

- What parts of the story stuck out to you? Why?

- What writer's craft moves did you notice the author using?

Say: *To show our understanding, we're going to write a response to our story. Let's get our page ready to write.*

Step 2: Choosing a Path to Respond

In this lesson, step 2 can follow a few different tracks.

If you want students simply to respond to reading (no prompt), follow step 2a.

Step 2a: Choosing a Text Structure

If you are doing this for the first time, we recommend using the "Basic Reading Response Text Structures" without a prompt.

To familiarize them with this process, give students only one structure and practice it a few times with multiple stories.

Choose the text structure that you would like the students to use and project it (write it on the board, write it on chart paper, or display it under a document camera). If your students are comfortable using these structures, let them choose their own.

Continue on to Steps 3–6.

Step 2b: Creating Questions

Show students the question stems for reading response.

Say: *We are going to create our own questions about this book. Here's an example of a question we might write for The Dot by Peter H. Reynolds. [Write this question on the board, write it on chart paper, or show it under the document camera: How does Vashti's attitude toward art change during the story?] I'm not going to answer this question right now. I'm just going to write a few questions that I could answer. Take a few minutes and write two or three questions about the story that you could answer using the question stems I've provided. You don't need to answer them right now.*

Give the students time to write a few questions in their journals or on sticky notes.

Say: *Now that we have all written some questions, who would like to share theirs?*

As students share, write five to eight of their questions on the board or on chart paper, or show them under the document camera.

Step 2c: Choosing a Question to Answer

Now you have a bank of questions for students to answer. Keep the questions visible for students to choose.

Say: *Now you have several questions you could choose to answer. Choose one and write it at the top of your page (next to where you have written "My Response to* The Dot *by Peter H. Reynolds). This is the question you will answer, using a text structure.*

Step 2d: Choosing a Text Structure

To familiarize them with this process, give students only one structure and practice it a few times with multiple stories.

Choose the text structure that you would like the students to use and project it on the board, write it on chart paper, or display it under a document camera. If your students are comfortable using these structures, let them choose their own.

Continue on to Steps 3–6.

Step 2e: Revealing the Question

For each book, we have provided you with some questions for short and extended responses. Feel free to use these or create your own using the question stems.

Say: *I want you to answer this question about the story: How does Vashti's attitude toward art change during the story? Write it at the top of your page (next to where you have written "My Response to* The Dot *by Peter H. Reynolds"). We will answer this question using a text structure.*

(Continued)

(Continued)

Step 2f: Choosing a Text Structure

To familiarize them with this process, give students only one structure and practice it a few times with multiple stories.

Choose the text structure that you would like the students to use and project it: Write it on the board, write it on chart paper, or display it under a document camera. If your students are comfortable using these structures, let them choose their own.

Continue on to Steps 3–6.

Step 3: Writing a Kernel Essay, One Box at a Time

Have students create a page in their journals that looks like this.

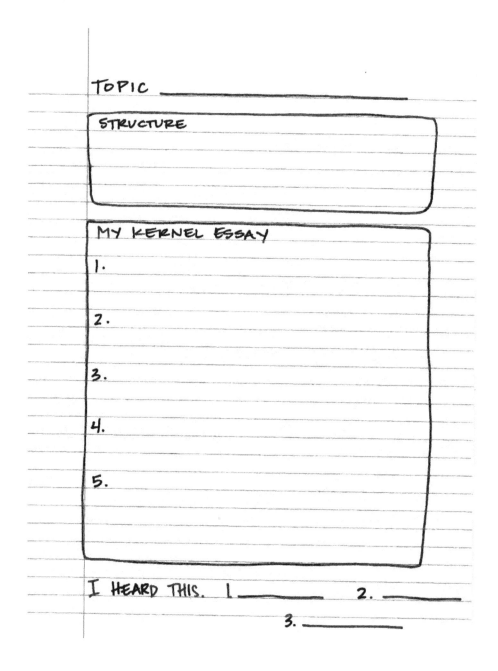

Say: *Now to write our kernel essay about our story* The Dot *by Peter H. Reynolds, we are going to use the text structure called "The Story of My Thinking," which has three boxes. [If you have allowed the students to choose their own structure, skip this part.] Remember that a kernel essay is small—you will only need to write one sentence per box. So how many sentences are we going to write? [We hope your students will tell you three sentences.] That's right, three. Remember that sentences start with a capital letter and end with some sort of punctuation. Now let's get started.*

We always recommend writing with your students, so you may wish to write your own kernel essay (on the board, chart paper, or on the document camera) as you walk them through the steps.

Say: *I'm going to write about how Vashti's thinking changed about how artists get better. The first box says, "I used to think . . . " So I'm going to write, "****Vashti*** *(not I)* ***used to think*** *that artists were just born with artistic talent." Go ahead and write your first sentence. If you need to change the words from the box in some way, go ahead.*

Give students time to write their sentences.

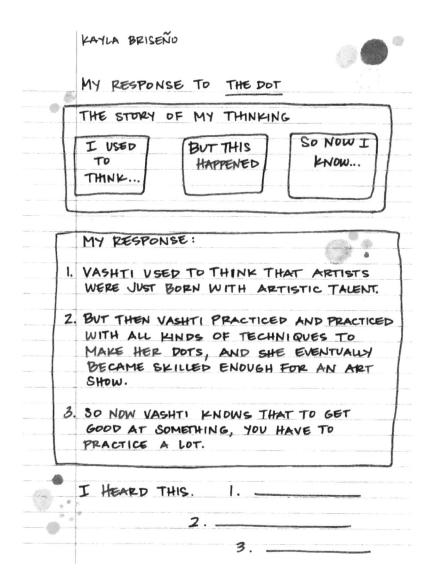

Say: *Now let's write our second sentence. The second box says, "But this happened . . ." I need to tell what happened in the story to change Vashti's thinking. So I'm going to write, "**But then** Vashti practiced and practiced with all kinds of techniques to make her dots, and she eventually became skilled enough for an art show." I don't need to use the words "But this happened." I'm just going to say what happened. Go ahead and write your next sentence.*

Give students time to write their sentences.

Say: *Now let's write our last sentence. The third box says, "So now I know . . ." I need to tell how Vashti's thinking changed. So I'm going to write, "**So now Vashti (not I) knows** that to get good at something, you have to practice it a lot." Hey! That's a truism. That last sentence is a great place to put a truism. You might want to try that, too. Go ahead and write your last sentence. If you need to change the words from the box in some way, go ahead.*

Give students time to write their sentences.

Step 4: Sharing the Kernel Essays (Don't Skip This Step!)

Writing should be social, and sharing is the main course, not the dessert, in the process, so *don't skip the sharing.* There will be students who think that they did not do the task correctly, or who didn't understand it at all, so their page might be blank. Sharing will help with that. They will have a chance to hear what other writers did with the structure.

Say: *We have written our kernel essays, and it's time to share what you wrote. Before I tell you how to move around, here are some ways not to do that sharing:*

1. **Say:** *"Here's my kernel essay. Read it."* [This is your chance to poke fun at—I mean, *imitate*—the lethargic behavior of your students when they just toss their notebooks at someone else when it's time to share. Ham it up. Have fun with this.] *What am I doing or not doing?*

   Students: *You're not sharing with your voice! You're just trading papers.*

   Say: *Exactly. We need to read our own writing, with our own voices.*

2. **Say:** *Here's the other wrong way to do it: "**Vashti used to think** that artists were just born with artistic talent. I mean, I thought that, too. My sister has always been good at art, and she's just good at everything. She's been into art ever since she was little. She was always drawing and painting and creating. She even sells her art now on her own website (www.maryreganart.com).* [It helps to do this part quickly, imitating that one student who always adds on a bunch of extra details. (You know the type.)] *What am I doing?*

   Students: *You're adding a whole bunch of details you didn't write. You're going on and on.*

   Say: *Yep. And while it is great to add details to your story (that's what we'll do when we pop and revise our kernel essays later), that's not the job for right now. Just read what you wrote, and then listen to your partner's essay.*

Say: *Now that you know what not to do, here's what you should do. Write "I heard this" at the bottom of your page. Then draw three lines next to it. When I say "go," I want you to stand up, find a partner, and take turns reading your kernel essays. Once someone has listened to your kernel essay, have the listener sign on one of the lines. Your job is to have three people listen to your kernel essay, get three signatures, listen to at least three kernel essays, and then sit down when you have finished. I'll know we are finished sharing when we have all returned to our seats.*

Allow students to move around the room and share their kernel essays. Once they have had a chance to get their signatures, gather them back together again and ask for volunteers to share with the class.

Say: *Now that you've had a chance to try out your writing on a few people's ears, who would like to share with the whole class? Did anyone hear a good one that we all need to hear?* [Watch as hands fly up after that question.]

Allow as many students to share as time allows. As students share their essays out loud, point to each step of the text structure to reinforce the structure.

If a student has changed the structure in some way, celebrate it by writing it on the board or chart paper. **You might say**: *Oh, I noticed that Francisco has used the words "Now Vashti believes . . ." instead of "Now Vashti knows . . ." and that Lily has added an extra "But this happened . . ." because she just couldn't keep it to one sentence. If you'd like to use Francisco's "Story of My Thinking" or Lily's "Story of My Thinking" next time we use this text structure, go ahead.*

Allowing students to make these structures their own has powerful results. Not only will students start tweaking the structures to make them work for their writing, but before long, many will start finding and/or inventing their own. If you keep the text structures you use and discover on the wall, it will be filled in no time with student-created ones. Students will quickly see themselves as writers who make choices.

Step 5: Repeating the Process (Often)

Once students have practiced writing and sharing a kernel essay, repeat this process often to give them practice with a variety of the other reading response structures.

If you really want them to internalize a certain structure, consider having them practice it three or more times in a week. You may choose to type the structure for them to glue to the top of the page of their journals or have them write it themselves (this helps with internalizing the structure).

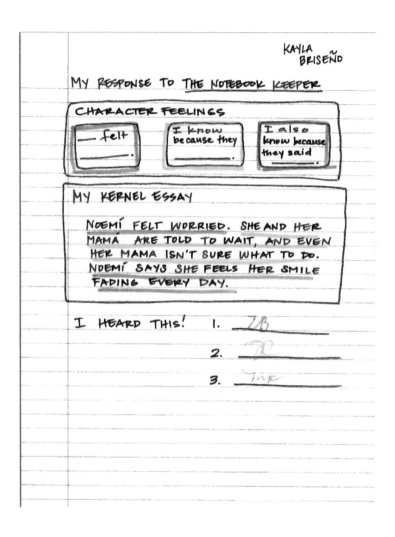

If you would like them to use a variety of structures, once you have practiced a few together, consider giving them a few to choose from and sharing what they come up with.

Step 6: Popping a Kernel Essay (Adding Details)

Once students have had some practice with writing kernel essays and they have a few to choose from, ask students to choose one they think they could pop (by adding more details—they might turn each sentence into at least one paragraph). If they are having trouble choosing, consider inviting them to choose two or three and trying them out on some listeners to see which one others find most compelling.

To develop a kernel essay, start by turning each sentence of the kernel essay into a paragraph. Here are some ideas for how to do that:

- Use the "like what" button. (After a statement, imagine a reader asking, "Like what?" The student will know what details to add.)

- Use jerk talk. (After a statement, imagine a real or imaginary listener who says, "No, it's not!" Prove it!")

- Add some ba-da-bings. (These are sentences that traditionally tell about circumstances and sensations: where your feet were, what you saw, and what you thought.)

- Add some pitchforks. (A pitchfork sentence or series of sentences takes one thing and branches it off into three or more.)

- Hunt for vague writing and change it into something specific.

- Add dialogue.

- Add (more) text evidence.

- Add a truism, and explain it.

- Add descriptions.

- Add metaphors, similes, or other writer's craft tools.

- Use the "three questions" technique. (Listeners write three questions, things they want to know about the writing.)

- Use the "Writer's Tools Chart" (found on the companion website) as a handy tool for revision.

TEACHER DEBRIEF

Why Should I Give My Students All This Choice?

No matter which way you decide to go (unprompted or prompted), it is important to give students choices. Providing a variety of choices leads them to really think about what they are answering and what they need to say.

Why These Kinds of Questions?

While we're not reinventing the wheel with these question types, we want thinking to be in the forefront. Taking students beyond the surface level requires them to really think.

Why Should I Have My Students Create Their Own Questions?

While we've provided you with some questions for each nonfiction picture book, it is important for students to go through the question creation phase. Students are more involved when they write their own questions. It builds confidence. When they face these types of questions on a test, the task won't be as daunting because they have walked down that road before.

The main reason students don't share their writing is that they lack confidence in their answers. *What if I'm wrong?* When they are the question creators, not only are they confident to share, but they have been given steps to express and support their thinking.

Can I Use These Structures for More Than Just Reading Response?

Just about all writing is argumentative. We make a claim and prove it. Whenever we ask students to answer a question about a text, their answer is a claim (something they believe is true), and they have to back it up with some sort of proof—text evidence, examples from their own life, or information or ideas from something else they've read, watched, or learned. This kind of writing and thinking can be applied to all sorts of genres.

QR Code 0.8
Gretchen teaches how to use text structures to respond to reading (Part 1)
qrs.ly/kkg7dvx

QR Code 0.9
Gretchen teaches how to use text structures to respond to short answer questions (Part 2)
qrs.ly/wzg7dvy

QR Code 0.10
Gretchen teaches how to use text structures to compose literary essays (Part 3)
qrs.ly/88g7dw0

Originally found in *Text Structures and Fables* by Gretchen Bernabei and Jayne Hover, a "3-Things Response" (also found on our book's companion website) is another useful tool to get your students to respond to reading (or to a video, a speaker, a field trip—anything), unprompted.

Lessons

Building an Orchestra of Hope
by Carmen Oliver and illustrated by Luisa Uribe

Summary: Favio Chávez loved music, but over time his focus changed to environmental science, which led him to Paraguay. While there, he discovered families who lived and worked in the landfills. Soon he combined his love of music and the environment to build an orchestra of instruments, which breathed new life and hope into the lives of many.

Why We Love It: This story brings new meaning to the phrase "from trash to treasure." Chávez's determination to use his skills and passions to better the lives of others is inspiring and thought-provoking. It leads the reader to think, "What trash can I turn to music?"

Topics: trash, landfills, Paraguay, South America, the environment, recycling, music, orchestras, musical instruments, music programs, people working in landfills, village life, subsistence living

Big Ideas: hope, determination, problem solving, dreaming for a better life, resourcefulness, caring for others, trash to treasure, teaching others, the power of music, lifting others, poverty, hope for the future, the power of performance

Back Matter:

- "More About Favio Chávez and the Recycled Orchestra of Cateura"
- Selected bibliography

LESSON STEPS:

1 QUICK WRITE.
(Choose One):

- Have you ever picked up a common, everyday object and turned it into something else?
- What are some problems (maybe make a list) that need a solution? What ideas do you have to fix or change one of them?
- Do you ever think about what happens to trash when we throw it out? What can you imagine might be the best thing to happen to it?

Write about this for 3 minutes and then set it aside.

2 READ.

Read the picture book *Building an Orchestra on Hope* by Carmen Oliver and discuss the story. Discuss parts of the story that stick out to you or that you connect with. What writer's craft moves do you notice the author using? Notice the parts of the story.

Building an Orchestra of Hope
by Carmen Oliver and illustrated by Luisa Uribe

3 SHARE THE STRUCTURE.

Show the students the structure found in the picture book. Reread the story, looking for chunks together and watching for how the author moves from one part to the other.

A Problem Solver's Journey				
The person's background and what brought them to the situation	What they noticed that gave them an idea	How the new idea started to take shape	A new problem that popped up and how they solved it	The result and who all benefitted

4 INVITATION TO WRITE.

Here are several ways you can get students to write.

- Have students use the text structure to write a kernel essay summary of the story. (Give them between 5 and 10 minutes to do this.)

- Have the students use the text structure to write their own piece in a kernel essay. (Give them between 5 and 10 minutes to do this.)

- See what students come up with. (Give them around 10 minutes.) Here are some possibilities:

  o A page of thoughts in their quick write

  o Examples of the author's craft moves

  o A text structure

Whatever they choose to write, let them know that they can change anything they need to and make it their own.

5 SHARE.

Invite students to try their writing on someone else's ears. This is a crucial step! The sharing is just as important as the writing.

Want to Go Deeper?
Try these options.

OPTION 1: CRAFT CHALLENGE

- **Noun + Verb Pitchfork**: This author uses a noun + verb pitchfork pattern where she creates a few two- or three-word sentences with a noun and verb in a row. Here's an example from the story:

    "Glass clinked. Metal pinged. Plastic bags rustled."

    Look through your piece to see where you can use a noun + verb pitchfork. After you write, try it out on someone's ears to see how it sounds in your writing.

- **Catalog:** In this story, the author creates a list of nouns, which is a rhetorical device called a catalog. Here's the example from the story:

    *"Colá collected oven **trays**, old **drainpipes**, door **keys**, metal **forks** and **spoons**, X-ray **films**, bottle **caps**, glue **canisters**, plastic **buttons**, paint **cans**, wooden **crates**, and oil **barrels**."*

    Look through your piece to see where you can use a catalog. After you write, try it out on someone's ears to see how it sounds in your writing.

- **Anaphork (Anaphora + Pitchfork)**: This author uses something we call an anaphork, a rhetorical device that combines anaphora—the repeating of a beginning word or phrase in successive phrases—and a pitchfork. Here's an example from the story:

    *"**He taught them how to** hold the bow at the right angle. **He taught them how to** hold the violin under the chin. **He taught them how to** read notes."*

    Look through your piece to see where you can try an anaphork. After you write, try it out on someone's ears to see how it sounds in your writing.

OPTION 2: ANALYZE

1. **Start with a big idea.**

    - If you want students to find the big ideas themselves, try asking, "What big ideas do you see in this story that tell you what it's really about?"

    - If students need a nudge, try using some of the big ideas from the list in this lesson's introduction and have students provide evidence from the story to support their answers. Ask, "How is this story about [the big idea]? How does the author explore [the big idea]? Where in the story do you see that?"

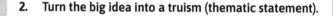

2. **Turn the big idea into a truism (thematic statement).**

    Once you have identified the big ideas, use one of them to create truisms for this story. Here are a few (found in the story) to get you started:

    - *When the world sends us garbage, we can choose to send back music.*

    - *Nothing can change your outlook as powerfully as music.*

    - *A person's skills are never wasted.*

    Have students write and share their own truisms.

    Ask them to prove their truisms by providing evidence from the text. They might imagine a listener saying, "Oh yeah? How do you know? How is that true in the story?"

Want to Go Deeper?
Try these options.

OPTION 3: READING RESPONSE

Students can compose short or extended responses to demonstrate understanding by answering any of these questions. Look in the appendix to find a list titled "Basic Reading Response Text Structures" and a list of "Useful Essay Question Stems for Nonfiction Texts."

Questions for Reading Response

- Explain how Favio's training contributed to the community.
- How does the setting influence the plot of this story?
- Explain how the people living and working in the landfill benefitted from the orchestra.
- How does the author show that Favio is resourceful?
- What happens in the story? (Retell the story.)

OPTION 4: EXTENSION IDEAS

- Dig into the back matter:
  - Use the "More About Favio Chávez and the Recycled Orchestra of Cateura" piece as a short nonfiction text to read, discuss, create and answer questions, and write.
  - Use the selected bibliography to jump-start research about this topic.
- Do an unconventional materials challenge: What useful thing can you make out of trash? Plan, create, write, and speak about it. It could be a classroom or a schoolwide challenge. Use it to bring awareness to the need to reduce waste and recycle properly.
- Put on a fashion show of trash: Bring in a variety of trash items and challenge groups of students to create clothing out of the materials to model in a fashion show. Consider inviting spectators to watch. Consider having students include some of their research about recycling and conservation in the show.
- Make music out of nontraditional materials and instruments.
- Talk to the music teacher about unusual instruments they have encountered and ask them to do a show and tell.
- Watch the YouTube video "Landfill Harmonic—the 'Recycled Orchestra,'" available at https://www.youtube.com/watch?v=yYbORpgSmjg&ab_channel=KeepAmericaBeautiful.
- Research recycling, creating things out of trash, and/or landfill living.
  - Create an infographic about that research.
  - Create a poem based on your research.
- Research other people or groups who have used things in an unconventional way.
  - Use the text structure "A Problem Solver's Journey" to write about your research.

Student Samples for
Building an Orchestra of Hope

QUICK WRITE

by **Hazel Gonzalez, 4th Grade**

Cancer is a problem we have in the world. Many people have died because of cancer. We need a cure for cancer soon!

QUICK WRITE

by **Luke Waun, 5th Grade**

I have turned a paper into a marble track. It was hard and confusing to stand it up. I was really focusing and got it done! It took me six days.

TRUISM

by **Sydney Hines, 12th Grade**

Hope can manifest and grow in various forms, much like the branches of a tree.

CRAFT CHALLENGE (NOUN + VERB PITCHFORK)

by **Hazel Gonzalez, 4th Grade**

Paper rustled. Books flew. Backpacks fell.

CRAFT CHALLENGE (NOUN + VERB PITCHFORK)

by **Luke Waun, 5th Grade**

Paper creased. Marbles binked. Pencils shook.

CRAFT CHALLENGE (CATALOG)

by **Luke Waun, 5th Grade**

I collected string, glistening beads, big charms, and leather.

Emmanuel's Dream: The True Story of Emmanuel Ofosu Yeboah

by Laurie Ann Thompson and illustrated by Sean Qualls

Summary: *Emmanuel's Dream* tells the story of Emmanuel Ofosu Yeboah, a boy born in Ghana with only one fully functioning leg. Raised by a single mother and taught the value of hard work from a young age, Emmanuel grows a passion to let others know that being a person with a disability does not mean that one is *unable*. He teaches himself to ride a bicycle and then uses it to raise awareness.

Why We Love It: This story is astounding. Emmanuel's story surpasses our imagination of the abilities of a child born into such challenging circumstances.

Topics: Ghana, West Africa, cyclists, bicycles, bike riding, Challenged Athletes Foundation, people with health conditions or impairments

Big Ideas: perseverance, resilience, tough love, supporting your family, working hard, overcoming obstacles, poverty, journey, raising awareness, breaking stereotypes, ability, strength, hope

Back Matter:

- Author's note

LESSON STEPS:

1 QUICK WRITE.
(CHOOSE ONE):

- What are some problems in the world (maybe make a list) that need a solution, and that people should know about? What ideas do you have to fix or change one of them?

- Think about a time you did something you didn't think you could do. What was it? Tell about that time.

- Think about a time you tried to learn something new. Was it easy? Did you stick with it? Why or why not?

Write about this for 3 minutes and then set it aside.

2 READ.

Read the picture book *Emmanuel's Dream: The True Story of Emmanuel Ofosu Yeboah* by Laurie Ann Thompson and discuss the story. Discuss parts of the story that stick out to you or that you connect with. What writer's craft moves do you notice the author using? Notice the parts of the story.

Emmanuel's Dream: The True Story of Emmanuel Ofosu Yeboah
by Laurie Ann Thompson and illustrated by Sean Qualls

3 SHARE THE STRUCTURE.

Show the students the structure found in the picture book. Reread the story, looking for chunks together and watching for how the author moves from one part to the other.

Outpowering a Challenge

When/where the person was born	How the person was different from others	Challenge(s) the person faced	How the person dealt with the challenge(s)	What the person did that made a difference

4 INVITATION TO WRITE.

Here are several ways you can get students to write.

- Have students use the text structure to write a kernel essay summary of the story. (Give them between 5 and 10 minutes to do this.)

- Have the students use the text structure to write their own piece in a kernel essay. (Give them between 5 and 10 minutes to do this.)

- See what students come up with. (Give them around 10 minutes.) Here are some possibilities:

  o A page of thoughts in their quick write

  o Examples of the author's craft moves

  o A text structure

Whatever they choose to write, let them know that they can change anything they need to and make it their own.

5 SHARE.

Invite students to try their writing on someone else's ears. This is a crucial step! The sharing is just as important as the writing.

Want to Go Deeper?
Try These Options.

OPTION 1: CRAFT CHALLENGE

- **Anaphork (Anaphora + Pitchfork):** This author uses the rhetorical device anaphora and adds a pitchfork. In other words, she repeats a word or phrase at the beginning of a sentence (anaphora) and does this three times (like a pitchfork). Kayla's students named this an "anaphork." Authors and speakers do this to create rhythm, to stir emotion, or to emphasize or bring focus to something. Here is an example from the story:

  *"Emmanuel **pedaled** through the bustling city of Accra. **He pedaled** through rain forests, over rolling hills, and across wide, muddy rivers. **He pedaled** past . . . **He pedaled** as . . . **He pedaled** through . . ."*

  Look through your piece to see where you can use an anaphork. After you write, try it out on someone's ears to see how it sounds in your writing.

- **Anaphork With an Antithetwist:** This author uses the rhetorical device anaphora and adds a pitchfork. In other words, she repeats a word or phrase at the beginning of a sentence (anaphora) and does this three times (like a pitchfork). However, after the word is repeated, the author surprises us with a twist by using the rhetorical device called antithesis (when two contrasting ideas are intentionally put next to each other, usually through parallel structure in a twist that plays on the repetition). We call this an antithetwist. Here is the example from the story:

  *"In Ghana, West Africa, a baby was born: **Two** bright eyes blinked in the light, **two** healthy lungs let out a powerful cry, **two** tiny fists opened and closed, **but only one** strong leg kicked."*

  Look through your piece to see where you can try an anaphork with an antithetwist. After you write, try it out on someone's ears to see how it sounds in your writing.

OPTION 2: ANALYZE

1. **Start with a big idea.**

   - If you want students to find the big ideas themselves, try asking, "What big ideas do you see in this story that tell you what it's really about?"

   - If students need a nudge, try using some of the big ideas from the list in this lesson's introduction and have students provide evidence from the story to support their answers. Ask, "How is this story about [the big idea]? How does the author explore [the big idea]? Where in the story do you see that?"

2. **Turn the big idea into a truism (thematic statement).**

   Once you have identified the big ideas, use one of them to create truisms for this story. Here are a few (found in the story) to get you started:

   - *"Being disabled does not mean being unable."*

   - *"One person is enough to change the world."*

   - *"In this world, we are not perfect. We can only do our best."* —Emmanuel Ofosu Yeboah

   Have students write and share their own truisms.

   Ask them to prove their truisms by providing evidence from the text. They might imagine a listener saying, "Oh yeah? How do you know? How is that true in the story?"

Want to Go Deeper?
Try these options.

OPTION 3: READING RESPONSE

Students can compose short or extended responses to demonstrate understanding by answering any of these questions. Look in the appendix to find a list titled "Basic Reading Response Text Structures" and a list of "Useful Essay Question Stems for Nonfiction Texts."

Questions for Reading Response

- Explain what may have caused Emmanuel to start working on his dream (of a bike journey).

- Explain why Emmanuel's dream (of a bike journey) was important to him or to others.

- Explain what Emmanuel's bike symbolizes.

- Explain how Emmanuel shows perseverance throughout the story.

- Explain how Emmanuel's goals change throughout the story.

OPTION 4: EXTENSION IDEAS

- Dig into the back matter:
  - Use the author's note as a short nonfiction text to read, discuss, create and answer questions, and write.
- Research more about Emmanuel Ofosu Yeboah, the Challenged Athletes Foundation, other athletes with disabilities, or the Special Olympics:
  - Create an infographic about your research.
  - Create a poem based on your research.
  - Use the text structure to write about your research.
- Watch the YouTube video "Emmanuel's Ride: An Inspiring True Story," available at https://www.youtube.com/watch?v=BHUDh82sZYs.
- Visit the Emmanuel Educational Foundation and Sports Academy (EEFSA) website at EmmanuelsDream.weebly.com.
- Research and map the route of Emmanuel's original bike journey.

QUICK WRITE

by Olivia Lyle, 2nd Grade

Algorithm subtraction was a little hard to learn, but I kept going on and working on it. After I said to my mom I was getting stuck, she bought me an algorithm book and it helped me. I do two pages a day and now I love math.

QUICK WRITE

by Joshua Paul Hidalgo, 2nd Grade

I kept trying to do a back flip, but I couldn't. But I kept trying and I did it.

QUICK WRITE

by Natalie Goings, 4th Grade

I cannot learn my multiplication facts! I have tried everything from flashcards to timing myself. It does not stick! They are so hard to memorize.

QUICK WRITE

by Scarlett Earle, 5th Grade

Pollution—We can find out ways to stop using gas.

Global Warming—Stop using up the Earth.

Trash—Start recycling.

Plants-Stop chopping them down.

KERNEL ESSAY (USING "OUTPOWERING A CHALLENGE")

by Arinya Moore, 2nd Grade

My grandma was born in Thailand a long time ago. She used to be in a Thailand school where her language was easy. Then her mom said they were moving to Texas (where I was born). She didn't understand English, so she couldn't communicate with anybody, and she was sad. But she showed that you can overcome a challenge!

KERNEL ESSAY (USING "OUTPOWERING A CHALLENGE")

by Hazel A. Cuny, 5th Grade

Taylor Swift was born in Pennsylvania in 1989. She loved writing music. When she got older, she became famous, and some people started hating her. She came out with the album *Reputation*. She taught people all over the world how strong and powerful you can be.

KERNEL ESSAY (USING "OUTPOWERING A CHALLENGE")

by Shiv Brazwell, 9th Grade

My dad was born in New York. He is Black and his family was poor. My dad faced racism and had to help out a lot because he also had a little brother and

a little sister. My dad grew up to be respectful and kind. Music helped him a lot as well and he got a scholarship to Ohio State University. Now, his parents could more easily afford college for his siblings. His image as a very respectful Black man disproves the racist ideas many people have. Also, he and his siblings are successful and maintain great relationships.

CRAFT CHALLENGE (ANAPHORK WITH AN ANTITHETWIST)

by Olivia Lyle, 2nd Grade

I had **two** cookies. I had **two** doughnuts. I had **two** cupcakes, **but only one** Oreo.

CRAFT CHALLENGE (ANAPHORK WITH AN ANTITHETWIST)

by Natalie Goings, 4th Grade

My adorable dog had **two** front legs, **two** back legs, two huge eyes, **and one** tiny, pumping heart.

CRAFT CHALLENGE (ANAPHORK WITH AN ANTITHETWIST)

by Scarlett Earle, 5th Grade

In a nest in my back yard, two little birds hatched, **two** little beaks chirped, **two** tiny wings flapped, **but only one** bird flew.

Finding My Dance
by Ria Thundercloud and illustrated by Kalila J. Fuller

Summary: Ria Thundercloud, Beautiful Thunder Woman, was introduced to dance in the powwow circle at a young age. Her love for dance grew as she continued to train and study, eventually leading to her career path as a professional dancer.

Why We Love It: We love this book because it demonstrates the universality of dancers and the power of dance, while also giving us insight into a culture and tradition that many don't know much about.

Topics: memoirs, Ria Thundercloud, Indigenous dancers, Indigenous women, jingle dance, jingle dress, Native Americans, "powwow trail," dance, powwow circle, travel, dance teams, professional dancers

Big Ideas: finding your place, identity, language, culture, tribes, ceremony, cultural inheritance, using art for expression, overcoming difficulties, following your passion, passing down traditions, commitment to celebration of heritage, becoming who you were meant to be, freedom through the arts

Back Matter:

- None

LESSON STEPS:

1 QUICK WRITE.
(CHOOSE ONE):

- What is an activity or hobby that you love to do?

- What is something you've always wanted to try doing (dance, sports, art, choir, cooking, etc.)? Why do you want to do it?

- Is there anything that you do that makes you feel the most like your real self? What is it?

- Does your culture or family have any special traditions that have been passed down? What are they?

Write about this for 3 minutes and then set it aside.

2 READ.

Read the picture book *Finding My Dance* by Ria Thundercloud and discuss the story. Discuss parts of the story that stick out to you or that you connect with. What writer's craft moves do you notice the author using? Notice the parts of the story.

3 Finding My Dance
by Ria Thundercloud and illustrated by Kalila J. Fuller

3 SHARE THE STRUCTURE.

Show the students the structure found in the picture book. Reread the story, looking for chunks together and watching for how the author moves from one part to the other.

Doing What You Love				
_____ loved _____.	Because they loved _____, they did _____.	They wanted to do/be/ create/go . . .	So they did/ were/created/ went . . .	This led them to _____.

4 INVITATION TO WRITE.

Here are several ways you can get students to write.

- Have students use the text structure to write a kernel essay summary of the story. (Give them between 5 and 10 minutes to do this.)

- Have the students use the text structure to write their own piece in a kernel essay. (Give them between 5 and 10 minutes to do this.)

- See what students come up with. (Give them around 10 minutes.) Here are some possibilities:

  o A page of thoughts in their quick write

  o Examples of the author's craft moves

  o A text structure

Whatever they choose to write, let them know that they can change anything they need to and make it their own.

5 SHARE.

Invite students to try their writing on someone else's ears. This is a crucial step! The sharing is just as important as the writing.

Want to Go Deeper?
Try These Options.

OPTION 1: CRAFT CHALLENGE

- **Isn't/Is Simile:** In this story, the author uses something we like to call an isn't/is simile. A simile is a comparison using *like* or *as*. An isn't/is simile follows this pattern:

    _____ isn't _____. It is _____, just like/as _____ [simile].

    Here is an example from the story:

    *"I was learning that dance **isn't** just one thing—**it is** fluid and evolves, **just as** a caterpillar becomes a butterfly."*

    Look through your piece to see where you can use an isn't/is simile. After you write, try it out on someone's ears to see how it sounds in your writing.

- **Ba-Da-Bing:** In this story, the author uses a ba-da-bing, which tells us what a character's body was doing (*ba*), what the character saw (*da*), and what the character thought (*bing*). Here is the example from the story:

    *"**We jumped** from time zone to time zone, region to region [**ba**], and **watched** the sun rise and set [**da**]. It felt magical to witness the changes of Mother Earth [**bing**]."*

    Look through your piece to see where you can use a ba-da-bing. After you write, try it out on someone's ears to see how it sounds in your writing.

- **Antithesis:** This author uses a rhetorical device called antithesis. Antithesis is when two contrasting ideas are intentionally put next to each other, usually through parallel structure. Here's an example from the story:

    *"Classical dance is **rigid and structured**, while traditional dance is more **grounded and expressive**."*

    Look through your piece to see where you can use antithesis. After you write, try it out on someone's ears to see how it sounds in your writing.

- **Translanguaging:** This author uses another language in the story. Here are a few examples from the story:

    *"My name is **Wakaja haja piiwiga**, which means 'Beautiful Thunder Woman.'"*

    *"**Yelihwaha-wíhta**, She Brings Good Energy."*

    Look through your piece to see where you might use another language. After you write, try it out on someone's ears to see how it sounds in your writing.

OPTION 2: ANALYZE

1. **Start with a big idea.**

   - If you want students to find the big ideas themselves, try asking, "What big ideas do you see in this story that tell you what it's really about?"

   - If students need a nudge, try using some of the big ideas from the list in this lesson's introduction and have students provide evidence from the story to support their answers. Ask, "How is this story about [the big idea]? How does the author explore [the big idea]? Where in the story do you see that?"

2. **Turn the big idea into a truism (thematic statement).**

   Once you have identified the big ideas, use one of them to create truisms for this story. Here are a few (found in the story) to get you started:

   - *The arts give us ways to express who we really are.*

   - *It's important to pass on our culture and traditions.*

   - *Most artists don't just learn one way to do something.*

   Have students write and share their own truisms.

   Ask them to prove their truisms by providing evidence from the text. They might imagine a listener saying, "Oh yeah? How do you know? How is that true in the story?"

Want to Go Deeper?
Try these options.

OPTION 3: READING RESPONSE

Students can compose short or extended responses to demonstrate understanding by answering any of these questions. Look in the appendix to find a list titled "Basic Reading Response Text Structures" and a list of "Useful Essay Question Stems for Nonfiction Texts."

Questions for Reading Response

- What does Ria's jingle dress symbolize in the story?
- What is the importance of the arena's circle shape?
- Explain whether Ria should have corrected people who were mispronouncing her name.
- Compare Ria's experience with jingle dance to her experience with classical dance.
- Explain why Ria felt she didn't fit in in high school.

OPTION 4: EXTENSION IDEAS

- Research more about Ria Thundercloud, Native Americans, powwows, the Ho-Chunk Nation, jingle dance, or other cultural dances.
  - Create an infographic about the topic.
  - Create a poem based on your research.
  - Use the text structure to write about your research (or another topic).
  - Watch Ria Thundercloud dance on YouTube: See "The Eagle Dance by Ria Thundercloud (Sandia, Ho-Chunk)," available at https://www.youtube.com/watch?v=tGDrr4z_e0w.
  - Watch the YouTube video "Reviving Native Languages—A Ho-Chunk Story," available at https://www.youtube.com/watch?v=_oQyl9dZIpA.
- Learn a few words from the Winnebago language (the language of the Ho-Chunk Nation).
- Make a map of the powwow trail.
- Learn a dance together as a class.
- Invite students to come prepared to teach everyone a few steps of their favorite kind of dance.

Student Samples for
Finding My Dance

QUICK WRITE

by Hattie Shipp, 3rd Grade

An activity I like to do is Legos. I want to be a house designer. I design houses with Legos.

QUICK WRITE

by Sejan Nagi, 4th Grade

Something that I've always wanted to do is cook because I want to be experienced at it.

QUICK WRITE

by Jaiden Adriella Cardenas, 5th Grade

A special tradition that my family celebrates is quinceañeras. My family and friends get together to celebrate quinceañeras, which are girls' 15th birthdays. She transitions from a girl to a woman. The symbol is usually her dad changing her shoes.

QUICK WRITE

by Madison Brown, 11th Grade

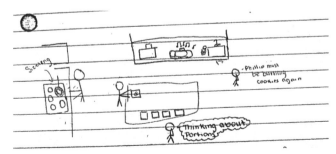

Figure 3.1

The sound of R and B could be heard for miles, but the sizzling in the pan was for my ears only. The only thing keeping me away was the steam that would heat my face. Turning toward the island was a cutting board soaked from the freshly washed vegetables. The feeling of the custom knife my grandmother got me rested on my fingers; the blade so clean you could see your reflection. The smell of outside and smoke lingering in my hair and clothes sometimes consuming my nostrils every time I looked down. The loud banging of the stairs as my brothers began to race to the table after their warning that Kobe would get to their food before they did and the kiss on my cheek from my mom walking in from her day at work.

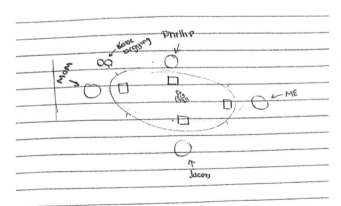

Figure 3.2

The screeching of the chairs and sometimes the table as my brothers finally make it to the table. The lingering feeling of my mother's kiss from before being wiped away with my smoke-covered sleeves. The chatter and loud R and B changed to quiet voices and jazz as I finally made my way to the table with two plates in my hand—the first one always going to my mom and then the brother that annoyed me the least that day. My second entrance lasted a short time as I was rushed into my seat so we could say grace and could finally dig in. The room was filled with the sound of whatever jazz artist was picked first in the shuffle of my playlist [and] when they say, "You could hear a pin drop," it was true at that moment. The sound of satisfaction and cutlery hitting the plate and in seconds the first question was asked: "Seconds?"

KERNEL ESSAY (USING "DOING WHAT YOU LOVE")

by Sejan Nagi, 4th Grade

I love art. Because I love art, I drew landscapes. I wanted to create art for my family. So I did really challenging pictures, which led me to painting.

KERNEL ESSAY (USING "DOING WHAT YOU LOVE")

by Blake Frankland, 4th Grade

I love to hunt in the woods with my dad. Because he loves to spend time with me, he taught me to hunt. When he was young, he was surrounded by the woods. He would play and hunt with his friends. He would practice his aim and improved

it, and he became a very good hunter, which led him to teach me how to hunt as well.

KERNEL ESSAY (USING "DOING WHAT YOU LOVE")

by Jaiden Adriella Cardenas, 5th Grade

I love to overhand when playing volleyball. Because I love volleyball, I go to private lessons. I want to go to the Olympics to play volleyball, so I train with my Coach Palmer. This will lead me to getting into the Olympics.

KERNEL ESSAY (USING "DOING WHAT YOU LOVE")

by Madison Brown, 11th Grade

Before my mom and dad got divorced, he would always barbecue for us, and we'd always have family over. With him not really in my life anymore, I picked up cooking and hosting those parties since my mom is always stressed with work and too busy.

I love cooking (alone) because it gives me time to create something for my family, and for them to try new flavors and new things. It's worth it after hours of standing in front of a stove or outside in front of a grill and catching the smell of it in my clothes. I love seeing them enjoy the food I made and pretending like I would keep my recipe away from them.

Student Samples for
Finding My Dance

3

Because I like cooking so much, I was able to get my baby brother into it and seeing him so excited warms my heart. We now have more things to talk about.

I wanted to learn how to cook so I could take the weight of coming home from work and helping kids with homework and then cook for all four of them. It also helps with finding peace for my family and I because even if my dad isn't there, I can still get the family together and make even more memories.

There are a lot of times when I'm working or at a practice, so I made little note cards with easy meals for my brothers so that even with me gone, my mom can still come home and rest.

This led me to wanting to cook for other people and helped me to form

bonds with my neighbors because I give them food and in return, they give us baked goods and ice cream.

CRAFT CHALLENGE (ISN'T/IS SIMILE)

by Krislyn Hines, 5th Grade

A classroom isn't a group of people. It is a family, just like mine.

CRAFT CHALLENGE (BA-DA-BING)

by Analeigh Moreno, 5th Grade

Abby Lee was going to the dance studio. She saw her dance students and thought, they will be stars.

4 Fish for Jimmy
by Katie Yamasaki

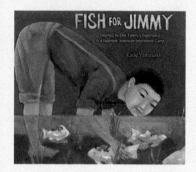

Summary: Based on the true story of the author's family, *Fish for Jimmy* tells of a Japanese American detained in an internment camp after the bombing of Pearl Harbor. While there, Taro's little brother Jimmy refuses to eat, so Taro takes a big risk to get his brother some fish, which he knows he will eat.

Why We Love It: This story highlights an important time in history. The more we hear stories of the people who lived through it, the more we understand different American experiences at that time.

Topics: World War II, Japanese Americans, Japanese internment, bombing of Pearl Harbor, imprisonment, internment camps, family separation, war, fish, food, American citizenship

Big Ideas: doing for others, survival, taking a risk, broken spirit, protecting your family

Back Matter:

- Author's note

LESSON STEPS:

1 QUICK WRITE.
(Choose One):

- Have you ever experienced a big change in your life? What happened?

- Have you ever had a problem that needed solving? What did you do?

- Have you ever had someone do something kind for you? What happened?

- Have you ever done something kind for someone else? What did you do?

Write about this for 3 minutes and then set it aside.

2 READ.

Read the picture book *Fish for Jimmy* by Katie Yamasaki and discuss the story. Discuss parts of the story that stick out to you or that you connect with. What writer's craft moves do you notice the author using? Notice the parts of the story.

Fish for Jimmy
by Katie Yamasaki

3 SHARE THE STRUCTURE.

Show the students the structure found in the picture book. Reread the story, looking for chunks together and watching for how the author moves from one part to the other.

Coping With a Bad Time

How life was before	Then this happened	How things became painful	One problem this caused	How someone solved that problem

4 INVITATION TO WRITE.

Here are several ways you can get students to write.

- Have students use the text structure to write a kernel essay summary of the story. (Give them between 5 and 10 minutes to do this.)

- Have the students use the text structure to write their own piece in a kernel essay. (Give them between 5 and 10 minutes to do this.)

- See what students come up with. (Give them around 10 minutes.) Here are some possibilities:
  - A page of thoughts in their quick write
  - Examples of the author's craft moves
  - A text structure

Whatever they choose to write, let them know that they can change anything they need to and make it their own.

5 SHARE.

Invite students to try their writing on someone else's ears. This is a crucial step! The sharing is just as important as the writing.

Want to Go Deeper?
Try these options.

OPTION 1: CRAFT CHALLENGE

- **Polysyndeton:** This author uses a rhetorical device called polysyndeton, which is the repeated use of coordinating conjunctions (instead of commas) to connect items. Here is an example from the story:

  *"Japan and America were at war, and Japanese people were forced to leave their homes **and** school **and** jobs.*

  Look through your piece to see where you can use polysyndeton. After you write, try it out on someone's ears to see how it sounds in your writing.

- **Ba-Da-Bing:** In this story, the author uses a ba-da-bing, which tells us what a character's body was doing (*ba*), what the character saw (*da*), and what the character thought (*bing*). Here is the example from the story:

  *"Taro **crept** from shadow to shadow until he arrived at the fence [**ba**].*

  *He **glanced** at the guards in the distance [**da**].*

  *Impossible as it was, he **feared** they could hear his heart pounding in his chest [**bing**]."*

  Look through your piece to see where you can use a ba-da-bing. After you write, try it out on someone's ears to see how it sounds in your writing.

OPTION 2: ANALYZE

1. **Start with a big idea.**

   - If you want students to find the big ideas themselves, try asking, "What big ideas do you see in this story that tell you what it's really about?"

   - If students need a nudge, try using some of the big ideas from the list in this lesson's introduction and have students provide evidence from the story to support their answers. Ask, "How is this story about [the big idea]? How does the author explore [the big idea]? Where in the story do you see that?"

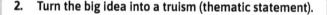

2. **Turn the big idea into a truism (thematic statement).**

   Once you have identified the big ideas, use one of them to create truisms for this story. Here are a few (found in the story) to get you started:

   - *Sometimes we must step out of our comfort zone to help others.*

   - *War can break our spirits.*

   - *When our spirits feel broken, one small thing can lift us up.*

   Have students write and share their own truisms.

   Ask them to prove their truisms by providing evidence from the text. They might imagine a listener saying, "Oh yeah? How do you know? How is that true in the story?"

Want to Go Deeper?
Try these options.

OPTION 3:
READING RESPONSE

Students can compose short or extended responses to demonstrate understanding by answering any of these questions. Look in the appendix to find a list titled "Basic Reading Response Text Structures" and a list of "Useful Essay Question Stems for Nonfiction Texts."

Questions for Reading Response

- What happened in the story?
- Explain whether it was right for Taro to leave the camp.
- Explain what fish symbolize in the story.
- Explain why the Japanese were forced to live in the camp.
- Explain what caused Jimmy not to eat.

OPTION 4:
EXTENSION IDEAS

- Dig into the back matter:
  - Use the author's note as a short nonfiction text to read, discuss, create and answer questions, and write.
- If you have one near you, take a field trip (or a virtual tour) to a World War II museum.
- If it is near you, visit the Granada Relocation Center (Camp Amache) in Amache, Colorado, which is now a National Historic Site. If it is not near you, consider a virtual tour: amache.org/virtual-pilgrimage/.
- Research more about World War II, Japanese internment, and the bombing of Pearl Harbor.
  - Create an infographic about the topic.
  - Create a poem based on your research.
  - Use the text structure to write about your research.
- Consider pairing this book with the following texts:
  - *Farewell to Manzanar* by James D. Houston and Jeanne Wakatsuki Houston (middle-grade memoir)
  - *They Called Us Enemy* by George Takei, Justin Eisinger, and Steven Scott (middle-grade graphic memoir)
  - *The Train to Crystal City: FDR's Secret Prisoner Exchange Program and America's Only Family Internment Camp During World War II* by Jan Jarboe Russell (written for adults)

QUICK WRITE

by Emilianna Junadi, 6th Grade

A big change that happened in my life was when I got glasses. You see, I lived my life until first grade not having any glasses. The rest of my family had glasses except for me at the time. When I was about seven years old, I got my first pair. It was a purple roundish pair.

I asked my mom, "Why do I have glasses?"

My mom replied, "It's because kids watch too much TV!"

I thought about that statement really hard (as hard as a seven-year-old can!). When I got to class the next day, I saw a bunch of kids with NO glasses that had even MORE screen time than me! I wondered, why do I have to wear glasses when other kids don't?

QUICK WRITE

by Alex Chen, 7th Grade

Fifth grade was a big change for me. I wasn't really focusing on grades and was virtual at that time. But when I moved to middle school, things really changed. I noticed that I would have to really focus if I actually wanted to have good grades and start getting used to working hard at home, just like college would be (at least that's what my dad said). I also had some behavioral changes since the punishments

were a little harsher and I had to actually try to stay quiet. Lastly, me getting into Pre-Algebra was a sign that I could be really smart, the smart person that I am today. I think that high school has much more homework and I would probably have to work a lot more in order to maintain my grades up to where I like them to be.

KERNEL ESSAY (USING "COPING WITH A BAD TIME")

by Corbett Hanzel, 5th Grade
(pictured and typed)

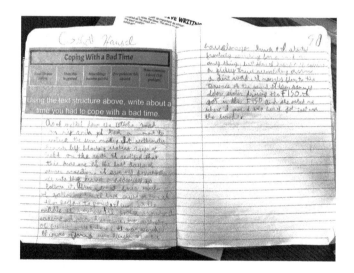

Figure 4.1

As I walked down Coliche Road on the ranch, I took a moment to notice the sun making its authority known by blasting valiant rays of light on the earth. I realized that this was one of the last days of summer vacation. I saw my dog Charlie run off into the brush and

decided to follow it. After about four minutes of following him, I lost sight of him. I then began to panic. I was in the middle of nowhere! I looked around and around and around some more. No sight of humans anywhere. I was scared I was going to miss lunch or be a javelina's lunch. I started frantically searching for a road or anything, but then I heard my savior: a pickup truck rumbling across a dirt road. I nearly flew to the source of the sound. I then saw my older sister driving the F-150. I got in and she asked me where I had been. I told her I had gotten lost in the woods.

KERNEL ESSAY (USING "COPING WITH A BAD TIME")

by Shivam Singh, 7th Grade

1. Life was decent. I was enjoying having free time during the pandemic, playing games all the time. I didn't understand how bad the virus was, until this.

2. My grandpa caught COVID and passed away. He had the virus for weeks and was only getting worse.

3. This was the first time I experienced a significant loss. I cried for hours because I never spent much time with him.

4. This caused me to feel horrible for the next few days. My mood was completely ruined.

5. Nobody solved the problem. Some of the pain went away with time and I

came to realize that everyone has to pass at one point or another.

KERNEL ESSAY RETELL (USING "COPING WITH A BAD TIME")

by Yuxuan Li, 7th Grade

1. Jimmy and his family lived in California in the 1940s. His parents had immigrated from Japan years ago to search for a better life. Jimmy's father owned a vegetable market. He would sell vegetables to owners of small vegetable stalls, sometimes with the help of Jimmy's mother. Life was simple, but **they were happy.**

2. Then, Japan bombed Pearl Harbor. That night, **the FBI showed up, and took Jimmy's father away.** They said because he was Japanese, he was a threat. Before he left, he told Taro that he was the man of the house now, and to look after Jimmy.

3. **Soon, Jimmy's family, along with anyone with Japanese ancestry, was forced to leave their old lives and live in internment camps.** They boarded buses with blacked out windows, and were dropped in dusty villages in the middle of the desert.

4. **Jimmy stopped eating.** He kept asking when they would be able to go home and eat the Pacific fish he always loved. Taro stayed up worrying about Jimmy.

5. Taro had an idea. He snuck some shears from the garden and clipped a hole in the fence. He slipped outside into the forest. He slipped his fingers in a pool of water in the forest, and wished he could help Jimmy. A fish swam into his fingers. Taro caught it and ran back to the camp. The next morning, he gave the fish to his mother, who cooked it to give to Jimmy. From then on, **Taro would sneak out every night through the hole in the fence to catch fish for Jimmy.**

KERNEL ESSAY RETELL (USING "COPING WITH A BAD TIME")

by Alex Chen, 7th Grade

Jimmy was a Japanese boy in the West Coast of America. He lived with his mom, dad, and his brother Taro. Life was very smooth and happy. They owned a vegetable stand, and they would always cook nice food from their mother's kitchen. Taro would always tell him stories about the ocean and how the Japanese were back then.

Life was great until Pearl Harbor was bombed by none other than the Japanese. Jimmy knew well that the Japanese were going to war with America. His mom and dad worried about what could happen. They worried that they would be taken away. A few hours later, Jimmy's dad was taken away by the Americans, just as they feared.

After Japan declared war on America, Jimmy and his mom and brother were all taken to a camp. The conditions were very crowded and dark while going to the camp. The camp was desolate in the middle of nowhere and it was very dirty, crowded, and lonely. Life would never be the same there. Jimmy's mom and his brother went with him into a camp while his dad went to another camp, making things even more painful.

Once they reached the camp, Jimmy suddenly lost his appetite and didn't eat for days on end. He also wouldn't play with the other kids and would just sit there and do nothing. The camp would become too traumatizing for Jimmy. After a few days of this, Jimmy's mother and brother were afraid that Jimmy was ill.

To solve this issue, Jimmy's brother Taro then escaped outside and went to a nearby stream. He then saw a few fish and noticed a way to maybe cure Jimmy. Taro came back to the camp with seven fish and his mother then started to cook the fish. Once Jimmy figured out that the fish was there, he actually started eating and his life started getting back to normal. Jimmy was happy for once and started playing with the other kids and drawing pictures in the mud.

Lastly, his dad then was able to go to the same camp as Jimmy and Taro showed him how he would always go to the river

to pick some fish for Jimmy. Then the camp didn't seem as painful to Jimmy anymore.

CRAFT CHALLENGE (POLYSYNDETON)

by Samuel Fleming, 4th Grade

When I go to HEB, I always buy eggs **and** milk **and** cheese.

CRAFT CHALLENGE (BA-DA-BING)

by Samuel Fleming, 4th Grade

I walked into my pantry, saw my dog was waiting in there, and I thought she must have smelled me eating late night snacks.

5 Free as a Bird: The Story of Malala
by Lina Maslo

Summary: Malala Yousafzai was born in a place and time that did not value girls' education. She and her family thought otherwise. When she spoke up about it, she was told to back down, but she didn't. And as a result, some people tried to silence her. This book tells the true story of Malala's mission to make sure everyone has an equal opportunity for education.

Why We Love It: Malala's story is a powerful one and should continue to be shared widely. Though the violence that she endured could make her story too graphic for young readers, Maslo's treatment of this atrocity is restrained enough to share with kindergartners. And the artwork is haunting enough for even more informed high school students to find chilling.

Topics: Malala Yousafzai, Pakistan, girls' education, Middle East, heroes, role models, parent–child relationships, education, terrorism, authoritarianism, propaganda, human rights

Big Ideas: courage, struggle, violence, persistence, oppression, suppression, human rights, gender inequality, equality, speaking up, standing for what is right

Back Matter:

- Author's note
- Timeline
- "Who Was Malalai of Maiwand [Malala's namesake]?"
- Further resources (books, films, websites)

LESSON STEPS:

1 QUICK WRITE.

Think of a time you saw someone speaking up about something they thought was wrong. It can be big or small. Who was it, what did they see, and what did they say and do?

Write about this for 3 minutes and then set it aside.

2 READ.

Read the picture book *Free as a Bird: The Story of Malala* by Lina Maslo and discuss the story. Discuss parts of the story that stick out to you or that you connect with. What writer's craft moves do you notice the author using? Notice the parts of the story.

Free as a Bird: The Story of Malala
by Lina Maslo

3 SHARE THE STRUCTURE.

Show the students the structure found in the picture book. Reread the story, looking for chunks together and watching for how the author moves from one part to the other.

A Hero's Journey				
How their journey began	What issues they noticed around them	What they wanted instead	What stood in their way and how they responded	What they became

4 INVITATION TO WRITE.

Here are several ways you can get students to write.

- Have students use the text structure to write a kernel essay summary of the story. (Give them between 5 and 10 minutes to do this.)
- Have the students use the text structure to write their own piece in a kernel essay. (Give them between 5 and 10 minutes to do this.)
- See what students come up with. (Give them around 10 minutes.) Here are some possibilities:
  - A page of thoughts in their quick write
  - Examples of the author's craft moves
  - A text structure

Whatever they choose to write, let them know that they can change anything they need to and make it their own.

5 SHARE.

Invite students to try their writing on someone else's ears. This is a crucial step! The sharing is just as important as the writing.

Want to Go Deeper?
Try these options.

OPTION 1: CRAFT CHALLENGE

- **Anaphork (Anaphora + Pitchfork):** This author uses the rhetorical device anaphora and adds a pitchfork. In other words, she repeats a word or phrase at the beginning of a sentence (anaphora) and does this three times (like a pitchfork). Kayla's students named this an "anaphork." Authors and speakers do this to create rhythm, to stir emotion, or to emphasize or bring focus to something. There are several examples of this in the book.

  *"And Malala did feel free **within the** doors at her school, **within the** covers of a book, **within the** patterned pages of calculus and chemistry."*

  Look through your piece to see where you can use an anaphork. After you write, try it out on someone's ears to see how it sounds in your writing.

- **Personified Reasons:** This author makes a statement and then provides a set of personified reasons (embodied with people) to support it.

  *"But she knew that girls and boys in many countries could not. **Some** of the countries were too poor. **Others** were always at war. **And still others** didn't think education was necessary, especially for girls."*

  Here's the pattern:

  Statement (claim, fact, problem, etc.)

  Personified Reasons: Some people . . . Others . . . And still others . . .

  Look through your piece to see where you can use personified reasons. You might even consider using this in an introductory paragraph. After you write, try it out on someone's ears to see how it sounds in your writing.

OPTION 2: ANALYZE

1. **Start with a big idea.**

   - If you want students to find the big ideas themselves, try asking, "What big ideas do you see in this story that tell you what it's really about?"

   - If students need a nudge, try using some of the big ideas from the list in this lesson's introduction and have students provide evidence from the story to support their answers. Ask, "How is this story about [the big idea]? How does the author explore [the big idea]? Where in the story do you see that?"

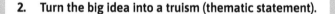

2. **Turn the big idea into a truism (thematic statement).**

   Once you have identified the big ideas, use one of them to create truisms for this story. Here are a few (found in the story) to get you started:

   - *"Speaking up is the only way things will get better."*

   - *"If we believe in something greater than our lives, then our voices will only multiply."*

   - *"When the whole world is silent, even one voice becomes powerful."* —Malala Yousafzai

   Have students write and share their own truisms.

   Ask them to prove their truisms by providing evidence from the text. They might imagine a listener saying, "Oh yeah? How do you know? How is that true in the story?"

Want to Go Deeper?
Try these options.

OPTION 3: READING RESPONSE

Students can compose short or extended responses to demonstrate understanding by answering any of these questions. Look in the appendix to find a list titled "Basic Reading Response Text Structures" and a list of "Useful Essay Question Stems for Nonfiction Texts."

Questions for Reading Response

- What is this story really about?
- What was the biggest conflict that Malala faced?
- Who is more courageous, Malala or her father?
- How does Malala change throughout the story?
- How does the setting influence the plot of the story?

OPTION 4: EXTENSION IDEAS

- Dig into the back matter:
  - Use the author's note, the timeline, and/or the "Who Was . . ." piece as a short nonfiction text to read, discuss, create and answer questions, and write.
  - Use the further resources to jump-start research about Malala's life and work.
- Choose another "hero" to research:
  - Create an infographic about that person.
  - Use the text structure to write about that person.
- Write a letter to Malala, the person you researched, or the person you wrote about in your quick write, using the same text structure (or not), to let them know what you admire about them.

Student Samples for
Free as a Bird

QUICK WRITE

by **Zayla O'Dell, 4th Grade**

When a girl was being bullied, my friends and I went to stand up for her. When we did, she was so happy.

QUICK WRITE

by **Lilliana Falcon, 5th Grade**

One time a girl named Jaiden, who is a really close friend of mine, saw me crying and asked what happened and I told her what happened and then she went up to that person and that person apologized to me.

KERNEL ESSAY (RETELL USING "A HERO'S JOURNEY")

by **Zinnia Briseño, 5th Grade**

Malala was a girl born in Pakistan, which was considered unlucky, but her father knew she would be strong. She realized that women in Pakistan didn't have the same rights as men and that education for girls was undervalued and prohibited. Malala and her father believed in education for everyone and knew that she would go on to do great things. An enemy came to Pakistan, [and] took away many freedoms, including her right to go to school, but she secretly went anyway. Because she continued to speak out, she was attacked and had to leave Pakistan, but that only made her stronger and she continued to speak up for others.

KERNEL ESSAY (USING "A HERO'S JOURNEY")

by **Fernando Lizcano, 5th Grade**

My friend saw my other friends being mean to one of the kids from the other class. They saw them being mean to them and that kid's face was looking sad. They wanted to be mean to make fun of them and just to act cool. They told them to stop, but they didn't, so they told the teacher. The teacher told them to stop and called the kids who told heroes.

CRAFT CHALLENGE (ANAPHORK)

by **Poppy Alston, 5th Grade**

Carl did not feel good **about** the pressure of his job, **about** the pressure of his schoolwork, **about** all of his stress.

CRAFT CHALLENGE (PERSONIFIED REASONS)

by **Zayla O'Dell, 4th Grade**

Some people think bullying is okay. **Others** don't. And **still others** continue to do it.

CRAFT CHALLENGE (PERSONIFIED REASONS)

by Poppy Alston, 5th Grade

Some people can't buy food because there are no stores near them. **Others** can't afford food. And **still others** can't get food because they don't have a car or any transportation to take them to the store.

Hidden Hope: How a Toy and a Hero Saved Lives During the Holocaust

by Elisa Boxer and illustrated by Amy June Bates

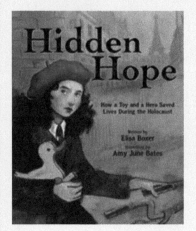

Summary: *Hidden Hope* tells the story of the French resistance to the Nazis' treatment of the Jews. Many people risked their lives to help—including Jacqueline Gauthier, who used a toy duck to sneak forged papers to people who needed them.

Why We Love It: For younger readers, this book serves as a gentle bridge into the topic of the Holocaust and what the Jews went through. It is an incredible story of grit, determination, risk-taking, and hope. Jacqueline's (or Judith's) story displays the power of hope in the darkest moments and the importance of caring for others, no matter how young you are.

Topics: World War II, the Holocaust, Nazis, German occupation of France, Jews, Jews in hiding, false papers, the French Resistance, anti-Semitism, young heroes

Big Ideas: hidden identity, fear, resistance, bravery, risking one's life for others, saving lives, caring for others, taking risks, overthrowing evil, heroism, resilience, freedom

Back Matter:

- Author's note
- Artist's note
- Author's bibliography

LESSON STEPS:

QUICK WRITE.
(Choose One):

- Have you ever helped someone else in a secret way? What did you do?

- Has someone ever helped you in a big way? Who were they, and what did they do for you?

- Have you ever needed to take a risk for a good reason? What was the reason, and what did you need to do?

Write about this for 3 minutes and then set it aside.

2 READ.

Read the picture book *Hidden Hope: How a Toy and a Hero Saved Lives During the Holocaust* by Elisa Boxer and discuss the story. Discuss parts of the story that stick out to you or that you connect with. What writer's craft moves do you notice the author using? Notice the parts of the story.

Hidden Hope: How a Toy and a Hero Saved Lives During the Holocaust

by Elisa Boxer and illustrated by Amy June Bates

3 SHARE THE STRUCTURE.

Show the students the structure found in the picture book. Reread the story, looking for chunks together and watching for how the author moves from one part to the other.

Risky Solution

What the problem was and why it was a problem	How some people were dealing with the problem	How one person helped with the problem	A setback that person faced	How that person kept going and how it turned out

4 INVITATION TO WRITE.

Here are several ways you can get students to write.

- Have students use the text structure to write a kernel essay summary of the story. (Give them between 5 and 10 minutes to do this.)
- Have the students use the text structure to write their own piece in a kernel essay. (Give them between 5 and 10 minutes to do this.)
- See what students come up with. (Give them around 10 minutes.) Here are some possibilities:
  - A page of thoughts in their quick write
  - Examples of the author's craft moves
  - A text structure

Whatever they choose to write, let them know that they can change anything they need to and make it their own.

5 SHARE.

Invite students to try their writing on someone else's ears. This is a crucial step! The sharing is just as important as the writing.

Want to Go Deeper?
Try these options.

OPTION 1: CRAFT CHALLENGE

- **Exclamations + Absolutes + Fragments:** In this story, the author uses a pattern of exclamations, absolutes (a combination of a noun and an -*ing* verb), and fragments. Here's the example from the story:

  "Hide! Quick! Hearts pounding, breath quickening, feet scrambling. Down into damp basements, up in old attics, crammed into dark closets."

  Look through your piece to see where you can use a combination like this. After you write, try it out on someone's ears to see how it sounds in your writing.

- **Onomatopoeia + Simple Sentence + Participial Phrases:** In this story, the author uses a pattern of onomatopoeias, a simple sentence, and participial phrases (a participle is a verb that ends with -*ed* or -*ing* and is used as an adjective; a participial phrase is a participle with a few more words tacked on to it). Here's an example from the story:

  "Bump, bump, bump went her bike over the cobblestone streets of Paris. Racing against time, hurrying against hate."

  Look through your piece to see where you can use a combination like this. After you write, try it out on someone's ears to see how it sounds in your writing.

OPTION 2: ANALYZE

1. **Start with a big idea.**

    - If you want students to find the big ideas themselves, try asking, "What big ideas do you see in this story that tell you what it's really about?"

    - If students need a nudge, try using some of the big ideas from the list in this lesson's introduction and have students provide evidence from the story to support their answers. Ask, "How is this story about [the big idea]? How does the author explore [the big idea]? Where in the story do you see that?"

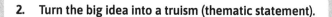

2. **Turn the big idea into a truism (thematic statement).**

    Once you have identified the big ideas, use one of them to create truisms for this story. Here are a few (found in the story) to get you started:

    - *"Hate has a way of bringing out heroes."*

    - *No one is too small, too weak, or not brave enough to make a difference.*

    - *A risk is worth it if it might save a life.*

    Have students write and share their own truisms.

    Ask them to prove their truisms by providing evidence from the text. They might imagine a listener saying, "Oh yeah? How do you know? How is that true in the story?"

Want to Go Deeper?
Try these options.

OPTION 3:
READING RESPONSE

Students can compose short or extended responses to demonstrate understanding by answering any of these questions. Look in the appendix to find a list titled "Basic Reading Response Text Structures" and a list of "Useful Essay Question Stems for Nonfiction Texts."

Questions for Reading Response

- What does the duck symbolize in the story?

- Explain whether it is OK to take a risk to help someone else.

- Explain why Judith might have been so committed to helping the Jewish people of France.

- Explain why it was important for the Jews to hide.

- Explain what the author means by "Hate has a way of bringing out heroes."

OPTION 4:
EXTENSION IDEAS

- Dig into the back matter:
  - Use the author's and artist's notes as short nonfiction texts to read, discuss, create and answer questions, and write.
- Research more about the Holocaust, Holocaust heroes, and the French Resistance.
  - Create an infographic about your research.
  - Create a poem based on your research.
  - Use the text structure "Risky Solution" to write about your research.
- Create something with a secret compartment.
- Visit a Holocaust museum, if there is one in your area.
- Consider pairing this book with *Martin & Anne* by Nancy Churnin.

Student Samples for
Hidden Hope

QUICK WRITE

by Catherine Millsap, 4th Grade

Once my brother and I were playing in the pool. He was doing a cool trick and he said he would teach me. It was scary, but when I did it, I had a lot of fun.

QUICK WRITE

by Robin Collette, 5th Grade

Someone who helped me in a big way is my mom because when I did dance, I was trying to get in the *Nutcracker*, and it was very hard. It was during COVID, and it was hard because it was on Zoom for auditions. That day, I was getting frustrated and sad, so my mom sat me down after the first Zoom and she was encouraging me and telling me, "You've got this." Then I got the role.

QUICK WRITE

by Kunjal Dangeti, 9th Grade

My brother always forgets his homework on his desk, so sometimes I take his homework and put it in his bag for him so he doesn't forget it and get in trouble.

KERNEL ESSAY (USING "RISKY SOLUTION")

by Cecily Cook, 8th Grade

Harry Potter's problem was that he was always in danger from Voldemort because he had defeated him. He had teachers and friends always helping and supporting him. Dumbledore always gave him advice and strategies that helped him defeat Voldemort again. A setback was that Dumbledore died in Harry's sixth year. Harry defeated Voldemort in the battle of Hogwarts in his seventh year.

KERNEL ESSAY RETELL (USING "RISKY SOLUTION")

by Rohan Agrawal, 6th Grade

1. The holocaust had to be stopped. The Nazis were storming through people's houses and checking if they were Jewish. If they were, they were shot on the spot. Their dead bodies littered the ground. This happened all over Europe, and a few million people were killed.

2. The Jews were terrified. Since they didn't want to be killed, they took to the streets. They hid in closets, bunkers, and anywhere they could find. There was also a French resistance, which helped the people however they could.

3. Jacqueline Geller, a Christian child helper, hid fake passports with fake names and non-Jewish identities in wooden ducks. She rode through the cobblestoned streets, going into people's houses and giving them the passport. If a Nazi saw her, they would think she was giving a toy to a child in need.

4. One problem Jacqueline Geller faced was that she wasn't Jacqueline Geller. She was Judith Gauthier. She was actually Jewish, not Christian. One day, as she was hurrying to get into a house, she was spotted and stopped by a Nazi. She thought she was dead, but as the Nazi searched her satchel, he only saw the wooden ducks. He was mad at her for wasting his time and stormed off.

5. Jacqueline knew that was a close call. If the soldier had taken more time to search the ducks, he would have found the fake passport and shot Judith on the spot. Nevertheless, she kept going, saving more than 200 people!

CRAFT CHALLENGE (EXCLAMATIONS + ABSOLUTES + FRAGMENTS)

by Catherine Millsap, 4th Grade

Dive! Swim! Whistles blowing, people screaming. Getting on the starting block. Diving into the water. Everything blacks out.

CRAFT CHALLENGE (EXCLAMATIONS + ABSOLUTES + FRAGMENTS)

by Robin Collette, 5th Grade

Ow! Oh! Leg hurting, arm aching, heart pounding. Down into the ground. Out of his chair. Over to help me up.

CRAFT CHALLENGE (ONOMATOPOEIA + SIMPLE SENTENCE + PARTICIPIAL PHRASE PATTERN)

by Catherine Millsap, 4th Grade

Boing, boing, boing went the ball as it was hitting the floor. Bouncing against the floor.

7 Joan Procter, Dragon Doctor
by Patricia Valdez and illustrated by Felicita Sala

Summary: This book tells the story of Joan Procter, who spent her lifetime researching reptiles, especially Komodo dragons. She shared her studies and passions with the world.

Why We Love It: Many have heard of Jane Goodall and her work with primates, but not many have heard of Joan Procter and her similar story with reptiles. From her childhood filled with curiosity to her path of introducing her research to the world, we find this woman fascinating.

Topics: reptiles, Komodo dragons, science, scientists, female scientists, zoos, national history museum, observation, animal study, lifelong passion, habitats, war, wartime conditions, how war changes the world

Big Ideas: lifelong passion, following your interests/passions, being different, being yourself, pursuing your passion, sharing knowledge, world-changing

Back Matter:

- Biography of Joan Procter
- Information on Komodo dragons
- Bibliography
- Some of Joan's original paintings of clown frogs

LESSON STEPS:

1 QUICK WRITE.
(Choose One):

- What is your favorite type of animal? Describe it. What do you like about it?
- If you could study something (for a living), what would it be, and why?

Write about this for 3 minutes and then set it aside.

2 READ.

Read the picture book *Joan Procter, Dragon Doctor* by Patricia Valdez and discuss the story. Discuss parts of the story that stick out to you or that you connect with. What writer's craft moves do you notice the author using? Notice the parts of the story.

Joan Procter, Dragon Doctor
by Patricia Valdez and illustrated by Felicita Sala

3 SHARE THE STRUCTURE.

Show the students the structure found in the picture book. Reread the story, looking for chunks together and watching for how the author moves from one part to the other.

A Curiosity That Changed the World

What someone was interested in	What that interest looked like at first	How that interest grew and brought about changes	The larger impact that it had on others

4 INVITATION TO WRITE.

Here are several ways you can get students to write.

- Have students use the text structure to write a kernel essay summary of the story. (Give them between 5 and 10 minutes to do this.)
- Have the students use the text structure to write their own piece in a kernel essay. (Give them between 5 and 10 minutes to do this.)
- See what students come up with. (Give them around 10 minutes.) Here are some possibilities:
  o A page of thoughts in their quick write
  o Examples of the author's craft moves
  o A text structure

Whatever they choose to write, let them know that they can change anything they need to and make it their own.

5 SHARE.

Invite students to try their writing on someone else's ears. This is a crucial step! The sharing is just as important as the writing.

Want to Go Deeper?
Try these options.

OPTION 1: CRAFT CHALLENGE

- **Alliterative Pitchfork:** This author uses an alliterative pitchfork. Alliteration is the repetition of the beginning sounds of words that are near each other. A pitchfork is a sentence (or series of sentences) that takes one thing and branches it off into three or more. Here's an example from the story:

  *"They **g**awked at the **g**eckos. They **p**eered at the **p**ythons. And they **m**arveled at the **m**onitors."*

  Look through your piece to see where you can use an alliterative pitchfork. After you write, try it out on someone's ears to see how it sounds in your writing.

- **Antithesis:** This author uses a rhetorical device called antithesis. Antithesis is when two contrasting ideas are intentionally put next to each other, usually through parallel structure. Here's an example from the story:

  *"While **other girls read stories about dragons and princesses, Joan read books about crocodiles**. Instead of **a favorite doll, a favorite lizard** accompanied her wherever she went."*

  Look through your piece to see where you can use antithesis. After you write, try it out on someone's ears to see how it sounds in your writing.

- **Myth Explosion:** This author uses a sentence that we call a myth explosion: She lists the myths or untruths that were spread about the dragons and dispels them in the same sentence. She even pitchforks it (not just one—but three!). Here's the example from the story:

  *"The reports of Komodo dragons were greatly exaggerated: They could grow to ten feet, **not thirty**. They ran fast, **but not as fast as a motorcar**. They could be fierce, **but they were mostly gentle**."*

  Look through your piece to see where you can use a myth explosion. After you write, try it out on someone's ears to see how it sounds in your writing.

OPTION 2: ANALYZE

1. **Start with a big idea.**

   - If you want students to find the big ideas themselves, try asking, "What big ideas do you see in this story that tell you what it's really about?"

   - If students need a nudge, try using some of the big ideas from the list in this lesson's introduction and have students provide evidence from the story to support their answers. Ask, "How is this story about [the big idea]? How does the author explore [the big idea]? Where in the story do you see that?"

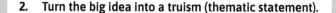

2. **Turn the big idea into a truism (thematic statement).**

   Once you have identified the big ideas, use one of them to create truisms for this story. Here are a few (found in the story) to get you started:

   - *Sometimes what we love can turn into something bigger that we can share with the world.*

   - *Being yourself and following your passions can impact the world around you.*

   Have students write and share their own truisms.

   Ask them to prove their truisms by providing evidence from the text. They might imagine a listener saying, "Oh yeah? How do you know? How is that true in the story?"

Want to Go Deeper?
Try these options.

OPTION 3: READING RESPONSE

Students can compose short or extended responses to demonstrate understanding by answering any of these questions. Look in the appendix to find a list titled "Basic Reading Response Text Structures" and a list of "Useful Essay Question Stems for Nonfiction Texts."

Questions for Reading Response

- Explain why it was unusual for Joan to have a passion for reptiles.

- How did Joan change the habitat for the lizards in the Natural History Museum?

- How did Joan change people's perceptions of the Komodo dragons?

- What surprised people when they saw the Komodo dragons?

- How were Joan and Sumbawa, the Komodo dragon, alike?

OPTION 4: EXTENSION IDEAS

- Dig into the back matter:
  - Use the biography of Joan Procter as a short nonfiction text to read, discuss, create and answer questions, and write.
  - Use the bibliography to jump-start research about this part of history and topic.
- Research the history of another reptile.
  - Create an infographic about that reptile.
  - Create a poem based on your research.
- Use the text structure to write about another person.

Student Samples for
Joan Procter, Dragon Doctor

QUICK WRITE

by Jackson Silva, 4th Grade

If I studied something for a living, it would be to study animals and what they do so I could know what is dangerous and what is not. Then I could help someone who thinks they are in danger, but is actually not.

QUICK WRITE

by Lorelei Mueller, 5th Grade

I would study the human body. Why? Because anatomy is very interesting. Seeing how small cells are. Also, I think the mitochondria is the powerhouse of the cell.

KERNEL ESSAY (USING "A CURIOSITY THAT CHANGED THE WORLD")

by Lorelei Mueller, 5th Grade

Mark Rober was interested in space. At first, he looked at books. Then he helped build the first Mars Rover. Later he started a YouTube channel and made Build Boxes for kids to learn STEM.

KERNEL ESSAY (USING "A CURIOSITY THAT CHANGED THE WORLD")

by Alex Leal, 5th Grade

My little brother was and is obsessed with lacrosse. At first he thought it was dumb, and he didn't want to do it. When he first tried it out, he loved it. He was aggressive and strong. Then it caused him to get more disciplined.

TRUISM

by Jack Biegler, 3rd Grade

Even though something could be rough on the outside, it could be soft on the inside.

CRAFT CHALLENGE (MYTH EXPLOSION)

by Alex Leal, 5th Grade

School is not that hard, as people say. As people say, it's a waste of time. But it actually helps you become smarter. If you fail a class, the teachers didn't fail you. You failed to get help as the teacher tries to teach you. The teachers try to make you learn new things, but it's mostly you who doesn't listen.

READING RESPONSE (USING THE TEXT STRUCTURE "RACE")

by Jack Biegler, 3rd Grade

Q: How did Joan change people's perceptions of the Komodo dragons?

A: Joan changed people's perceptions of dragons by showing people that Komodo dragons are calm and don't go as fast as they thought. In the story, it states how she went into the enclosure and touched Sumbawa when people thought the Komodo dragons were scary. Even though people were scared of him, when Joan went and touched him, people were surprised.

José Feeds the World: How a Famous Chef Feeds Millions of People in Need Around the World

by David Unger and illustrated by Marta Álvarez Miguéns

Summary: Born in Spain, José Andrés learns the value of service, cooking, and creating community—and the power of sharing food—from a young age. As he grows older and becomes a famous chef, he sees the needs and the hunger of those around him, so he gets to work. Through his organization, World Central Kitchen, he has been able to care for and feed thousands who have been in crisis.

Why We Love It: José Andrés is a modern-day superhero, and his story needs to be heard by everyone. So many of our books about people are about people from history, but José Andrés is currently doing this work, and he is making history. We think he deserves a Nobel Prize! Upon hearing about his work, readers will be inspired to get involved, help others, and find out what gifts they have that can change the world.

Topics: food, chefs, cooking, food activism, humanitarianism, disaster relief, natural disasters, Haiti earthquake, Hurricane Maria (Puerto Rico), Hurricane Dorian (Bahamas), Fire Volcano (Guatemala), Navajo Nation, COVID-19 pandemic, war in Ukraine, World Central Kitchen

Big Ideas: community, caring for others, volunteering, finding a need and meeting it, feeding people, acts of service, the power of food to nourish and heal, relief, humanitarian aid, persistence, problem solving, sharing your passion, people in crisis, not hesitating to help

Back Matter:

- José Andrés's recognitions
- Quote by José Andrés
- Glossary

LESSON STEPS:

1 QUICK WRITE.
(CHOOSE ONE):

- Have you ever been through a natural disaster (hurricane, earthquake, blizzard) or a long power outage? What happened? What did it feel like?

- Have you ever done some volunteer work? What did you do?

- What kind of food brings you comfort? Who makes it?

- Has anyone ever helped you in a big way? What did they do?

Write about this for 3 minutes and then set it aside.

2 READ.

Read the picture book *José Feeds the World: How a Famous Chef Feeds Millions of People in Need Around the World* by David Unger and discuss the story. Discuss parts of the story that stick out to you or that you connect with. What writer's craft moves do you notice the author using? Notice the parts of the story.

8 José Feeds the World: How a Famous Chef Feeds Millions of People in Need Around the World
by David Unger and illustrated by Marta Álvarez Miguéns

3 SHARE THE STRUCTURE.

Show the students the structure found in the picture book. Reread the story, looking for chunks together and watching for how the author moves from one part to the other.

A Hero's Journey

How their journey began	What issues they noticed around them	What they wanted instead	What stood in their way and how they responded	What they became

4 INVITATION TO WRITE.

Here are several ways you can get students to write.

- Have students use the text structure to write a kernel essay summary of the story. (Give them between 5 and 10 minutes to do this.)

- Have the students use the text structure to write their own piece in a kernel essay. (Give them between 5 and 10 minutes to do this.)

- See what students come up with. (Give them around 10 minutes.) Here are some possibilities:

  o A page of thoughts in their quick write

  o Examples of the author's craft moves

  o A text structure

Whatever they choose to write, let them know that they can change anything they need to and make it their own.

5 SHARE.

Invite students to try their writing on someone else's ears. This is a crucial step! The sharing is just as important as the writing.

Want to Go Deeper?
Try These Options.

OPTION 1: CRAFT CHALLENGE

- **Anaphork (Anaphora + Pitchfork):** This author uses something we call an anaphork, a rhetorical device that combines anaphora—the repeating of a beginning word or phrase in successive phrases—and a pitchfork. Here's an example from the story:

  *"**By** truck, **by** train, **by** car, **by** van: People are being fed."*

  Look through your piece to see where you can try an anaphork. After you write, try it out on someone's ears to see how it sounds in your writing.

- **Translanguaging:** This author uses another language (Spanish) in the story. Here are a few examples from the story:

  o *"When José was three, he liked helping his parents cook by peeling onions and scrubbing carrots in the **cocina**—the kitchen—after school."*

  o *"When José was fifteen, he moved to Barcelona, Spain, to enter a cooking school to become a **cocinero**—the person who cooks in the **cocina**."*

  Look through your piece to see where you can use another language. After you write, try it out on someone's ears to see how it sounds in your writing.

- **Antithesis:** This author uses a rhetorical device called antithesis. Antithesis is when two contrasting ideas are intentionally put next to each other, usually through parallel structure. Here's an example from the story:

  *"He **saw opportunities** where people **saw problems**."*

  Look through your piece to see where you can use antithesis. After you write, try it out on someone's ears to see how it sounds in your writing.

OPTION 2: ANALYZE

1. **Start with a big idea.**

   - If you want students to find the big ideas themselves, try asking, "What big ideas do you see in this story that tell you what it's really about?"

   - If students need a nudge, try using some of the big ideas from the list in this lesson's introduction and have students provide evidence from the story to support their answers. Ask, "How is this story about [the big idea]? How does the author explore [the big idea]? Where in the story do you see that?"

2. **Turn the big idea into a truism (thematic statement).**

   Once you have identified the big ideas, use one of them to create truisms for this story. Here are a few (found in the story) to get you started:

   - *Food can make people feel better.*

   - Everyone has their own way to help.

   - *No one should ever go hungry.*

   - *Some people see opportunities where others see problems.*

   Have students write and share their own truisms.

   Ask them to prove their truisms by providing evidence from the text. They might imagine a listener saying, "Oh yeah? How do you know? How is that true in the story?"

Want to Go Deeper?
Try these options.

OPTION 3: READING RESPONSE

Students can compose short or extended responses to demonstrate understanding by answering any of these questions. Look in the appendix to find a list titled "Basic Reading Response Text Structures" and a list of "Useful Essay Question Stems for Nonfiction Texts."

Questions for Reading Response

- Explain your opinion on whether José's organization is necessary.

- Explain the importance of volunteering in the story.

- Explain the effect that José's parents' profession (nursing) had on his life.

- What is the reason the author repeated the line, "Food could make people feel better"?

- Explain what the author means by "He realized he needed to find a way to get people who were in trouble to feel their own power."

OPTION 4: EXTENSION IDEAS

- Spend some time learning more about José Andrés:

  o If it is age appropriate, watch the documentary *We Feed People* (about José Andrés; the trailer is available at https://wck.org/wefeedpeople). It is marked for ages 13 and up.

  o Watch the YouTube video "Waffles + Mochi 'Tomato' Full Episode 1: Netflix Jr" (18:15–22:57), available at https://www.youtube.com/watch?v=0GypJISaCS4, to see José Andrés cook and teach about food.

  o Read "Why Aren't We Teaching More Kids to Cook in Schools?" by José Andrés (from his Substack called Longer Tables With José Andrés), available at https://joseandres.substack.com/p/why-arent-we-teaching-more-kids-to.

- Choose another "hero" to research or learn more about World Central Kitchen, humanitarian aid, or natural disasters:

  o Create an infographic about your research.

  o Use the text structure to write about your research.

- Write a letter to José Andrés, the person you researched, or the person you wrote about in your quick write, using the same text structure (or not), to let them know what you admire about them.

- As a class, volunteer in your area.

- If you have one in your area, consider visiting (and possibly volunteering at) a soup kitchen.

Student Samples for *José Feeds the World*

QUICK WRITE

by Douglas Mueller, 4th Grade

A food that brings me comfort is Big Red cake. It is plain vanilla cake with Big Red poured into it and topped with vanilla pudding and Cool Whip. Me and my mom make it together.

QUICK WRITE

by Henry Wommack, 4th Grade

A food that makes me comfortable is Hamburger Helper. It is pasta with ground beef. It is super good, like all my mom's cooking (unless you don't like that type of food).

KERNEL ESSAY RETELL (USING "A HERO'S JOURNEY")

by Henry Wommack, 4th Grade

I got in for four-square and Holden wasn't yelling, "Get Henry out!" like everyone else. He noticed that the ball touched Eason's foot while he tried to get me out, but it bounced off his foot and went out. Holden said Eason was out and he wanted Eason to stop cheating. Holden kept saying Eason was out, but Lukus was saying I was out. Holden became a better friend after that because he stood up for me.

KERNEL ESSAY RETELL (USING "A HERO'S JOURNEY")

by Zayd Ehab Samir Zabaneh, 6th Grade

1. José's journey began where he started cutting onions at three. Then at five, he wanted to become a chef. He wanted to feed people.

2. José noticed people that were not fortunate who needed food. He knew he could help, so he traveled the world.

3. José and WCK realized the people wanted food the way they liked it and they also wanted it quick and easy.

4. Most packets didn't have the right materials to be able to cook, so he tried to start his organization.

5. He made a world global center for food. His business was successful and now he is feeding the people in need.

TRUISM

by Mateo Nelson, 6th Grade

It's important to know that true heroes don't do it for fame or power, but because it is the right thing to do.

TRUISM

by Dixon Weber, 6th Grade

One dream can save millions of lives.

Student Samples for *José Feeds the World*

TRUISM

by Catarina Caruso, 6th Grade

Sometimes it's the little things that count.

READING RESPONSE (USING THE TEXT STRUCTURE "RACE")

by Mateo Nelson, 6th Grade

Q: Explain your opinion on whether José's organization is necessary.

A: José's organization is necessary because the text says, "He helped in Haiti, Puerto Rico, the Abaco Islands, Guatemala, Navajo reserves, California, New York City, and Ukraine." This means that he has helped people all around the world, even when wars and natural disasters were happening around him. He put others before himself even at the cost of his safety.

READING RESPONSE (USING THE TEXT STRUCTURE "BA-DA-BING-ING THE EVIDENCE")

by Catarina Caruso, 6th Grade

Q: Explain the effect that José's parents' profession (nursing) had on his life.

A: Nurses work a lot, and I know how hard it can be to provide for your family when you are working hard to keep them under a roof. This is when José had to step up and help. Ever since then, he has learned that doing small things are big. Now he helps people all over the world.

At the beginning of the book, the narrator is talking about how José saw doctors helping people at his parents' job. This helped him see what big and little things can impact someone's life just by helping. This made him want to start.

Seeing his parents help means that he will help. This impacted his life forever.

READING RESPONSE (USING THE TEXT STRUCTURE "RACE")

by George Ahl, 3rd Grade

Q: Explain your opinion on whether José's organization is necessary.

A: I think José's organization is necessary because he feeds people around the world and it made him happy, too. In the book, it states that he was, "Cooking for people who need help [and it] filled his heart with joy." This means that José loves cooking because it helps people and he grew up cooking and helping in his childhood.

Magic Ramen: The Story of Momofuku Ando

by Andrea Wang and illustrated by Kana Urbanowicz

9

Summary: Momofuku Ando looked around after World War II and saw long lines of hungry people waiting for a little bit of food. This image never left his mind as he sought a solution—one that would be fast, affordable, and available to everyone. This is the story of how he created instant ramen to meet the needs he saw around him.

Why We Love It: Most of us have had instant ramen. Many of us may have even needed it to get through college or a tough time. But have you ever thought about its invention? The story behind it has a great heart, and we know our students will enjoy learning about it just as much as we did.

Topics: ramen, inventions, inventors, Japan, poverty, post–World War II, Japanese food, experiments, nutrition, cooking, processes

Big Ideas: innovation, feeding the hungry, meeting the needs of others, observation, experimentation, trial and error, perseverance, serving others, helping, balance, food insecurity

Back Matter:

- Short author's note
- Pronunciation guide
- Afterword

LESSON STEPS:

1 QUICK WRITE.
(CHOOSE ONE):

- What are some useful inventions that already exist?
- Do you know the story of how something was invented?
- What is something you think the world needs that doesn't already exist (an invention)?
- If you could invent something to make a process go faster and maybe cheaper, what would it be?

Write about this for 3 minutes and then set it aside.

2 READ.

Read the picture book *Magic Ramen: The Story of Momofuku Ando* by Andrea Wang and discuss the story. Discuss parts of the story that stick out to you or that you connect with. What writer's craft moves do you notice the author using? Notice the parts of the story.

# 9 Magic Ramen: The Story of Momofuku Ando
by Andrea Wang and illustrated by Kana Urbanowicz

3 SHARE THE STRUCTURE.

Show the students the structure found in the picture book. Reread the story, looking for chunks together and watching for how the author moves from one part to the other.

Cooking Up a New Idea

The inventor: Who the inventor was	The catalyst: What sparked the idea	The vision: What the inventor tried (that didn't work)	The aha moment: What the inventor tried (that *did* work)	The impact: How the invention was received

4 INVITATION TO WRITE.

Here are several ways you can get students to write.

- Have students use the text structure to write a kernel essay summary of the story. (Give them between 5 and 10 minutes to do this.)

- Have the students use the text structure to write their own piece in a kernel essay. (Give them between 5 and 10 minutes to do this.)

- See what students come up with. (Give them around 10 minutes.) Here are some possibilities:
  - A page of thoughts in their quick write
  - Examples of the author's craft moves
  - A text structure

Whatever they choose to write, let them know that they can change anything they need to and make it their own.

5 SHARE.

Invite students to try their writing on someone else's ears. This is a crucial step! The sharing is just as important as the writing.

Want to Go Deeper?
Try These Options.

OPTION 1: CRAFT CHALLENGE

- **Translanguaging:** This author uses another language (Japanese) in the story. Here are a few examples from the story:
  - *"'Yatta!' he cried. 'That's it!'"*
  - *"'Maho no ramen!' . . . 'Magic ramen!'"*

  Look through your piece to see where you can use another language. After you write, try it out on someone's ears to see how it sounds in your writing.

- **Anaphork (Anaphora + Pitchfork):** This author uses the rhetorical device anaphora and adds a pitchfork. In other words, she repeats a word or phrase at the beginning of a sentence (anaphora) and does this three times (like a pitchfork). Kayla's students named this an "anaphork." Authors and speakers do this to create rhythm, to stir emotion, or to emphasize or bring focus to something. Here's an example from the story:

  "**No more** *waiting in line in the cold.* **No more** *high prices.* **No more** *empty stomachs."*

  Look through your piece to see where you can use an anaphork. After you write, try it out on someone's ears to see how it sounds in your writing.

- **When–What Pattern:** This author uses what we like to call a when–what pattern, in which she first tells when something happened and then tells what happened. Here's an example from the story:

  "Day after day, Ando experimented.

  Night after night, he failed.

  Month after month, he kept trying.

  Nothing worked."

  Here's the pattern that the author repeats: _____ after _____, noun/pronoun + verb. Look through your piece to see where you can use a when–what pattern. After you write, try it out on someone's ears to see how it sounds in your writing.

OPTION 2: ANALYZE

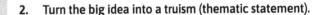

1. **Start with a big idea.**

   - If you want students to find the big ideas themselves, try asking, "What big ideas do you see in this story that tell you what it's really about?"

   - If students need a nudge, try using some of the big ideas from the list in this lesson's introduction and have students provide evidence from the story to support their answers. Ask, "How is this story about [the big idea]? How does the author explore [the big idea]? Where in the story do you see that?"

2. **Turn the big idea into a truism (thematic statement).**

   Once you have identified the big ideas, use one of them to create truisms for this story. Here are a few (found in the story) to get you started:

   - *"The world is peaceful only when everyone has enough to eat."*

   - *Some solutions take time and lots of trial and error.*

   Have students write and share their own truisms.

   Ask them to prove their truisms by providing evidence from the text. They might imagine a listener saying, "Oh yeah? How do you know? How is that true in the story?"

Want to Go Deeper?
Try these options.

OPTION 3: READING RESPONSE

Students can compose short or extended responses to demonstrate understanding by answering any of these questions. Look in the appendix to find a list titled "Basic Reading Response Text Structures" and a list of "Useful Essay Question Stems for Nonfiction Texts."

Questions for Reading Response

- Explain why Ando wanted to create instant ramen.
- Explain how Ando shows determination throughout the story.
- What obstacles did Ando face as he worked to create his ramen?
- Explain why the setting (time and place) is important to this story.
- Explain whether the instant ramen was a good solution for the long lines of hungry people.

OPTION 4: EXTENSION IDEAS

- Dig into the back matter:
  - Use the afterword as a short text to read, discuss, create and answer questions, and write.
- Consider showing videos about how ramen is made traditionally (the long way).
- Consider making instant ramen together as a class.
- Research the history of another inventor and/or invention.
  - Use the text structure "Cooking Up a New Idea" to write about the research.
  - Create an infographic about the topic.
  - Create a poem based on your research.

Student Samples for
Magic Ramen

QUICK WRITE

by **Kyron McWilliams, 3rd Grade**

The world needs shoes that when you have grown out of them, you just have to click a button and change the shoe size and it only costs 50 dollars.

QUICK WRITE

by **Helen Boies, 4th Grade**

Some useful inventions that exist are pencils, calendars, and water bottles. Though they are very different, they all help us. Pencils help us write important information, and calendars tell us what year, month, and day it is. Water bottles hold a large or small amount of water, and they help us drink.

KERNEL ESSAY RETELL (USING "COOKING UP A NEW IDEA")

by **Jordyn Gamez, 3rd Grade**

The inventor of ramen was Momofuku Ando. He loved feeding the homeless, so he invented ramen so that they had food to eat. He tried to make the noodles out of flour, but it did not work, so he kept trying. His wife was cooking, and he said, "Aha!" He knew what he had to do. He put oil in a pot. Today, people like ramen and it is hard not to like it because it is so fast to make.

CRAFT CHALLENGE (ANAPHORK)

by **Azalea Andrade, 3rd Grade**

More trees. More air. More life.

CRAFT CHALLENGE (ANAPHORK)

by **Skyler Richardson, 3rd Grade**

One last time, I see home. One last time, I see Springfield. One last time, I see Mary Todd Lincoln. (from Abraham Lincoln's perspective)

CRAFT CHALLENGE (ANAPHORK)

by **Helen Boies, 4th Grade**

Go change the world. Go change lives. Go live your dreams.

CRAFT CHALLENGE (WHEN-WHAT PATTERN)

by **Addy Eichholtz, 3rd Grade**

Drama after drama, parents watched. Horror after horror, they got terrified. Comedy after comedy, they laugh. Movie night is the best!

CRAFT CHALLENGE (WHEN-WHAT PATTERN)

by **Hailey Cole, 5th Grade**

Day after day, I read. Night after night, I wrote. Month after month, I kept working. I finished.

Student Samples for *Magic Ramen*

READING RESPONSE (USING THE TEXT STRUCTURE "RACE")

by Dixon Weber, 6th Grade

Q: Explain why Ando wanted to create instant ramen.

A: Ando wanted to create instant ramen because he saw a long line of people waiting to get a single bowl and thought that he could do better. In the book, it says that he "could not forget the hungry people," so he started cooking. This means that he could not ignore the struggles so he started preparing to help.

Martin & Anne: The Kindred Spirits of Dr. Martin Luther King, Jr. and Anne Frank

by Nancy Churnin and illustrated by Yevgenia Nayberg

Summary: *Martin & Anne* tells the story of Dr. Martin Luther King Jr. and Anne Frank—born in different countries, but in the same year. At first glance, their lives seem completely different, but they are actually pretty similar.

Why We Love It: Dr. Martin Luther King Jr. and Anne Frank are such well-known figures, but the pairing of their stories in this book is eye-opening. The parallel structure highlights the theme of using one's voice in the face of injustice and brings new insights into two important people whose lives were cut short but had a long-lasting impact on so many.

Topics: Dr. Martin Luther King Jr., Anne Frank, World War II, Holocaust, Hitler, Jews, Jews in hiding, civil rights movement, racism, history, historical figures, segregation, Rosa Parks, the "I Have a Dream" speech, Gandhi, nonviolent protest, historically Black colleges and universities (HBCUs)

Big Ideas: kindness, equality, the power of words, the power of writing, inequality, prejudice, anti-Semitism, mistreatment, hate (the effects of), human rights, inspiring others, speaking out against hate, racism, genocide, using one's voice in the face of injustice, character

Back Matter:

- Timeline (1929–1986)
- Selected bibliography

LESSON STEPS:

1 QUICK WRITE.
(CHOOSE ONE):

- Who is someone that is famous for something they said?

- Who is someone you think has had a big impact on the world? What do you know about that person? How have they made positive changes in the world?

Write about this for 3 minutes and then set it aside.

2 READ.

Read the picture book *Martin & Anne: The Kindred Spirits of Dr. Martin Luther King, Jr. and Anne Frank* by Nancy Churnin and discuss the story. Discuss parts of the story that stick out to you or that you connect with. What writer's craft moves do you notice the author using? Notice the parts of the story.

Martin & Anne: The Kindred Spirits of Dr. Martin Luther King, Jr. and Anne Frank

by Nancy Churnin and illustrated by Yevgenia Nayberg

3 SHARE THE STRUCTURE.

Show the students the structure found in the picture book. Reread the story, looking for chunks together and watching for how the author moves from one part to the other.

A Powerful Life

Where and when the person was born	How the person was different from other people	What the person did that made a difference then	Challenges the person faced	What else the person did that made a difference (even now)

4 INVITATION TO WRITE.

Here are several ways you can get students to write.

- Have students use the text structure to write a kernel essay summary of the story. (Give them between 5 and 10 minutes to do this.)

- Have the students use the text structure to write their own piece in a kernel essay. (Give them between 5 and 10 minutes to do this.)

- See what students come up with. (Give them around 10 minutes.) Here are some possibilities:

  o A page of thoughts in their quick write

  o Examples of the author's craft moves

  o A text structure

Whatever they choose to write, let them know that they can change anything they need to and make it their own.

5 SHARE.

Invite students to try their writing on someone else's ears. This is a crucial step! The sharing is just as important as the writing.

Want to Go Deeper?
Try These Options.

10

OPTION 1: CRAFT CHALLENGE

- **Different–Different–Alike Pattern:** This author uses what we like to call a different-different-alike sentence pattern. Here is an example from the story:

  "They never met. They didn't speak the same language. But their hearts beat with the same hope."

  Here's the pattern: They didn't _____ [how they were different]. They didn't _____ [how they were different]. But they _____ [how they were the same].

  Look through your piece to see where you can use a different-different-alike sentence pattern. After you write, try it out on someone's ears to see how it sounds in your writing.

OPTION 2: ANALYZE

1. **Start with a big idea.**

   - If you want students to find the big ideas themselves, try asking, "What big ideas do you see in this story that tell you what it's really about?"

   - If students need a nudge, try using some of the big ideas from the list in this lesson's introduction and have students provide evidence from the story to support their answers. Ask, "How is this story about [the big idea]? How does the author explore [the big idea]? Where in the story do you see that?"

2. **Turn the big idea into a truism (thematic statement).**

   Once you have identified the big ideas, use one of them to create truisms for this story. Here are a few (found in the story) to get you started:

   - *"Light can brighten the deepest darkness."*
   - *"Kindness can heal the world."*
   - *"Love is stronger than hate."*
   - *Our words have power.*

   Have students write and share their own truisms.

   Ask them to prove their truisms by providing evidence from the text. They might imagine a listener saying, "Oh yeah? How do you know? How is that true in the story?"

Want to Go Deeper?
Try these options.

OPTION 3: READING RESPONSE

Students can compose short or extended responses to demonstrate understanding by answering any of these questions. Look in the appendix to find a list titled "Basic Reading Response Text Structures" and a list of "Useful Essay Question Stems for Nonfiction Texts."

Questions for Reading Response

- Explain why the author chose to put these two stories together.

- What is one word you would use to describe Martin?

- What is one word you would use to describe Anne?

- How are Martin and Anne alike/different?

- How do both stories convey the same message that words have power?

- What is a conflict that both characters faced?

OPTION 4: EXTENSION IDEAS

- Dig into the back matter:
  - Use the timeline as a short text to read, discuss, create and answer questions, and write.
- Consider showing videos about Martin and Anne's lives.
  - Research other unlikely pairs from history whose stories need to be told and use the text structure "A Powerful Life" to write about the research. Try using "famous people born at the same time" as a search term.
- Research the history of other world-changers.
  - Use the text structure "A Powerful Life" to write about the research.
  - Create a timeline about that person's life.
  - Create an infographic about the topic.
  - Create a poem based on your research.

Student Samples for
Martin & Anne

QUICK WRITE

by Zachary Oblitas, 9th Grade

Martin Luther King, Jr. is a very important figure in American history due to his contribution to desegregation and basic civil rights for the Black population in the US, and for his inspirational speech, "I Have a Dream."

CRAFT CHALLENGE (DIFFERENT-DIFFERENT-ALIKE PATTERN)

by Catherine Millsap, 4th Grade

They didn't know each other. They didn't go to the same shelter. But they both loved animals.

CRAFT CHALLENGE (DIFFERENT-DIFFERENT-ALIKE PATTERN)

by Zachary Oblitas, 9th Grade

Both countries had different goals. They both had different people. But they shared the same enemy.

KERNEL ESSAY (USING "A POWERFUL LIFE")

by Catherine Millsap, 4th Grade

My friend Jack was born in 2013 in Texas. Jack is different than other people because I can be myself around him. Jack has helped me chill and have more fun. He can never tell when I lie and

that's a problem. Jack can change my mood in a second.

KERNEL ESSAY (USING "A POWERFUL LIFE")

by Jackson Guenther, 5th Grade

Abraham Lincoln was born in the 19th century in America. He saw that slavery was dirty and strived against it. He led the union in the civil war to abolish slavery and free the people of his country. He faced many hard battles in the south for Robert E. Lee, a formidable general. But Lincoln pushed through. His actions helped make this country into what it is today.

TRUISM

by John Kothmann, 5th Grade

Just because a group of people look or act different, doesn't mean they should be hated or treated differently.

READING RESPONSE (USING THE TEXT STRUCTURE "RACE")

by John Kothmann, 5th Grade

Q: What is a conflict that both characters faced?

A: The conflict that both characters faced was that both had evil in their countries that discriminated against them because they were viewed as less

important. In the book, it states, "Martin couldn't go to school with his best friend," and, "Anne's school closed its doors to her. Suddenly, her friends didn't want to play with her anymore." This means that the hatred of Adolf Hitler and racism spread, affected everyone and it turned friends against each other.

Mr. Crum's Potato Predicament

by Anne Renaud and illustrated by Felicita Sala

Summary: Restaurant owner and chef George Crum was known for his delicious cooking. One day, a picky customer came in wanting only potatoes for a meal. Each dish that Crum made him was sent back until George jokingly sliced the potato ultra-thin and smothered it in salt. The finicky guest loved it, and the potato chip became an instant hit.

Why We Love It: We love this creative take on George Crum's story. Dripping with strong diction, alliteration, and craft, it makes a great read-aloud. The back matter is also a useful informational text to learn more about George Crum and the history of the potato chip.

Topics: food, potatoes, potato chips, cooking, restaurants, inventions, inventors, African American inventors, Native American inventors, George "Crum" Speck

Big Ideas: trial and error, creating something new, persistence, creativity, unexpected discoveries, pushing through setbacks, failure leads to success

Back Matter:

- Author's note

- Author's sources

LESSON STEPS:

1 QUICK WRITE.
(CHOOSE ONE):

- Can you imagine a world without potato chips? What would it be like?

- What is your favorite kind (and flavor) of chip? Describe it. Why do you like it?

- Have you ever cooked something with your family or friends? What did you make? Describe the experience.

- Do you know the story of how something was invented?

- What is something you think the world needs that doesn't already exist (an invention)?

Write about this for 3 minutes and then set it aside.

2 READ.

Read the picture book *Mr. Crum's Potato Predicament* by Anne Renaud and discuss the story. Discuss parts of the story that stick out to you or that you connect with. What writer's craft moves do you notice the author using? Notice the parts of the story.

Mr. Crum's Potato Predicament
by Anne Renaud and illustrated by Felicita Sala

3 SHARE THE STRUCTURE.

Show the students the structure found in the picture book. Reread the story, looking for chunks together and watching for how the author moves from one part to the other.

Cooking Up a New Idea

The inventor: Who the inventor was	The catalyst: What sparked the idea	The vision: What the inventor tried (that didn't work)	The aha moment: What the inventor tried (that *did* work)	The impact: How the invention was received

4 INVITATION TO WRITE.

Here are several ways you can get students to write.

- Have students use the text structure to write a kernel essay summary of the story. (Give them between 5 and 10 minutes to do this.)

- Have the students use the text structure to write their own piece in a kernel essay. (Give them between 5 and 10 minutes to do this.)

- See what students come up with. (Give them around 10 minutes.) Here are some possibilities:
  - A page of thoughts in their quick write
  - Examples of the author's craft moves
  - A text structure

Whatever they choose to write, let them know that they can change anything they need to and make it their own.

5 SHARE.

Invite students to try their writing on someone else's ears. This is a crucial step! The sharing is just as important as the writing.

Want to Go Deeper?
Try These Options.

OPTION 1: CRAFT CHALLENGE

- **Alliterative Pitchfork:** This author uses an alliterative pitchfork to pitchfork some strong verbs. Alliteration is the repetition of the beginning sounds of words that are near each other. A pitchfork is a sentence (or series of sentences) that takes one thing and branches it off into three or more. Here are some examples from the story:

    *"He **fricasséed** and **flambéed**, **boiled** and **braised**, **poached** and **puréed**."*

    *"He made **sorbets** and **soufflés**, **stews** and **succotashes**, ragouts and goulashes."*

    Look through your piece to see where you can use an alliterative pitchfork. After you write, try it out on someone's ears to see how it sounds in your writing.

- **Polysyndeton:** This author uses a rhetorical device called polysyndeton, which is the repeated use of coordinating conjunctions (instead of commas) to connect items. Here are some examples from the story:

    *"He fricasséed **and** flambéed, boiled **and** braised, poached **and** puréed."*

    *"He made sorbets **and** soufflés, stews **and** succotashes, ragouts **and** goulashes."*

    Look through your piece to see where you can use polysyndeton. After you write, try it out on someone's ears to see how it sounds in your writing.

- **Anaphork (Anaphora + Pitchfork):** This author uses something we call an anaphork, a rhetorical device that combines anaphora—the repeating of a beginning word or phrase in successive phrases—and a pitchfork. Here's an example from the story (it even uses alliteration!):

    *"Everyone loves my spuds. **They are** scrumptious. **They are** succulent. **They are** sublime."*

    Look through your piece to see where you can try an anaphork. After you write, try it out on someone's ears to see how it sounds in your writing.

OPTION 2: ANALYZE

1. **Start with a big idea.**

   - If you want students to find the big ideas themselves, try asking, "What big ideas do you see in this story that tell you what it's really about?"

   - If students need a nudge, try using some of the big ideas from the list in this lesson's introduction and have students provide evidence from the story to support their answers. Ask, "How is this story about [the big idea]? How does the author explore [the big idea]? Where in the story do you see that?"

2. **Turn the big idea into a truism (thematic statement).**

   Once you have identified the big ideas, use one of them to create truisms for this story. Here are a few (found in the story) to get you started:

   - *Sometimes when you're frustrated, it can turn into something delightful.*

   - *Persistence, creativity, and a sense of humor are the recipe for success.*

   Have students write and share their own truisms.

   Ask them to prove their truisms by providing evidence from the text. They might imagine a listener saying, "Oh yeah? How do you know? How is that true in the story?"

Want to Go Deeper?
Try these options.

OPTION 3: READING RESPONSE

Students can compose short or extended responses to demonstrate understanding by answering any of these questions. Look in the appendix to find a list titled "Basic Reading Response Text Structures" and a list of "Useful Essay Question Stems for Nonfiction Texts."

Questions for Reading Response

- What happened in this story?

- Explain how George showed persistence in the story.

- Explain why the author included the line, "Now George was known to his customers to be a bit of a prankster."

- Explain the effect the unsatisfied customer had on George's success.

- Explain how George's chips became so popular.

OPTION 4: EXTENSION IDEAS

- Dig into the back matter:
  - Use the author's note as a short nonfiction text to read, discuss, create and answer questions, and write.
  - Use the author's sources to conduct further research.
- Research more about potato chips, snack foods, the origin of certain foods, inventors, and inventions.
  - Create an infographic about your research.
  - Create a poem based on your research.
  - Use the "Cooking Up a New Idea" text structure to write about your research.
- Make (or just eat!) potato chips as a class.
- Try different ways to cook potatoes as a class.
- If you live near one, take a field trip to a potato chip factory.
- Watch the YouTube video "George 'Crum' Speck: The Inventor of Potato Chips," available at https://www.youtube.com/watch?v=J4fXYk5hlUU. (This video suggests that George Crum's sister was the actual inventor of the potato chip. This would be a great source for discussion, research, and argument writing.)
- Watch the YouTube video "How It's Made—Potato Chips," available at https://www.youtube.com/watch?v=eXI-hQ9UMGU.
- Graph and chart different kinds of potato chips by flavor, favorite kind, price, and so on.
- Do a living museum presentation. Assign each student a different person from history to research, study, and impersonate (dress like them, talk like them, respond to questions about them).

QUICK WRITE

by Kinsey Coronado, 4th Grade

One time my sister, Oma, and I got the chance to bake some homemade cinnamon rolls. Now this was very fun. We got to mix all kinds of things and sometimes even taste test. But there was a part I didn't like which was how long we had to wait, and then let sit. But altogether, by the end, the result was amazing and yummy. I really like how cinnamony it was and how the icing was so sweet, but not too sweet, yet it was the perfect amount. So that is definitely my favorite baking experience.

QUICK WRITE

by Lucy Padilla, 4th Grade

One time I was cooking some cake with my mom in the kitchen. It was chocolate cake. First, we put in the flour, then the two large eggs. After I put all the ingredients in, my mom set the whisk thing to five so everything—all the flour—flew into my face. After we cleaned, we had to start all over again. We punched the dough and punched, then yummy chocolate cake!

QUICK WRITE

by Layla Rubal, 4th Grade

The one thing I cooked was eggs and rice. You have to be careful to cook because you don't want to burn yourself. You have to follow the steps on the box for rice, so you don't do something wrong. And be careful with the eggs, too. You have to wash your hands when you break an egg to bake or cook.

QUICK WRITE

by Kavya Kannan, 9th Grade

Personally, I think Sun Chips Garden Salsa are the best kind of chips to exist. They are whole wheat, baked, and they taste so good! They are sweet, a little spicy, and have a little tomato tanginess to them. They go well with any dip: guac, salsa, cheese, or just the chips by themselves. You cannot go wrong when it is Sun Chips. They are just so good.

KERNEL ESSAY RETELL (USING "COOKING UP A NEW IDEA")

by Hattie Shipp, 3rd Grade

The person was Mr. Crum. When a customer returned his plate, the potatoes got skinny and hard. He tried to make the potatoes even better, but it did not work. It finally worked when he sent the plate back to the table and the person liked it. Word spread and people from far, far away enjoyed his potato chips.

KERNEL ESSAY RETELL (USING "COOKING UP A NEW IDEA")

by Camilynn Schneider, 4th Grade

A customer did not like his food, so he had to cut it thinner every time. He tried to cut it thinner, but it just would not work.

Then he cut it as thin as paper. He was just trying to make a customer happy when he accidently made potato chips.

KERNEL ESSAY (USING "COOKING UP A NEW IDEA")

by Thaila Gonzales, 4th Grade
Ruth Wakefield wanted to make chocolate cookies. She wanted the chocolate to melt. Instead, it stayed in little chunks of chocolate. It made delicious tasting cookies for everyone to enjoy.

TRUISM

by Hattie Shipp, 3rd Grade
If you keep trying, you will finally get it.

TRUISM

by Anthony Cardamone, 6th Grade
The more you try, the better you get.

CRAFT CHALLENGE (ALLITERATIVE PITCHFORK)

by Helen Boies, 4th Grade
She jumped and jogged, sprinted and skipped, ran and rode.

CRAFT CHALLENGE (ALLITERATIVE PITCHFORK)

by Chevelle White-Hill, 6th Grade
Mrs. Wakefield watched as her assistant gave Mr. Straindomer his second plate of chocolate chip cookies. When he was done, he let out a sigh, then shouted at Mrs. Wakefield, "What an astonishing, astounding, awe-inspiring, unbelievable, unusual batch of cookies you made!"

CRAFT CHALLENGE (POLYSYNDETON)

by Gracie Garcia, 4th Grade
George Crum sliced and diced, cracked and coiled, salted and served.

READING RESPONSE (USING THE TEXT STRUCTURE "RACE")

by Anthony Cardamone, 6th Grade
Q: Explain the effect the unsatisfied customer had on George's success.

A: The unsatisfied customer had an effect on George's success. When Filbert kept making George make new potato dishes, George eventually made thin-crispy-potatoes which led to the invention of the potato chips. "Delectable and delicious!" declared George after he, too, ate a few. "I'll call them Crum's Crisp Crispies and put a plateful on every table." This means that George had the idea of making Filbert's requests into his own food.

One Plastic Bag: Isatou Ceesay and the Recycling Women of the Gambia
by Miranda Paul and illustrated by Elizabeth Zunon

Summary: This is the true story of Isatou Ceesay and how she turned the trash in her village into something that helped many thrive—including the animals who were being hurt from ingesting the plastic waste.

Why We Love It: We love purses. We hate garbage. We love women who turn garbage into purses. We love the power and agency in this story and how it gives us hope.

Topics: Gambia, West Africa, women creators, women entrepreneurs, plastic, trash, recycling, reusing, plastic bags, litter, harm to animals, the dangers of litter

Big Ideas: seeing a need and meeting it, caring for one's community, ingenuity, community, creativity, working together, resourcefulness, entrepreneurship, taking action as a group

Back Matter:

- Author's note
- Wolof glossary and pronunciation guide
- Timeline
- "For Further Reading"

LESSON STEPS:

1 QUICK WRITE.
(CHOOSE ONE):

- Did you ever notice a problem and you ignored it, but it grew and grew until you had to do something? What was it?

- What are some problems (maybe make a list) that need a solution? What ideas do you have to fix or change one of them?

- Do you ever think about what happens to trash when we throw it out? What can you imagine might be the best thing to happen to it?

Write about this for 3 minutes and then set it aside.

2 READ.

Read the picture book *One Plastic Bag: Isatou Ceesay and the Recycling Women of the Gambia* by Miranda Paul and discuss the story. Discuss parts of the story that stick out to you or that you connect with. What writer's craft moves do you notice the author using? Notice the parts of the story.

12 One Plastic Bag: Isatou Ceesay and the Recycling Women of the Gambia

by Miranda Paul and illustrated by Elizabeth Zunon

3 SHARE THE STRUCTURE.

Show the students the structure found in the picture book. Reread the story, looking for chunks together and watching for how the author moves from one part to the other.

A Growing Problem and a Solution

Where _____ was when they first noticed the problem	How _____ saw the problem growing bigger	How things got worse	How a solution was born	How the solution changed things (or what they hoped)

4 INVITATION TO WRITE.

Here are several ways you can get students to write.

- Have students use the text structure to write a kernel essay summary of the story. (Give them between 5 and 10 minutes to do this.)

- Have the students use the text structure to write their own piece in a kernel essay. (Give them between 5 and 10 minutes to do this.)

- See what students come up with. (Give them around 10 minutes.) Here are some possibilities:

  o A page of thoughts in their quick write

  o Examples of the author's craft moves

  o A text structure

Whatever they choose to write, let them know that they can change anything they need to and make it their own.

5 SHARE.

Invite students to try their writing on someone else's ears. This is a crucial step! The sharing is just as important as the writing.

Want to Go Deeper?
Try These Options.

OPTION 1: CRAFT CHALLENGE

- **Personification:** This author uses personification, which is giving nonhuman objects human capabilities. Here is an example from the story:

   *"She barely notices the ugliness growing around her . . . **until the ugliness finds its way to her.**"*

   Look through your piece to see where you can use personification. After you write, try it out on someone's ears to see how it sounds in your writing.

- **Translanguaging:** This author uses another language (Wolof) in the story. Here are a few examples from the story:

   o   *"'Can you help me?'*

   'Waaw—yes.' Her sister shows Isatou the stiches, then hands her a metal tool. Isatou's fingers busy themselves . . . in . . . out . . . around.

   'Jerejef—thank you.'"

   Look through your piece to see where you can use another language. After you write, try it out on someone's ears to see how it sounds in your writing.

- **Beg-to-Differ Sentence Pattern:** This author uses a beg-to-differ sentence pattern. Here is the example from the story:

   *"**Some people** in the village laugh at us. **Others** call us 'dirty.' **But I** believe what we are doing is good."*

   Look through your piece to see where you can use this sentence pattern: Some people _____. Others _____. But I _____. After you write, try it out on someone's ears to see how it sounds in your writing.

OPTION 2: ANALYZE

1.   **Start with a big idea.**

   - If you want students to find the big ideas themselves, try asking, "What big ideas do you see in this story that tell you what it's really about?"

   - If students need a nudge, try using some of the big ideas from the list in this lesson's introduction and have students provide evidence from the story to support their answers. Ask, "How is this story about [the big idea]? How does the author explore [the big idea]? Where in the story do you see that?"

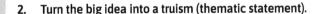

2.   **Turn the big idea into a truism (thematic statement).**

   Once you have identified the big ideas, use one of them to create truisms for this story. Here are a few (found in the story) to get you started:

   - *When we work together, we all benefit.*

   - *Big changes start with small steps.*

   - *Some problems grow until they can't be ignored.*

   - *People have the power to both ruin and heal the earth.*

   Have students write and share their own truisms.

   Ask them to prove their truisms by providing evidence from the text. They might imagine a listener saying, "Oh yeah? How do you know? How is that true in the story?"

Want to Go Deeper?
Try these options.

OPTION 3: READING RESPONSE

Students can compose short or extended responses to demonstrate understanding by answering any of these questions. Look in the appendix to find a list titled "Basic Reading Response Text Structures" and a list of "Useful Essay Question Stems for Nonfiction Texts."

Questions for Reading Response

- Explain how Isatou contributed to her community.
- Explain your opinion about why people should or should not reuse trash.
- Explain who benefitted from the ladies' handmade bags.
- How does the author show Isatou's ingenuity?
- What happens in the story? (Retell the story.)

OPTION 4: EXTENSION IDEAS

- Dig into the back matter:
  - Use the author's note as a short nonfiction text to read, discuss, create and answer questions, and write.
  - Use the "For Further Reading" section to jump-start further research.
- Do an unconventional materials challenge: What useful thing can you make out of trash? Plan, create, write, and speak about it. It could be a classroom or a schoolwide challenge. Use it to bring awareness to the need to reduce waste and recycle properly.
- Put on a fashion show of trash: Bring in a variety of trash items and challenge groups of students to create clothing out of the materials to model in a fashion show. Consider inviting spectators to watch. Consider having students include some of their research about recycling and conservation in the show.
- Watch the YouTube video "How to Recycle Plastic Bags Into Purses: Isatou Ceesay—Njau, Gambia," available at https://www.youtube.com/watch?app=desktop&v=r354rs7aYzI.
- Research recycling, creating things out of trash, and/or the effects of plastic on the earth.
  - Create an infographic about that research.
  - Create a poem based on your research.

Student Samples for
One Plastic Bag

QUICK WRITE

by Zayla O'Dell, 4th Grade

I noticed a problem. My friend was being really rude to me so my friends and my friend that was being rude made my other friend cry. I didn't do anything, and the problem got bigger.

QUICK WRITE

by Bryanna Rieken, 4th Grade

There was a time when we started using too much plastic or harmful products. This turned into harming animals or even killing them, and in a lot of places people continue these bad habits, and that is just making the problem worse, so I think we should start picking up the trash, or even making things out of these harmful products and plastic. We should make something other than plastic that is not very harmful because we should always protect animals. It can also eventually affect us, too. So, remember to always protect animals and stop using too many harmful things.

QUICK WRITE

by Ali Anne Ryan, 5th Grade

I think about what will happen to our ecosystem and world if this continues. Yes, people talk about it, but we need to do something. Our beaches are awesome and from a beach girl, I want to help. Just two weeks ago, there was a huge piece of plastic in the water at the beach. People barely noticed it, but I did. It was horrible and we need to do something.

QUICK WRITE

by Trevor Baptist, 9th Grade

Sometimes when I notice I need to clean my room, I ignore it. I say, "I will do it later," or, "It's not that messy." Then I wait and wait until I notice that I can barely walk without stepping on something. I realize I now have to clean my whole room, which takes a lot longer than if I had just put stuff away, instead of leaving it out.

KERNEL ESSAY RETELL (USING "A GROWING PROBLEM AND A SOLUTION")

by Harper Kovarik, 4th Grade

In Gambia, Isatou broke her basket and found a plastic bag. She brought it to her village where everyone was using plastic. The plastic was thrown onto the ground and started to pile up. The goats would jump into the pile of plastic and ingest the garbage. More goats ate the plastic and died. So, Isatou started to gather friends to recycle the plastic and they crocheted the plastic trash into purses and sold them. When they got enough money to buy more goats, not only did they get more goats, but they got rid of the plastic.

Student Samples for
One Plastic Bag

KERNEL ESSAY (USING "A GROWING PROBLEM AND A SOLUTION")

by Filip Jovanović, 5th Grade

Once there was a girl named Lana. She loved the beach, but sometimes there was trash. As she got older, she saw more trash fill up to the point that she couldn't swim. Two years later, she saw a dead turtle and that stuck with her. As she thought, she got an idea. She would gather an organization to help her clean the ocean. It took some time, but eventually she got the beach clean and started cleaning more beaches.

TRUISM

by Ford Selig, 3rd Grade

It's important not to litter and to throw away trash when you see it.

CRAFT CHALLENGE (PERSONIFICATION)

by Lillian LaBryer, 5th Grade

The trash's ugliness goes unnoticed, until it grows too big to ignore.

CRAFT CHALLENGE (BEG-TO-DIFFER SENTENCE PATTERN)

by Zayla O'Dell, 4th Grade

Some people bully me. **Others** call me names. **But I** know I have true friends.

CRAFT CHALLENGE (BEG-TO-DIFFER SENTENCE PATTERN)

by Lillian LaBryer, 5th Grade

Some people made fun of them. **Others** were grossed out. **But Lily** knew that eventually she would make a difference, one step at a time.

CRAFT CHALLENGE (BEG-TO-DIFFER SENTENCE PATTERN)

by Lillian LaBryer, 5th Grade

Some people think that a kid can't make a difference. **Others** know even one impact helps. **But I** think we can all make change.

CRAFT CHALLENGE (BEG-TO-DIFFER SENTENCE PATTERN)

by Kartik Sapre, 9th Grade

Some people just throw it out. **Others** don't care. **But I** want to give it a new purpose.

READING RESPONSE (USING THE TEXT STRUCTURE "RACE")

by Luke Bright, 7th Grade

Q: Why are the goats important in the story?

A: I think that the goats were important because they were the call to action, making Isatou have the idea to make purses out of plastic. "Isatou must be

strong and do something. But what?" This proves that she felt the call to do something about the problem.

READING RESPONSE (USING THE TEXT STRUCTURE "RACE")

by **Ford Selig, 3rd Grade**

Q: Explain your opinion about why people should or should not reuse trash.

A: I think people should reuse trash because they have nowhere else to put it and it is a creative solution. On page eight it says, "She drops it in the dirt as everyone else does. There's nowhere to put it." This shows that she is doing what everyone else is doing at first, but then she does the right thing by reusing the trash.

13 Queen of Leaves: The Story of Botanist Ynes Mexia

by Stephen Briseño and illustrated by Isabel Muñoz

Summary: Ynes Mexia was a woman who pursued her education and her interests later in life. As a botanist, her curiosity and exploration led to a life of adventure and several scientific discoveries—most notably the mysterious wax palm, whose story is told in parallel to Mexia's in this book.

Why We Love It: We love the dual narrative and the intertwining of Ynes's story with the wax palm's. We especially love learning about her unique experiences around the world.

Topics: women in STEM, female scientists, the environment, science, botany, plants, plant specimens, specimen collecting, wax palm, endangered plants, nature, Mexican Americans, travel, California, Texas, Mexico, Ecuador, Alaska, Brazil, Colombia

Big Ideas: curiosity, exploration, nature's beauty, appreciating nature, adventure, blooming later in life, finding your passion, forging a new path, preservation, study, risk-taking

Back Matter:

- Author's note
- Bibliography

LESSON STEPS:

1 QUICK WRITE.
(Choose One):

- Have you ever gone through something difficult? What happened? What did you do?

- What is something that you are interested in—something that you are curious about and would like to study?

- What is your favorite plant? Describe it. What do you know about it?

Write about this for 3 minutes and then set it aside.

2 READ.

Read the picture book *Queen of Leaves: The Story of Botanist Ynes Mexia* by Stephen Briseño and discuss the story. Discuss parts of the story that stick out to you or that you connect with. What writer's craft moves do you notice the author using? Notice the parts of the story.

Queen of Leaves: The Story of Botanist Ynes Mexia

by Stephen Briseño and illustrated by Isabel Muñoz

3 SHARE THE STRUCTURE.

Show the students the structure found in the picture book. Reread the story, looking for chunks together and watching for how the author moves from one part to the other.

Discovering a Life Purpose			
How life was hard for _____	How life got harder for _____	How _____ discovered something they loved	How that changed things

4 INVITATION TO WRITE.

Here are several ways you can get students to write.

- Have students use the text structure to write a kernel essay summary of the story. (Give them between 5 and 10 minutes to do this.)

- Have the students use the text structure to write their own piece in a kernel essay. (Give them between 5 and 10 minutes to do this.)

- See what students come up with. (Give them around 10 minutes.) Here are some possibilities:

  ○ A page of thoughts in their quick write

  ○ Examples of the author's craft moves

  ○ A text structure

Whatever they choose to write, let them know that they can change anything they need to and make it their own.

5 SHARE.

Invite students to try their writing on someone else's ears. This is a crucial step! The sharing is just as important as the writing.

Want to Go Deeper?
Try these options.

OPTION 1: CRAFT CHALLENGE

- **Personification:** This author uses personification to describe the wax palm. Personification is giving nonhuman objects human capabilities. Here is an example from the story:

  "The wax palm knows what it's like to be lonely."

  Look through your piece to see where you can use personification. After you write, try it out on someone's ears to see how it sounds in your writing.

- **Extended Simile + a Pitchforked Description:** In this story, the author uses a simile (a comparison using *like* or *as*) and then extends and explains it with a pitchfork. Here's the example from the story:

  *"Ynes's family lived **like** plants in separate pots. **Father** busy with work in Washington, D. C. **Mother and sister**, Adele, rubbing elbows with the wealthy. And **Ynes**? She was alone with her books, in the shade of trees."*

  Look through your piece to see where you can use a simile + a pitchforked description. After you write, try it out on someone's ears to see how it sounds in your writing.

- **Metaphor:** In this story, the author uses a metaphor, which is a figure of speech that describes something by saying it is something else—like a simile, but without *like* or *as*. Here's an example from the story:

  *"Every plant **was** a promise. Each seed a possibility."*

  Look through your piece to see where you can use a metaphor. After you write, try it out on someone's ears to see how it sounds in your writing.

- **Antithesis:** This author uses a rhetorical device called antithesis. Antithesis is when two contrasting ideas are intentionally put next to each other, usually through parallel structure. Here's an example from the story:

  *"**She didn't always know what it was like to be** accepted. Or to have friends. Or to feel important. **But Ynes did know what it was like to be** a trailblazer, a groundbreaker, a late bloomer."*

  Look through your piece to see where you can use antithesis. After you write, try it out on someone's ears to see how it sounds in your writing.

OPTION 2: ANALYZE

1. **Start with a big idea.**

   - If you want students to find the big ideas themselves, try asking, "What big ideas do you see in this story that tell you what it's really about?"

   - If students need a nudge, try using some of the big ideas from the list in this lesson's introduction and have students provide evidence from the story to support their answers. Ask, "How is this story about [the big idea]? How does the author explore [the big idea]? Where in the story do you see that?"

2. **Turn the big idea into a truism (thematic statement).**

   Once you have identified the big ideas, use one of them to create truisms for this story. Here are a few (found in the story) to get you started:

   - *There is so much beauty in nature to be explored.*

   - *"There [isn't] any place, any field of study, or any age at which a woman [can] not excel."*

   - *Sometimes loneliness can be a gift.*

   Have students write and share their own truisms.

   Ask them to prove their truisms by providing evidence from the text. They might imagine a listener saying, "Oh yeah? How do you know? How is that true in the story?"

Want to Go Deeper?
Try these options.

OPTION 3:
READING RESPONSE

Students can compose short or extended responses to demonstrate understanding by answering any of these questions. Look in the appendix to find a list titled "Basic Reading Response Text Structures" and a list of "Useful Essay Question Stems for Nonfiction Texts."

Questions for Reading Response

- Explain whether Ynes's loneliness in the beginning of her life contributed to her future career.

- Explain how both Ynes and the wax palm defied the odds.

- Explain how the wax palm is important in the story.

- Explain whether it is beneficial to go back to school when you're older.

- Explain how Ynes shows tenacity throughout the story.

OPTION 4:
EXTENSION IDEAS

- Dig into the back matter:
  - Use the author's note as a short nonfiction text to read, discuss, create and answer questions, and write.
  - Use the bibliography to jump-start research about Ynes Mexia.
- Research more about plants, botany, the wax palm, or another woman in STEM.
  - Create an infographic about your research.
  - Create a poem based on your research.
  - Use the text structure "Discovering a Life Purpose" to write about your research on a person.
- Contact a local gardener or botanist to talk about plants and gathering specimens.
- Take a field trip to a local garden center, botanical garden, or nursery to learn more about plants.
- Watch the PBS *American Masters* special called "Ynés Mexía: Mexican-American Botanist and Adventurer," available at https://www.pbs.org/wnet/americanmasters/ynes-mexia-accomplished-latina-botanist-k6bggm/13948/.

QUICK WRITE

by Carlotta Febres, 4th Grade

I would like to learn Greek because many words in English use Greek roots. Greek also sounds like a fun language to learn.

QUICK WRITE

by Vrisan Shah, 6th Grade

Space fascinates me. The science behind atoms, galaxies, black holes, stars, and the universe is something that I've always been curious about. Astrophysics is one topic that sparks my interest and curiosity. The theories about how and why our universe exists like it does, and other cosmic phenomena are what I'm going to pursue in further studies.

The exploration, discovery, and inhabitation of planets is another such topic that I am interested in. I research the designs of rockets and try to improve them. One of my ideas is creating an infinite loop of asteroid mining, which could make trillions of dollars.

KERNEL ESSAY (USING "DISCOVERING A LIFE PURPOSE")

by Carlotta Febres, 4th Grade

Life was hard for J. K. Rowling because she was very poor. Life got harder for her because she was still poor, and she had to take care of her young daughter and she wanted to get her books published. J. K. Rowling discovered that she loves writing because she started writing at a young age. It changed things because she wrote books so famous they changed the world.

KERNEL ESSAY (USING "DISCOVERING A LIFE PURPOSE")

by Zinnia Briseño, 5th Grade

When Joan Procter was young, she was a girl who loved animal science, specifically reptiles. She was not accepted for that. When she grew up, she went to school to learn more about animals. Only men were with her. She found out that even if she was a girl, she could love reptiles, too! She became very famous and worked at a zoo with the reptiles.

CRAFT CHALLENGE (ANTITHESIS)

by Carlotta Febres, 4th Grade

The little doe never would play near the river. Or the lions' field. Or the tigers' tree. The little doe did play at home.

CRAFT CHALLENGE (ANTITHESIS)

by Zinnia Briseño, 5th Grade

I did not know what it was going to be like to study animals. But I did know I wanted to be a zoologist.

TRUISM

by Winnie Parish, 2nd Grade

If you listen to what everyone else says, you will never discover anything new.

READING RESPONSE (USING THE TEXT STRUCTURE "QA12345")

by Saisha Davinder, 6th Grade

Q: What made Ynes Mexia different?

A: Ynes Mexia is different in so many good ways! She was a trailblazer in botany, proved that anything can be done no matter the age, showed that you can face many hardships, and that with perseverance you can achieve your goals.

I know this because throughout the book, I saw many things she overcame. Like in the beginning her parents split and her father died. In the middle, she went to a botany class in her 50s, despite her age.

In the end, she had to go through many challenges to get over 150,000 samples.

This means that Ynes Mexia did not only persevere through the hard times, but she was also brave throughout her time as a botanist. She didn't care what other people thought of her and she did what she wanted to accomplish her dreams.

I know this because during the book, she had troubles. Like when she was stuck in a whirlpool and when she ate poisonous berries. She knew that what she was doing was worth her time and her life.

This means that no matter the obstacle that Ynes had, she believed that it would pay off in the end, and it did! After all of the hardships that she had, she was happy while doing it. She lived her life the way she wanted to.

My answer is that Ynes is courageous and persevered when times were tough.

Sweet Justice: Georgia Gilmore and the Montgomery Bus Boycott

by Mara Rockliff and illustrated by R. Gregory Christie

Summary: This book tells a story about a woman who isn't well known, but who did what she could with the little she had to bring about big changes during the Montgomery bus boycott.

Why We Love It: We all know of Rosa Parks and Dr. Martin Luther King Jr., but what about the others who did their part to bring about real change? This is a book about an unsung hero and her story of courage and perseverance that deserves to be shared widely. It also illustrates the Montgomery bus boycott.

Topics: Georgia Gilmore, Montgomery bus boycott, Rosa Parks, Dr. Martin Luther King Jr., incarceration, civil rights movement, segregation, protests, Montgomery, Alabama

Big Ideas: racial inequality, justice, equality, racism, taking a stand, oppression, working together, change, persistence, teamwork, courage, nonviolent protest

Back Matter:

- "After the Boycott"
- Author's note on sources
- Sources

LESSON STEPS:

1 QUICK WRITE.

Think of someone (maybe someone you know or someone you've learned about) who has helped to make the world a better place. Who was it? What did they do?

Write about this for 3 minutes and then set it aside.

2 READ.

Read the picture book *Georgia Gilmore and the Montgomery Bus Boycott* by Mara Rockliff and discuss the story. Discuss parts of the story that stick out to you or that you connect with. What writer's craft moves do you notice the author using? Notice the parts of the story.

Sweet Justice: Georgia Gilmore and the Montgomery Bus Boycott

by Mara Rockliff and illustrated by R. Gregory Christie

3 SHARE THE STRUCTURE.

Show the students the structure found in the picture book. Reread the story, looking for chunks together and watching for how the author moves from one part to the other.

Making a Change				
The problem	How things needed to change	Who worked together and how	What stood in their way and how they responded	How change happened

4 INVITATION TO WRITE.

Here are several ways you can get students to write.

- Have students use the text structure to write a kernel essay summary of the story. (Give them between 5 and 10 minutes to do this.)

- Have the students use the text structure to write their own piece in a kernel essay. (Give them between 5 and 10 minutes to do this.)

- See what students come up with. (Give them around 10 minutes.) Here are some possibilities:

  o A page of thoughts in their quick write

  o Examples of the author's craft moves

  o A text structure

Whatever they choose to write, let them know that they can change anything they need to and make it their own.

5 SHARE.

Invite students to try their writing on someone else's ears. This is a crucial step! The sharing is just as important as the writing.

Want to Go Deeper?
Try these options.

OPTION 1: CRAFT CHALLENGE

- **Pitchforked Metaphor:** A pitchfork is a sentence (or a series of sentences) that takes one thing and branches it off into three or more. It takes something from being vague to being crystal clear. A metaphor is a comparison of two different things, without using *like* or *as*. This author used a pitchfork of metaphors to describe the term *segregation*.

  *"**Segregation was** a long, hot summer dragging wishful children past the shady park with the Whites Only sign. **It was the** pale pink hands. . . . And **the city buses**!"*

  Look through your piece to see where you can use a metaphor or a pitchfork of metaphors. After you write, try it out on someone's ears to see how it sounds in your writing.

OPTION 2: ANALYZE

1. **Start with a big idea.**

   - If you want students to find the big ideas themselves, try asking, "What big ideas do you see in this story that tell you what it's really about?"

   - If students need a nudge, try using some of the big ideas from the list in this lesson's introduction and have students provide evidence from the story to support their answers. Ask, "How is this story about [the big idea]? How does the author explore [the big idea]? Where in the story do you see that?"

2. **Turn the big idea into a truism (thematic statement).**

   Once you have identified the big ideas, use one of them to create truisms for this story. Here are a few (found in the story) to get you started:

   - *"You cannot be afraid if you want to accomplish anything."* —Georgia Gilmore

   - *It takes many dedicated people to make real change happen.*

   Have students write and share their own truisms.

   Ask them to prove their truisms by providing evidence from the text. They might imagine a listener saying, "Oh yeah? How do you know? How is that true in the story?"

Want to Go Deeper?
Try these options.

OPTION 3:
READING RESPONSE

Students can compose short or extended responses to demonstrate understanding by answering any of these questions. Look in the appendix to find a list titled "Basic Reading Response Text Structures" and a list of "Useful Essay Question Stems for Nonfiction Texts."

Questions for Reading Response

- What was the biggest conflict that Georgia faced?
- Explain how cooking plays an important part in this story.
- How does the setting influence the plot of the story?
- Why was the bus boycott necessary?
- Explain how Georgia helped make change in her city.
- Explain how Georgia shows courage through the story.

OPTION 4:
EXTENSION IDEAS

- Dig into the back matter:
  - Use the "After the Boycott" piece as a short nonfiction text to read, discuss, create and answer questions, and write.
  - Use the sources to jump-start research about this part of history.
- Choose other key players from the civil rights movement to research:
  - Create an infographic about that person.
  - Use the text structure to write about that person.
- Write a letter to Georgia, or the person you researched, or the person you wrote about in your quick write, using the same text structure (or not), to let them know what you admire about them.
- Write a letter as Georgia at some point in the story.
- Make a timeline of the Montgomery bus boycott.
- Write a play about this story and act it out as a class.
- Do more research on Georgia and create an infographic or a poster about her to share with others.
- Make a newspaper about this time period and include sections like letters to the editor, advertisements, front-page headlines, and so on.

Student Samples for *Sweet Justice*

QUICK WRITE

by Hanley Bahl, 6th Grade

Joan of Arc made the world a better place. She made the world a better place by showing that women can do everything that men can. Joan of Arc also led the French to victory over England. Even though she was killed painfully, her legacy will always be a symbol to the French. She is a symbol of peace and power.

QUICK WRITE

by Kathryn Taylor, 6th Grade

My dad has made the world a better place. My dad is a firefighter; he works long hours to help coworkers, too. Firefighters work around the clock. They also do a lot of training for their jobs such as carrying all of their equipment, climbing buildings, and carrying people. My dad saves lives all he can.

QUICK WRITE

by Lillian Broihahn, 6th Grade

One of the people I learned about is Zeb Powell, a professional snowboarder. He is the first black snowboarder to compete in X Games. Zeb helped motivate other African American snowboarders to compete. Zeb Powell motivated and influenced many lives.

QUICK WRITE

by Astoria Graham, 6th Grade

Joseph Swan made the world a better place by inventing the lightbulb. Usually, people think of someone more famous like Thomas Edison or Albert Einstein, but nobody ever thinks about the people who did it first. Just like Claudette Colvin was the first to refuse her seat to a white person and all the credit went to Rosa Parks. So, next time you hear a story about someone famous, don't forget who did it first.

KERNEL ESSAY (USING "MAKING A CHANGE")

by Leah Langner, 6th Grade

Claudette Colvin didn't give up her seat and got arrested, kind of like Rosa Parks. Most people know about Rosa, but Claudette kind of gets forgotten in the shadows. Rights were inequal on buses and they needed to change. Claudette Colvin, a 15-year-old girl, worked together with Martin Luther King, Jr. and other civil rights activists by starting the Montgomery Bus Boycott and other peaceful protests. The government's laws stood in the way of having equal rights for all skin colors. The laws changed and African American citizens had more rights and got closer to being equal.

Student Samples for *Sweet Justice*

KERNEL ESSAY (USING "MAKING A CHANGE")

by Vivian Gruetzmacher, 6th Grade

Paige Buecker's problem is that she gets a lot of hate. People need to be kind. Paige works with her teammates such as Nika Mühl, Aaliyah Edwards, Azzi Fudd, Caroline Ducharme, [and] Jana El Alfy. They help, not hate. Paige Bueckers dealt with all of the hate by just brushing it off and playing like she always does. She has made change happen by donating $50,000 to charity.

Swimming With Sharks: The Daring Discoveries of Eugenie Clark

by Heather Lang and illustrated by Jordi Solano

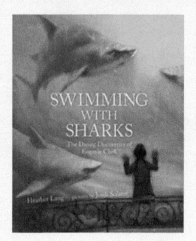

Summary: This is the story of Dr. Eugenie Clark, a fish scientist who turned her curiosity and love of marine life into a career. In the process, she learned a great deal about sharks and shared her knowledge with the world.

Why We Love It: Eugenie did so much to educate the world about something we knew little about and therefore feared. Her story is fascinating and left us wanting to do more research!

Topics: sharks, marine life, scientists, zoology, oceanography, ichthyology, ocean fish, women in science

Big Ideas: passion, discovery, exploration, curiosity, study, misunderstood creatures, misconceptions, advocacy

Back Matter:

- Author's note
- "More About Sharks"
- Selected sources

LESSON STEPS:

1 QUICK WRITE.
(Choose One):

- What is something that you like that other people don't?

- What is something that you are interested in—something that you are curious about and would like to study?

- What is your favorite animal? Describe it. What do you know about it?

Write about this for 3 minutes and then set it aside.

2 READ.

Read the picture book *Swimming With Sharks: The Daring Discoveries of Eugenie Clark* by Heather Lang and discuss the story. Discuss parts of the story that stick out to you or that you connect with. What writer's craft moves do you notice the author using? Notice the parts of the story.

Swimming With Sharks: The Daring Discoveries of Eugenie Clark

by Heather Lang and illustrated by Jordi Solano

3 SHARE THE STRUCTURE.

Show the students the structure found in the picture book. Reread the story, looking for chunks together and watching for how the author moves from one part to the other.

A Curiosity That Changed the World

What someone was interested in	What that interest looked like at first	How that interest grew and brought about changes	The larger impact that it had on others

4 INVITATION TO WRITE.

Here are several ways you can get students to write.

- Have students use the text structure to write a kernel essay summary of the story. (Give them between 5 and 10 minutes to do this.)

- Have the students use the text structure to write their own piece in a kernel essay. (Give them between 5 and 10 minutes to do this.)

- See what students come up with. (Give them around 10 minutes.) Here are some possibilities:
  - A page of thoughts in their quick write
  - Examples of the author's craft moves
  - A text structure

Whatever they choose to write, let them know that they can change anything they need to and make it their own.

5 SHARE.

Invite students to try their writing on someone else's ears. This is a crucial step! The sharing is just as important as the writing.

Want to Go Deeper?
Try these options.

OPTION 1: CRAFT CHALLENGE

- **Antithesis:** This author uses a rhetorical device called antithesis. Antithesis is when two contrasting ideas are intentionally put next to each other, usually through parallel structure. Here's an example from the story:

  *"**Most people saw** piercing eyes . . . rows of sharp teeth . . . vicious bloodthirsty killers! **Not Eugenie Clark. She saw** sleek, graceful fish gliding through the water."*

  Look through your piece to see where you can use antithesis. After you write, try it out on someone's ears to see how it sounds in your writing.

- **Catalog:** In this story, the author creates a list of nouns, which is a rhetorical device called a catalog. Here's the example from the story:

  "Genie caught hammerheads, blacktip sharks, dogfish sharks, lemon sharks, nurse sharks, bull sharks, and tiger sharks."

  Look through your piece to see where you can use a catalog. After you write, try it out on someone's ears to see how it sounds in your writing.

- **Refrain:** This author uses a refrain, which is a line that is repeated on purpose. Writers sometimes do this to create humor (make it funny), create rhythm, engage their reader, or reveal something. The author repeats the following:

  "She observed. She sketched. She took detailed notes."

  Look through your piece and see where you can add a refrain of your own. Try it out on someone's ears to see how it sounds in your writing.

- **Anaphork (Anaphora + Pitchfork):** This author uses something we call an anaphork, a rhetorical device that combines anaphora—the repeating of a beginning word or phrase in successive phrases—and a pitchfork. Here's an example from the story:

  *"**People killed them** out of fear. **People killed them** for their fins. **People killed them** thinking it would make beaches safer."*

  Look through your piece to see where you can try an anaphork. After you write, try it out on someone's ears to see how it sounds in your writing.

OPTION 2: ANALYZE

1. **Start with a big idea.**

   - If you want students to find the big ideas themselves, try asking, "What big ideas do you see in this story that tell you what it's really about?"

   - If students need a nudge, try using some of the big ideas from the list in this lesson's introduction and have students provide evidence from the story to support their answers. Ask, "How is this story about [the big idea]? How does the author explore [the big idea]? Where in the story do you see that?"

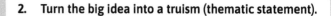

2. **Turn the big idea into a truism (thematic statement).**

   Once you have identified the big ideas, use one of them to create truisms for this story. Here are a few (found in the story) to get you started:

   - *"There will always be more to learn."*

   - *People fear what they do not understand.*

   - *When we take time to learn about something, our fear melts away.*

   Have students write and share their own truisms.

   Ask them to prove their truisms by providing evidence from the text. They might imagine a listener saying, "Oh yeah? How do you know? How is that true in the story?"

Want to Go Deeper?
Try these options.

OPTION 3: READING RESPONSE

Students can compose short or extended responses to demonstrate understanding by answering any of these questions. Look in the appendix to find a list titled "Basic Reading Response Text Structures" and a list of "Useful Essay Question Stems for Nonfiction Texts."

Questions for Reading Response

- How did Eugenie change the perception of sharks?

- Explain how the repeated line "She observed. She sketched. She took detailed notes" affects the reader's understanding of Eugenie's process.

- Why did people listen when Eugenie talked about sharks?

- Explain what Eugenie's research showed about sharks.

- Explain whether Eugenie should have gone into the shark's cave alone.

OPTION 4: EXTENSION IDEAS

- Dig into the back matter:
  - Use the author's note and "More About Sharks" piece as short nonfiction texts to read, discuss, create and answer questions, and write.
  - Use the selected sources (found on the copyright page) to jump-start research about Dr. Eugenie Clark.
- Research more about sharks.
  - Create an infographic about your research.
  - Create a poem based on your research.
  - Create a class aquarium to contain paper sharks that each student researched.
- Research another scientist.
  - Create an infographic about your research.
  - Create a poem based on your research.
  - Use the text structure "A Curiosity That Changed the World" to write about that person.
- Pair this book with *Joan Procter, Dragon Doctor* by Patricia Valdez to compare and contrast two women scientists.

Student Samples for *Swimming With Sharks*

QUICK WRITE

by Hattie Shipp, 3rd Grade

My favorite animal is a puppy. I like them because they are soft. I like that they can be lots of different colors.

KERNEL ESSAY RETELL (USING "A CURIOSITY THAT CHANGED THE WORLD")

by Zinnia Briseño, 5th Grade

Eugenie Clark loved sharks. At first, she only had fish and a notebook. She grew up and started to study sharks. People started to believe that sharks were not savage killers because of her research.

KERNEL ESSAY (USING "A CURIOSITY THAT CHANGED THE WORLD") + CRAFT CHALLENGE (ANAPHORK)

by Lillian LaBryer, 5th Grade

Louis Pasteur was interested in finding the rabies vaccine. Many people thought he couldn't do it. **They told him** it was impossible. **They told him** he was wasting his time. They were wrong. After six years of trial and error, he found it. There was a kid named Joseph, and Louis Pasteur treated Joseph's rabies. The rest of the world used it. There was finally a vaccine to rabies!

KERNEL ESSAY (USING "A CURIOSITY THAT CHANGED THE WORLD")

by Ali Anne Ryan, 5th Grade

Bethany Hamilton was interested in surfing. She started out as a kid and moved on to being a pro. When she was a kid, many people thought surfing wasn't that popular. But Bethany showed them cool tricks and became very popular, and the population of girl surfers grew.

KERNEL ESSAY (USING "A CURIOSITY THAT CHANGED THE WORLD") + CRAFT CHALLENGE (ANAPHORK)

by Aubrielle Osborne, 5th Grade

Simone Biles was interested in gymnastics. **Some people thought** it was a waste of time. **Some people thought** she wouldn't make it. **Some people thought** she wasn't good enough. But she got better and started competing. People got inspired by her.

TRUISM

by Cuate Saunders, 7th Grade

It's important to do what you want in life no matter what your peers say.

TRUISM

by Paul Duncan, 3rd Grade

It's important to listen to the experts.

CRAFT CHALLENGE (ANTITHESIS)

by Ali Anne Ryan, 5th Grade

Most people see vicious dogs, **but I see a** sweet, cuddly Doberman looking out for its family.

READING RESPONSE (USING THE TEXT STRUCTURE "RACE")

by Paul Duncan, 3rd Grade

Q: Why did people listen when Eugenie talked about sharks?

A: People listened when Eugenie talked about sharks because she was a shark expert. In the book, it says, "She knew sharks are magnificent and misunderstood." This means she knew what she was doing because she was an expert who had studied sharks.

READING RESPONSE (USING THE TEXT STRUCTURE "FIGURING OUT THE READING")

by Robert Cross, 6th Grade

Q: How did Eugenie change the perception of sharks?

A: I read the words, "Genie loved learning about all kinds of fish, but there wasn't much information about sharks. She dreamed she'd discover their secrets, too." This told me that sharks weren't studied much because they were misunderstood, and people just thought they were inept, bloodthirsty creatures. Genie was going to prove them wrong. Then I read, "Genie spoke out to the world: 'Sharks are magnificent and misunderstood!' When Genie talked, people listened. Dr. Eugenie Clark had become one of the most respected fish scientists in the world." This told me that people believe that Dr. Eugenie Clark was right. This means that she was respected, and people trusted her. So then I knew that Genie was an influencer and that she changed people's view on sharks.

16 Tamales for Christmas
by Stephen Briseño and illustrated by Sonia Sánchez

Summary: At Christmastime, Grandma makes and sells tamales to buy gifts for her many children, grandchildren, and great grandchildren. This Christmas, she decides to make 1,000 dozen—all out of her humble kitchen and with the help of her *familia*.

Why We Love It: Besides being personally fond of the author, we love the warmth in every page of this story. We appreciate this celebration of the tamale tradition for so many, but also love that everybody can relate to special ways to celebrate the holidays.

Topics: tamales, Christmas, cooking, Mexican Americans, grandparents, homemade food

Big Ideas: family/*familia*, Hispanic culture, serving others, helping others, making sacrifices, hard work, working together, generosity, resourcefulness, tenacity

Back Matter:

- Author's note
- "Making Tamales at Home"
- Tamale recipe

LESSON STEPS:

1 QUICK WRITE.
(Choose One):

- Do your parents, grandparents, or guardians make food that you love? What is it? When do they make it?

- Do you know how to make some food? What is it? What are the steps to making it?

- Has someone ever done something big for you because they care about you? Who was it? What did they do?

Write about this for 3 minutes and then set it aside.

2 READ.

Read the picture book *Tamales for Christmas* by Stephen Briseño and discuss the story. Discuss parts of the story that stick out to you or that you connect with. What writer's craft moves do you notice the author using? Notice the parts of the story.

Tamales for Christmas
by Stephen Briseño and illustrated by Sonia Sánchez

3 SHARE THE STRUCTURE.

Show the students the structure found in the picture book. Reread the story, looking for chunks together and watching for how the author moves from one part to the other.

Accomplishing a Big Task					
When _____, this person does this because _____.	First this person does this.	Then this person does this.	When _____, this person does this.	Before _____, this person does this.	When this person finishes, I know this.

4 INVITATION TO WRITE.

Here are several ways you can get students to write.

- Have students use the text structure to write a kernel essay summary of the story. (Give them between 5 and 10 minutes to do this.)

- Have the students use the text structure to write their own piece in a kernel essay. (Give them between 5 and 10 minutes to do this.)

- See what students come up with. (Give them around 10 minutes.) Here are some possibilities:

  o A page of thoughts in their quick write

  o Examples of the author's craft moves

  o A text structure

Whatever they choose to write, let them know that they can change anything they need to and make it their own.

5 SHARE.

Invite students to try their writing on someone else's ears. This is a crucial step! The sharing is just as important as the writing.

Want to Go Deeper?
Try these options.

OPTION 1: CRAFT CHALLENGE

- **Metaphor With a Pitchforked Description:** In this story, the author uses a metaphor, which is a comparison of two different things, without using *like* or *as*, and then follows it with a pitchfork (one thing branched into three or more) description. Here's an example from the story.

  *"Her **kitchen is the heartbeat** of our familia, **loud and cramped and perfumed** with delicious smells."*

  Look through your piece to see where you can use a metaphor with a pitchforked description. After you write, try it out on someone's ears to see how it sounds in your writing.

- **Varied Refrain:** In this story, the author uses a refrain, which is a line that is repeated throughout the book. Usually, a refrain uses the same words every time; however, while this author always starts the refrain the same, he changes the ending a little each time. Here are some examples from the story:

  *"With masa in one hand, corn husks in the other, **Grandma's just getting started**."*

  *"With masa in one hand, corn husks in the other, **Grandma is tenacious**."*

  *"With masa in one hand, corn husks in the other, **Grandma's just warming up.**"*

  Look through your piece to see where you can use a varied refrain. After you write, try it out on someone's ears to see how it sounds in your writing.

- **AAAWWUBBIS[1] Opener:** In this book, the author uses an AAAWWUBBIS opener. AAAWWUBBIS stands for *After, Although, As, When, While, Until, Because, Before, If, Since.* Here is an example from the story:

  *"**As** Grandma strings the lights and hoists up the tree, the fridge fills up, too, every nook and cranny shiny with foil."*

  Look through your piece and see where you can use an AAAWWUBBIS opener. It is a great way to combine two sentences and add some sentence variety to your writing. Try it out on someone's ears to see how it sounds in your writing.

OPTION 2: ANALYZE

1. **Start with a big idea.**

   - If you want students to find the big ideas themselves, try asking, "What big ideas do you see in this story that tell you what it's really about?"

   - If students need a nudge, try using some of the big ideas from the list in this lesson's introduction and have students provide evidence from the story to support their answers. Ask, "How is this story about [the big idea]? How does the author explore [the big idea]? Where in the story do you see that?"

2. **Turn the big idea into a truism (thematic statement).**

   Once you have identified the big ideas, use one of them to create truisms for this story. Here are a few (found in the story) to get you started:

   - *We work hard for the ones we love.*

   - *Generosity is an important ingredient.*

   - *Sometimes the best gift we can give is ourselves.*

   - *We can decide that we want to make memories.*

   Have students write and share their own truisms.

   Ask them to prove their truisms by providing evidence from the text. They might imagine a listener saying, "Oh yeah? How do you know? How is that true in the story?"

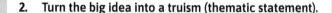

[1]AAAWWUBBIS originated in Jeff Anderson's book *Mechanically Inclined* (2005). See Anderson, J. (2005). *Mechanically inclined: Building grammar, usage, and style into writer's workshop.* Taylor & Francis, p. 31.

Want to Go Deeper?
Try these options.

OPTION 3: READING RESPONSE

Students can compose short or extended responses to demonstrate understanding by answering any of these questions. Look in the appendix to find a list titled "Basic Reading Response Text Structures" and a list of "Useful Essay Question Stems for Nonfiction Texts."

Questions for Reading Response

- Explain what happens in the story (retell).
- What do tamales symbolize in the story?
- How does Grandma show generosity in the story?
- Explain why Grandma made so many tamales.
- Explain the importance of teamwork in the story.

OPTION 4: EXTENSION IDEAS

- Dig into the back matter:
  - Use the author's note and "Making Tamales at Home" piece as short nonfiction texts to read, discuss, create and answer questions, and write.
- Research more about tamales, foods made by Mexican Americans, holiday traditions, or other cultural foods.
  - Create an infographic about the topic.
  - Create a poem based on your research.
  - Use the text structure to write about your research (or another topic).
  - Watch the YouTube video "Como Hacer Los Tamales Esponjaditos De Mi Rancho a Tu Cocina," available at https://www.youtube.com/watch?v=h_kbN4cLmJI. (We love this YouTuber! Her video is all in Spanish, and she shows the tamale-making process from start to finish.)
- Invite a tamale maker to your school to talk about their work (and hopefully bring samples!).
- Have students gather recipes from home and put them together in a class cookbook.
- Make tamales together as a class.
- Host a potluck and have everyone bring some food from home (bought or made).
- For a unit on food and making things, consider pairing this book with one of the following:
  - *Fry Bread: A Native American Family Story* by Kevin Noble Maillard
  - *The Only Way to Make Bread* by Cristina Quintero
  - *Magic Ramen: The Story of Momofuku Ando* by Andrea Wang

QUICK WRITE

by Hattie Shipp, 3rd Grade

My mom makes cinnamon bread. She makes it every Christmas morning. It tastes good because it is like a cinnamon roll. She adds fruit on the top.

QUICK WRITE

by Zinnia Briseño, 5th Grade

When I first got my dog, I didn't know it. My parents made it a big surprise and kept it a secret for weeks. We drove for two hours to "go to lunch with old friends," but it was really to get our puppy Molly.

CRAFT CHALLENGE (METAPHOR WITH A PITCHFORKED DESCRIPTION)

by Luke Waun, 5th Grade

The rides are the wrath of my adrenaline, loud and rickety with fun drops and spins.

KERNEL ESSAY (USING "ACCOMPLISHING A BIG TASK") + CRAFT CHALLENGE (AAAWWUBBIS OPENERS)

by Luke Waun, 5th Grade

When my friend Hank plays baseball, he is good at it. First, Hank can pitch. He can also hit. **When** Hank hits it, he runs to first or second base. **Before** the game, he listens to music. **When** Hank finishes pitching, I know he will win.

KERNEL ESSAY (USING "ACCOMPLISHING A BIG TASK") + CRAFT CHALLENGE (AAAWWUBBIS OPENERS)

by Zinnia Briseño, 5th Grade

When my dad wrote his first book, *The Notebook Keeper,* he said it was because he loved writing. First, he thought of an idea and wrote it down. Then he finished it and sent it to an agent. **When** it got sent to publishers, it got rejected a few times. **Before** too long, somebody chose it and it got published. **When** he finished, we were really proud of him.

The Boo-Boos That Changed the World: A True Story About an Accidental Invention (Really!)

by Barry Wittenstein and illustrated by Chris Hsu

Summary: Most inventions start with a problem. For Earle Dickson, his problem was that his wife was accident-prone. Luckily for him, his father was a doctor, and he worked for a manufacturer of medical supplies. Those three things became the catalyst for one of the world's most useful inventions: the Band-Aid.

Why We Love It: We love the playfulness of the writing style in this book, which makes it really fun to read out loud. We also love learning how something so simple came to be, both because of the humanness of Dickson's wife's kitchen mishaps and because of his boss's determination to bring his invention to market. They all knew it would change the world, and it's fun to see how it did.

Topics: Band-Aids, inventions, inventors, accidents, problem and solution, first aid, Boy Scouts, injuries, World War II

Big Ideas: trial and error, problem solving, ideas becoming popular, meeting a need

Back Matter:

- Author's note
- Earle Dickson timeline
- List of other inventions in the 1920s–1930s
- "Learn More"

LESSON STEPS:

1 QUICK WRITE.

What is a little invention that nobody thinks much about, but is still pretty important? Look around the room. What's one small item in this room that is important?

Write about this for 3 minutes and then set it aside.

2 READ.

Read the picture book *The Boo-Boos That Changed the World: A True Story About an Accidental Invention (Really!)* by Barry Wittenstein and discuss the story. Discuss parts of the story that stick out to you or that you connect with. What writer's craft moves do you notice the author using? Notice the parts of the story.

17 The Boo-Boos That Changed the World: A True Story About an Accidental Invention (Really!)

by Barry Wittenstein and illustrated by Chris Hsu

3 SHARE THE STRUCTURE.

Show the students the structure found in the picture book. Reread the story, looking for chunks together and watching for how the author moves from one part to the other.

An Inventor and the Invention					
Who the person was	What sparked the idea for the invention	The process: What happened first?	The process: What happened next?	The process: What happened last?	How it was received or How it changed things

4 INVITATION TO WRITE.

Here are several ways you can get students to write.

- Have students use the text structure to write a kernel essay summary of the story. (Give them between 5 and 10 minutes to do this.)

- Have the students use the text structure to write their own piece in a kernel essay. (Give them between 5 and 10 minutes to do this.)

- See what students come up with. (Give them around 10 minutes.) Here are some possibilities:

  o A page of thoughts in their quick write

  o Examples of the author's craft moves

  o A text structure

Whatever they choose to write, let them know that they can change anything they need to and make it their own.

5 SHARE.

Invite students to try their writing on someone else's ears. This is a crucial step! The sharing is just as important as the writing.

Want to Go Deeper?
Try These Options.

OPTION 1: CRAFT CHALLENGE

- **Hyphenated Adjectives:** This author uses several hyphenated adjectives to describe the Boy Scouts. Adjectives are words that describe nouns, and hyphenated adjectives are two words that are glued together with a hyphen. Here are some examples from the story:

  *"All those **fall-down**, **climb-up**, **scratched-elbows**, **scraped-knees** boys got plenty of cuts."*

  Look through your piece to see where you can use a hyphenated adjective. After you write, try it out on someone's ears to see how it sounds in your writing.

- **Geographic Pitchfork:** This author uses a list (or pitchfork) of people, including their geography (the places they are from). We call that a geographic pitchfork. Here is the example from the story:

  "From boisterous hot-dog vendors in Brooklyn, fancy French winemakers, tired taxi drivers in Denmark, and English bobbies on bicycles to daredevil skateboarders in Saskatchewan, king-crab fishermen in Alaska, sweaty Ugandan soccer players, and applauding audiences at the Bolshoi Theatre in Moscow . . ."

  Look through your piece to see where you can use a geographic pitchfork. After you write, try it out on someone's ears to see how it sounds in your writing.

OPTION 2: ANALYZE

1. **Start with a big idea.**

   - If you want students to find the big ideas themselves, try asking, "What big ideas do you see in this story that tell you what it's really about?"

   - If students need a nudge, try using some of the big ideas from the list in this lesson's introduction and have students provide evidence from the story to support their answers. Ask, "How is this story about [the big idea]? How does the author explore [the big idea]? Where in the story do you see that?"

2. **Turn the big idea into a truism (thematic statement).**

   Once you have identified the big ideas, use one of them to create truisms for this story. Here are a few (found in the story) to get you started:

   - *Much of our best work starts with paying attention to our family and friends and their needs.*

   - *A solution for one person might just benefit everybody.*

   Have students write and share their own truisms.

   Ask them to prove their truisms by providing evidence from the text. They might imagine a listener saying, "Oh yeah? How do you know? How is that true in the story?"

Want to Go Deeper?
Try these options.

OPTION 3: READING RESPONSE

Students can compose short or extended responses to demonstrate understanding by answering any of these questions. Look in the appendix to find a list titled "Basic Reading Response Text Structures" and a list of "Useful Essay Question Stems for Nonfiction Texts."

Questions for Reading Response

- Explain the benefits of Earle's invention.
- What led to the invention of the Band-Aid?
- Explain why the inventing process took so long.
- What does Earle's boss's reaction show about his character?
- What is a turning point in the story?

OPTION 4: EXTENSION IDEAS

- Dig into the back matter:
  - Use the author's note or the timeline as short nonfiction texts to read, discuss, create and answer questions, and write.
- Research the history of another invention.
  - Create an infographic about that invention.
  - Create a poem based on your research.
  - Make a timeline of that invention.
- Do further research on Band-Aids using the "Learn More" section.
- Use the text structure "An Inventor and the Invention" to write about an invention that you have researched.

Consider pairing this book with other books about inventions, such as the following:

- *The Crayon Man: The True Story of the Invention of Crayola Crayons* by Natascha Biebow
- *Magic Ramen: The Story of Momofuku Ando* by Andrea Wang

Student Samples for *The Boo-Boos That Changed the World*

QUICK WRITE

by **Samuel Fleming, 4th Grade**

One invention that is small but useful is the magnet. The magnet is amazing. You can stick papers to your fridge or stick schedules to a whiteboard.

QUICK WRITE

by **Haley Carol Magilke, 8th Grade**

One invention that people think little about are shoes. This is important because they make sure that your feet do not get injured while you are walking. I think that most people overlook the importance of shoes because they are a fashion statement now. It is just the norm to put on shoes in the morning, but no one really stops to think why.

KERNEL ESSAY (USING "AN INVENTOR AND THE INVENTION")

by **Samuel Fleming, 4th Grade**

Benjamin Franklin invented the lightning rod. He wanted to protect people. When lightning hits, it will hit the rod and go to the ground. Then the lightning won't hurt anybody. The ground channels the lightning. It changed peoples' lives because people would have died.

KERNEL ESSAY (USING "AN INVENTOR AND THE INVENTION")

by **Pablo Micah Cortez, 8th Grade**

John Harvey Kellogg invented peanut butter. He marketed it as a nutritious protein substitute for people who could hardly chew on solid food. Peanuts are roasted and then blanched, then they are ground and finally mixed. Then, they will be put in a jar. They will be shipped out to grocery stores. Peanut butter changed things by being an easy source of protein and being useful during war time.

KERNEL ESSAY (USING "AN INVENTOR AND THE INVENTION")

by **Lorelai Dressell, 8th Grade**

Christiaan Huygens was a Dutch polymath. His interest, as an astronomer, in the accurate measurement of time then led him to his discovery. He had an idea that he thought would work to help people tell time much faster. He did some research on how things would work and got some test pieces and started building the first clock. He showed people he said were smarter than him to see what they said and to help and finally they made one that worked great. It changed things by letting people be able to tell time much faster and provided a reliable way to measure time. Clocks have also influenced the way we work.

Student Samples for
The Boo-Boos That Changed the World

KERNEL ESSAY (USING "AN INVENTOR AND THE INVENTION")

by Cohen Watson, 8th Grade

Samuel Morse, along with a group of other people, had invented the "language" of the telegraph. This is known as Morse code.

Morse came up with this idea when he'd overheard a conversation about electromagnetism while on a ship from the United States to Europe. He made a group that were all willing to aid in his crazy idea.

Between 1832 and 1837, he'd successfully made a working model of the telegraph, which was the device that used Morse code. They had finally got it to work, after many attempts of trial and error. The first message ever sent was, "What hath God wrought?"

Morse Code was a huge hit! It paved the way for more advanced communication in the future, not to mention the key role this could play in wars over long distances!

TRUISM

by Grayson Austin, 7th Grade

Sometimes the simplest and smallest ideas can lead to big and popular inventions.

TRUISM

by Jem Moore, 8th Grade

All things are important.

TRUISM

by Lainey Dixon, 8th Grade

There's always more to achieve if you keep pushing.

CRAFT CHALLENGE (GEOGRAPHIC PITCHFORK)

by Maija Clevenger, 8th Grade

From teachers in Brazil, to golfing dads in America, students in Germany, and checkout workers in Japan-all use shoes in their daily lives.

READING RESPONSE (USING THE TEXT STRUCTURE "RACE")

by Asher Leonhart, 7th Grade

Q: Explain the benefits of Earle's invention.

A: The advantage to this invention is the easy coverage of smaller wounds. This is shown when Earle cut "Small squares of sterile gauze," and, "Now all Josephine had to do was cut off a piece of the longer strip and put it on." This shows how easy it was to cover small wounds.

The Boy Who Harnessed the Wind

by William Kamkwamba and Bryan Mealer and illustrated by Elizabeth Zunon

Summary: Born in Malawi and living through a drought, William Kamkwamba sees the need for a water solution. Utilizing his love of how mechanical things work, he teaches himself how to build a windmill. Many of his fellow villagers doubt and tease him at first, but once he is able to use items from the junkyard to build a windmill and generate electricity to bring water, their jeers become cheers.

Why We Love It: This is a powerful story of problem solving, ingenuity, and resourcefulness. It has deservedly been retold for many different audiences and makes a great addition to any STEM, growth mindset, or inventor unit.

Topics: William Kamkwamba, wind power, electricity, Malawi, Africa, farming, drought, famine, village life, science, engineering, inventions, inventors, windmills, water, water scarcity, food scarcity

Big Ideas: resourcefulness, seeing a need and meeting it, serving your community, poverty, helping others, creativity, determination, hard work, challenge, problem solving, wonder, hunger, perseverance, impact, self-teaching

Back Matter:

- William's story (untitled)

LESSON STEPS:

1 QUICK WRITE.
(CHOOSE ONE):

- What are some serious problems (maybe make a list) that need a solution? What ideas do you have to fix or change one of them?

- What is an invention that you are glad that we have?

- Do you know the story of how something was invented? What is it?

- What is something you think the world needs that we don't already have (an invention)?

Write about this for 3 minutes and then set it aside.

2 READ.

Read the picture book *The Boy Who Harnessed the Wind* by William Kamkwamba and Bryan Mealer and discuss the story. Discuss parts of the story that stick out to you or that you connect with. What writer's craft moves do you notice the author using? Notice the parts of the story.

The Boy Who Harnessed the Wind
by William Kamkwamba and Bryan Mealer and illustrated by Elizabeth Zunon

3 SHARE THE STRUCTURE.

Show the students the structure found in the picture book. Reread the story, looking for chunks together and watching for how the author moves from one part to the other.

An Inventor and the Invention					
Who the person was	What sparked the idea for the invention	The process: What happened first?	The process: What happened next?	The process: What happened last?	How it was received or How it changed things

4 INVITATION TO WRITE.

Here are several ways you can get students to write.

- Have students use the text structure to write a kernel essay summary of the story. (Give them between 5 and 10 minutes to do this.)

- Have the students use the text structure to write their own piece in a kernel essay. (Give them between 5 and 10 minutes to do this.)

- See what students come up with. (Give them around 10 minutes.) Here are some possibilities:

  o A page of thoughts in their quick write

  o Examples of the author's craft moves

  o A text structure

Whatever they choose to write, let them know that they can change anything they need to and make it their own.

5 SHARE.

Invite students to try their writing on someone else's ears. This is a crucial step! The sharing is just as important as the writing.

Want to Go Deeper?
Try These Options.

OPTION 1: CRAFT CHALLENGE

- **Ba-Da-Boom:** In this story, the author uses a ba-da-boom, which tells us what a character's body was doing (*ba*), what the character saw (*da*), and a reaction their body had (*boom*). Here is the example from the story:

  *"Now William stood on the road [**ba**] and watched the lucky students pass [**da**], alone with the monster in his belly and the lump in his throat [**boom**]."*

  Look through your piece to see where you can use a ba-da-boom. After you write, try it out on someone's ears to see how it sounds in your writing.

- **More-Than Metaphor:** This author uses something we like to call a more-than metaphor. A metaphor is a comparison of two different things, without using *like* or *as*. A more-than metaphor follows this pattern:

  _____ is more than _____ [this metaphor]. It is _____ [this stronger metaphor].

  Here is an example from the story:

  *"This windmill was **more than a machine**. It was **a weapon** to fight hunger."*

  Look through your piece to see where you can use a more-than metaphor. After you write, try it out on someone's ears to see how it sounds in your writing.

- **Beg-to-Differ Sentence Pattern:** This author uses a beg-to-differ sentence pattern. Here is the example from the story:

  *"**Some** giggled, **others** teased, **but William** waited for the wind."*

  Look through your piece to see where you can use this beg-to-differ sentence pattern:

  Some people _____. Others _____. But I/the character _____.

After you write, try it out on someone's ears to see how it sounds in your writing.

OPTION 2: ANALYZE

1. **Start with a big idea.**

   - If you want students to find the big ideas themselves, try asking, "What big ideas do you see in this story that tell you what it's really about?"

   - If students need a nudge, try using some of the big ideas from the list in this lesson's introduction and have students provide evidence from the story to support their answers. Ask, "How is this story about [the big idea]? How does the author explore [the big idea]? Where in the story do you see that?"

2. **Turn the big idea into a truism (thematic statement).**

   Once you have identified the big ideas, use one of them to create truisms for this story. Here are a few (found in the story) to get you started:

   - *"Heroes can be any age."*

   - *Creativity, determination, and hard work can help save our world.*

   - *Every community suffers and has problems that need solving.*

   Have students write and share their own truisms.

   Ask them to prove their truisms by providing evidence from the text. They might imagine a listener saying, "Oh yeah? How do you know? How is that true in the story?"

Want to Go Deeper?
Try these options.

OPTION 3: READING RESPONSE

Students can compose short or extended responses to demonstrate understanding by answering any of these questions. Look in the appendix to find a list titled "Basic Reading Response Text Structures" and a list of "Useful Essay Question Stems for Nonfiction Texts."

Questions for Reading Response

- Explain how the community's feelings about William's work change throughout the story.
- What leads to William's invention?
- Explain how William shows resourcefulness throughout the story.
- How does the setting influence the plot of this story?
- Explain how William's community benefits from his work.

OPTION 4: EXTENSION IDEAS

- Dig into the back matter:
  - Use William's story (untitled) as a short nonfiction text to read, discuss, create and answer questions, and write.
- Research more about William Kamkwamba, electricity, windmills, wind power, or other inventors.
  - Create an infographic about the topic.
  - Create a poem based on your research.
  - Use the text structure to write about your research (or another topic).
  - Watch the Netflix movie *The Boy Who Harnessed the Wind* (this is marked for 13 and up).[2]
  - Read the middle-grade memoir *The Boy Who Harnessed the Wind*.[3]
  - Watch William Kamkwamba's TED Talk on YouTube, available at https://www.youtube.com/watch?v=6QkNxt7MpWM.
- For a unit on ingenuity, resourcefulness, inventors, and inventions, consider pairing this book with one of the following:
  - *Building an Orchestra of Hope* by Carmen Oliver
  - *Emmanuel's Dream: The True Story of Emmanuel Ofosu Yeboah* by Laurie Ann Thompson
  - *Magic Ramen: The Story of Momofuku Ando* by Andrea Wang
  - *One Plastic Bag: Isatou Ceesay and the Recycling Women of the Gambia* by Miranda Paul
  - *The Boo-Boos That Changed the World: A True Story About an Accidental Invention (Really!)* by Barry Wittenstein
  - *The Crayon Man: The True Story of the Invention of Crayola Crayons* by Natascha Biebow
  - *The Secret Kingdom: Nek Chand, a Changing India, and a Hidden World of Art* by Barb Rosenstock
  - *Whoosh!: Lonnie Johnson's Super-Soaking Stream of Inventions* by Chris Barton

---

[2]Ejiofor, C. (Director & Screenwriter). (2019). *The boy who harnessed the wind* [Film]. Netflix; Participant Media; BBC Films; British Film Institute; Potboiler Productions.

[3]Kamkwamba, W., & Mealer, B. (2010). *The boy who harnessed the wind: Creating currents of electricity and hope* [Young readers paperback edition]. Rocky Pond Books.

Student Samples for *The Boy Who Harnessed the Wind*

QUICK WRITE

by Leila Kirkpatrick, 3rd Grade

An invention I'm glad we have is the lightbulb. Because if we didn't have the lightbulb, there wouldn't be light. And if we didn't have light, it would get harder and harder to see as it gets darker.

QUICK WRITE

by Hannah Gagliano, 4th Grade

This is how bubble gum was invented. One day scientists were trying to make some sort of rubber. Then they found out that you could cut it, so they made it a candy.

KERNEL ESSAY (USING "AN INVENTOR AND HIS INVENTION")

by Hannah Gagliano, 4th Grade

The Egyptians invented marshmallows. They made it so the royalty and gods could have a sweet treat. They squeezed sap from the mallow plant. They mixed it with nuts and honey. Then they put it in a mold. It changed things by giving people a new dessert.

CRAFT CHALLENGE (MORE-THAN METAPHOR)

by Hannah Gagliano, 4th Grade

My book is more than a book. It is a ticket that brings me into a new world.

TRUISM

by Foster Shipp, 6th Grade

Dreams are only dreams until you live them out.

READING RESPONSE

by Foster Shipp, 6th Grade

Q: Explain how the community's feelings about William's work changes throughout the story.

A: The community called him crazy since they didn't know what he was doing, at the beginning of the story when he started building. Finally, they realized he was being smart, so two people started helping him. He was closed up at first, then when he opened up, they wanted to help.

19 The Crayon Man: The True Story of the Invention of Crayola Crayons

by Natascha Biebow and illustrated by Steven Salerno

Summary: Edwin Binney listened, he experimented, and at times, he failed. But together with his team at Crayola, the crayon came to be. This is the colorful true story of crayons.

Why We Love It: Crayons are a part of so many lives, which makes this story so interesting. Not only do we get to learn about the invention of crayons, but the back matter in this book is incredible! It can be useful, too.

Topics: crayons, Crayola, color, inventors, inventions, experiments

Big Ideas: history, discovery, invention, ingenuity, curiosity, creativity, seeing a need and meeting it, listening to others, problem solving, seeing beyond

Back Matter:

- "How Crayola Crayons Are Made Today" (how-to infographic)
- "A Man Who Loved Color" (one-page biography of Edwin Binney)
- Selected bibliography of primary and secondary sources

LESSON STEPS:

1 QUICK WRITE.
(Choose One):

- What are some useful inventions that already exist?
- Do you know the story of how something was invented?
- What is something you think the world needs that we don't already have (an invention)?

Write about this for 3 minutes and then set it aside.

2 READ.

Read the picture book *The Crayon Man: The True Story of the Invention of Crayola Crayons* by Natascha Biebow and discuss the story. Discuss parts of the story that stick out to you or that you connect with. What writer's craft moves do you notice the author using? Notice the parts of the story.

The Crayon Man: The True Story of the Invention of Crayola Crayons

by Natascha Biebow and illustrated by Steven Salerno

3 SHARE THE STRUCTURE.

Show the students the structure found in the picture book. Reread the story, looking for chunks together and watching for how the author moves from one part to the other.

An Inventor and the Invention					
Who the person was	What sparked the idea for the invention	The process: What happened first?	The process: What happened next?	The process: What happened last?	How it was received or How it changed things

4 INVITATION TO WRITE.

Here are several ways you can get students to write.

- Have students use the text structure to write a kernel essay summary of the story. (Give them between 5 and 10 minutes to do this.)

- Have the students use the text structure to write their own piece in a kernel essay. (Give them between 5 and 10 minutes to do this.)

- See what students come up with. (Give them around 10 minutes.) Here are some possibilities:

  o A page of thoughts in their quick write

  o Examples of the author's craft moves

  o A text structure

Whatever they choose to write, let them know that they can change anything they need to and make it their own.

5 SHARE.

Invite students to try their writing on someone else's ears. This is a crucial step! The sharing is just as important as the writing.

Want to Go Deeper?
Try these options.

OPTION 1: CRAFT CHALLENGE

- **Microscope Sentence:** This author uses a type of sentence that we call a microscope sentence, which is a sentence that zooms out, then zooms in, and then focuses on someone or something. Here's an example from the story:

  "In a small stone mill in Pennsylvania, in a top-secret lab, Edwin's team experimented."

  Look through your piece to see where you can use a microscope sentence. After you write, try it out on someone's ears to see how it sounds in your writing.

- **Hypophora:** This author uses a rhetorical device called hypophora. This is when the author asks a question and then immediately provides an answer to said question.

  Here are a few examples from the story:

  "How could they make better, stronger crayons? Melted paraffin wax? Perhaps!"

  "Would children like them? Children did!"

  Look through your piece to see where you can use hypophora. After you write, try it out on someone's ears to see how it sounds in your writing.

- **Hyphenated Adjectives:** This author uses several hyphenated adjectives to describe colors. Adjectives are words that describe nouns, and hyphenated adjectives are two words that are glued together with a hyphen. Here are some examples from the story:

  *"He noticed the **yellow-orange** petals of the **black-eyed** Susans in his garden. He marveled at the rich **scarlet-red** tones of the cardinal's feathers. He admired the deep **blue-green** of the waves in the sea."*

  Look through your piece to see where you can use some hyphenated adjectives. After you write, try it out on someone's ears to see how it sounds in your writing.

OPTION 2: ANALYZE

1. **Start with a big idea.**

   - If you want students to find the big ideas themselves, try asking, "What big ideas do you see in this story that tell you what it's really about?"

   - If students need a nudge, try using some of the big ideas from the list in this lesson's introduction and have students provide evidence from the story to support their answers. Ask, "How is this story about [the big idea]? How does the author explore [the big idea]? Where in the story do you see that?"

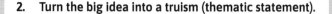

2. **Turn the big idea into a truism (thematic statement).**

   Once you have identified the big ideas, use one of them to create truisms for this story. Here are a few (found in the story) to get you started:

   - *Curiosity can be a key to invention.*

   - *Much of our best work starts with listening to other people.*

   - *The world is full of color.*

   Have students write and share their own truisms.

   Ask them to prove their truisms by providing evidence from the text. They might imagine a listener saying, "Oh yeah? How do you know? How is that true in the story?"

Want to Go Deeper?
Try these options.

OPTION 3: READING RESPONSE

Students can compose short or extended responses to demonstrate understanding by answering any of these questions. Look in the appendix to find a list titled "Basic Reading Response Text Structures" and a list of "Useful Essay Question Stems for Nonfiction Texts."

Questions for Reading Response

- Why does the author choose to mention all the black that Edwin saw at work right after describing how he saw color everywhere?

- What led to the invention of the crayon?

- Explain why the inventing process took so long.

- The author mentions a few times that "Edwin listened." Explain how his listening contributed to the invention of the crayon.

- Explain the impact of Edwin's invention.

OPTION 4: EXTENSION IDEAS

- Dig into the back matter:
  - Use the "How Crayola Crayons Are Made Today" piece as a short how-to/infographic text to read, discuss, create and answer questions, and write.
  - Consider pairing the "How Crayola Crayons Are Made Today" piece with the YouTube video "How Crayons Are Made," available at https://www.youtube.com/watch?v=lmiRjmbnn8Q.
  - Use the "A Man Who Loved Color" piece as a nonfiction biography text to read, discuss, create and answer questions, and write.
  - Use the selected bibliography of primary and secondary resources to jump-start research about this part of history.
- Research the history of another inventor and/or invention.
  - Use the text structure "An Inventor and the Invention" to write about the research.
  - Create an infographic about the topic.
  - Create a poem based on your research.
- Possible Text Pairings:
  - *The Day the Crayons Quit* by Drew Daywalt
  - *Blue* by Nana Ekua Brew-Hammond
  - *The Color Collector* by Nicholas Solis
  - *The Boo-Boos That Changed the World* by Barry Wittenstein

Student Samples for
The Crayon Man

QUICK WRITE

by Payton West, 6th Grade

Something I think is useful that's not been invented is windshield wipers for your glasses. These would be helpful because they get rained on and they get foggy way too easily.

KERNEL ESSAY (USING "AN INVENTOR AND THE INVENTION")

by Khavir Patel, 4th Grade

Alexander Graham Bell was an inventor. The idea that was sparked was the telephone. He really wanted unlimited talk with friends. He tried his best to make it, [but] the invention failed. He finally finished and got an award. His invention changed things so everyone could talk for as long as they wanted.

KERNEL ESSAY RETELL (USING "AN INVENTOR AND THE INVENTION")

by Karma Nay, 7th Grade

Edward Binney was the first one to make crayons. His wife was complaining about the crayons being too expensive and that they smudged too easily. So, he made colored wax. He asked his wife what the crayons names should be and she came up with the name. He got an award for the crayons and everyone loved them.

CRAFT CHALLENGE (HYPOPHORA)

by Khavir Patel, 4th Grade

How could they make robots better? They could make it faster.

CRAFT CHALLENGE (MICROSCOPE SENTENCE)

by Aryanna McBee, 8th Grade

In the loaded city of Dallas, in the crowded restaurant, at the small table, people were eating.

TRUISM

by Joshua Carillo, 6th Grade

It can take a small or insignificant difference to change the world. It might be hard, but anyone can change the world for the better.

TRUISM

by Luke Bright, 7th Grade

Sometimes when you shut your mouth and just listen, extraordinary things can come.

READING RESPONSE (USING THE TEXT STRUCTURE "QA12"[4])

by Molly Jimenez, 4th Grade

Q: Explain the impact of Edwin's invention.

A: The impact of Edwin's invention was that children could now color and draw better with the crayons. I know this because his other inventions couldn't be used to color well. In the text it says, "Now they could draw a tiny green caterpillar or the big blue sky. Their drawings wouldn't smudge and they wouldn't rub out." This means that they couldn't draw well before but now they could.

READING RESPONSE (USING THE TEXT STRUCTURE "RACE")

by Luke Bright, 7th Grade

Q: Why did the author write this story?

A: The author chose to write this story, in my eyes, because Crayola is used so much that people often overlook how and why it was made, because they take the simple stuff for granted. But at the time it was invented, it was special. In the text it said, "Excitement over the new, colorful invention spread like a wildfire." It spread so quickly because no one had it, and they appreciated something that they didn't have before, which shows what an important invention it was.

READING RESPONSE (USING THE TEXT STRUCTURE "RACE")

by Joshua Carillo, 6th Grade

Q: Why does the author choose to mention all the black that Edwin saw at work right after describing how he saw color everywhere?

A: The author chose to mention the black because the author shows his liking for color and his dislike for black. On pages 3-4, the author states, "But all day long, all he saw was black." The illustrator shows how Edwin disliked his job. This means that Edwin wanted to find color where he worked. He also wanted to make people happy.

---

[4]The text structure "QA12" is a shortened version of "QA12345."

20 Whoosh!: Lonnie Johnson's Super-Soaking Stream of Inventions
by Chris Barton and illustrated by Don Tate

Summary: The Super Soaker water gun was almost never invented! Lonnie Johnson was a tinkerer, an inventor, and an engineer. He came up with the idea for the Super Soaker—by accident! However, when he looked for someone to help him create and sell it, he was turned down by many companies. Never one to give up, Lonnie pushed through, he found someone to produce it, and the rest is history.

Why We Love It: This accidental invention has created a lot of fun for so many, and the story behind it is worth reading! This is a story of determination in the face of failure, of problem solving, and of ingenuity. Because Lonnie was not just a tinkerer, but a NASA engineer, this would be perfect in any STEM classroom.

Topics: inventions, inventors, African American inventors, failed inventions, accidental inventions, scientists, science fairs, engineers, NASA, Super Soaker, toy companies, building things, STEM, technology

Big Ideas: failure, success, grit, ingenuity, tenacity, curiosity, trial and error, problem solving, facing challenges, setbacks, creating, perseverance, overcoming obstacles, pursuing passion

Back Matter:

- Author's note

LESSON STEPS:

1 QUICK WRITE.
(Choose One):

- What is a toy that you love (or loved when you were younger)?
- What is an invention that you are glad that we have?
- Do you know the story of how something was invented? What is it?
- What is something you think the world needs that we don't already have (an invention)?
- Did someone ever tell you that you wouldn't be able to do something, but you did it anyway? What was it? Why were you told that? What did you do?

Write about this for 3 minutes and then set it aside.

2 READ.

Read the picture book *Whoosh!: Lonnie Johnson's Super-Soaking Stream of Inventions* by Chris Barton and discuss the story. Discuss parts of the story that stick out to you or that you connect with. What writer's craft moves do you notice the author using? Notice the parts of the story.

Whoosh!: Lonnie Johnson's Super-Soaking Stream of Inventions
by Chris Barton and illustrated by Don Tate

3 SHARE THE STRUCTURE.

Show the students the structure found in the picture book. Reread the story, looking for chunks together and watching for how the author moves from one part to the other.

Doing What You Love				
_____ loved _____.	Because they loved _____, they did _____.	They wanted to do/be/create/go . . .	So they did/were/created/went . . .	This led them to _____.

4 INVITATION TO WRITE.

Here are several ways you can get students to write.

- Have students use the text structure to write a kernel essay summary of the story. (Give them between 5 and 10 minutes to do this.)

- Have the students use the text structure to write their own piece in a kernel essay. (Give them between 5 and 10 minutes to do this.)

- See what students come up with. (Give them around 10 minutes.) Here are some possibilities:

  o A page of thoughts in their quick write

  o Examples of the author's craft moves

  o A text structure

Whatever they choose to write, let them know that they can change anything they need to and make it their own.

5 SHARE.

Invite students to try their writing on someone else's ears. This is a crucial step! The sharing is just as important as the writing.

Want to Go Deeper?
Try these options.

OPTION 1: CRAFT CHALLENGE

- **Shaka-Laka-Boom:** This author uses something we call a shaka-laka-boom. This kind of sentence tells what someone **said** (*shaka*), what someone **did** (*laka*), and what immediately **happened** (*boom*). Here is an example from the story:

  *"'Sure,' Lonnie said. 'Wanna see?' [**shaka**]"*

  *Lonnie worked the pump [**laka**], which squeezed air into a chamber [**boom**]. When he pulled the trigger [**laka**], the air escaped [**boom**], forcing water out with a WHOOSH! [**boom**]"*

  Look through your piece to see where you can use a shaka-laka-boom. After you write, try it out on someone's ears to see how it sounds in your writing.

- **Pitchforked Verbs:** A pitchfork represents the act of taking one thing and branching it into a few more things. In this story, the author pitchforks some of his verbs. Here is an example from the story:

  *"He **unpacked** it, **filled** the tank with water, **pumped** the gun until the air pressure was good and high . . ."*

  Look through your piece to see where you can pitchfork some verbs. After you write, try it out on someone's ears to see how it sounds in your writing.

- **Wasn't–Wasn't–Was Pattern:** This author uses a wasn't–wasn't–was sentence pattern. Here is the example from the story:

  *"**It wasn't** easy. **It wasn't** obvious. **But** Lonnie found a solution."*

  Look through your piece to see where you can use this sentence pattern: It wasn't _____. It wasn't _____. But _____. After you write, try it out on someone's ears to see how it sounds in your writing.

OPTION 2: ANALYZE

1. **Start with a big idea.**

   - If you want students to find the big ideas themselves, try asking, "What big ideas do you see in this story that tell you what it's really about?"

   - If students need a nudge, try using some of the big ideas from the list in this lesson's introduction and have students provide evidence from the story to support their answers. Ask, "How is this story about [the big idea]? How does the author explore [the big idea]? Where in the story do you see that?"

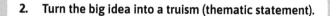

2. **Turn the big idea into a truism (thematic statement).**

   Once you have identified the big ideas, use one of them to create truisms for this story. Here are a few (found in the story) to get you started:

   - *It's important not to give up on your dream.*

   - *Sometimes success is right on the other side of a setback—we will only find it if we keep going.*

   - *Following your curiosity can you lead you to surprising outcomes.*

   Have students write and share their own truisms.

   Ask them to prove their truisms by providing evidence from the text. They might imagine a listener saying, "Oh yeah? How do you know? How is that true in the story?"

Want to Go Deeper?
Try these options.

OPTION 3:
READING RESPONSE

Students can compose short or extended responses to demonstrate understanding by answering any of these questions. Look in the appendix to find a list titled "Basic Reading Response Text Structures" and a list of "Useful Essay Question Stems for Nonfiction Texts."

Questions for Reading Response

- What led to the invention of the Super Soaker?

- Explain why it took so long for his idea for the Super Soaker to be made into a product.

- Explain how Lonnie shows determination throughout the story.

- Explain why you think Lonnie's mom didn't make him stop when he set a fire in the kitchen.

- Explain why Lonnie didn't let the results of the exam stop his dream of becoming an engineer.

OPTION 4:
EXTENSION IDEAS

- Dig into the back matter:
  - Use the author's note as a short nonfiction text to read, discuss, create and answer questions, and write.

- Do an engineering challenge: What useful thing can you create? Plan, create, write, and speak about it. It could be a STEM challenge.

- Watch the YouTube video "Meet the Man Who Invented the Super Soaker," available at https://www.youtube.com/watch?v=-1zAO1WkG58.

- Write a thank-you letter to Lonnie Johnson.

- Research the history of another inventor and/or invention.
  - Use the text structure "Doing What You Love" to write about the research.
  - Create an infographic about the topic.
  - Create a poem based on your research.

Student Samples for *Whoosh!*

QUICK WRITE

by Jacob Wong, 4th Grade

I think we need a car that people cannot get hurt in. A car made out of a Jell-O substance, so cars just bump off each other.

KERNEL ESSAY RETELL (USING "DOING WHAT YOU LOVE")

by Donghwa Lee, 9th Grade

Lonnie Johnson loved inventing. Because he loved inventing, he made a lot of inventions, like a water gun. He wanted toy companies to make his new invention. He visited some companies until one accepted the water gun. He called his water gun the Super Soaker and from there, he made even more inventions in his new workshop.

READING RESPONSE (USING THE TEXT STRUCTURE "RACE")

by Kevin Gradillas, 6th Grade

Q: Explain why it took so long for his idea for the Super Soaker to be made into a product.

A: The reason why it took so long for his idea to become a product is because many toy companies rejected his ideas, and he had no money. From pages 20 to 23, it says many toy companies rejected his ideas. Also, it says he quit his job and lost all his money. These pages explain how he had a difficult time to find someone to accept his idea. He had to go through many companies for one to say yes.

READING RESPONSE (USING THE TEXT STRUCTURE "RACE")

by CD Vardiman, 7th Grade

Q: What led to the invention of the Super Soaker?

A: Johnson accidentally invented the Super Soaker while trying to make an environmentally friendly refrigerator. While Johnson was in his bathroom trying to make a better way to keep food frozen in a fridge without using bad chemicals, he tried putting water with pressurized air but instead of cooling, it shot out and even made a gust of wind. He then had a new idea to make money for himself. I know this because eventually he gets a company to produce his machine and eventually it sells. This means he could get a bigger workshop and make more inventions. So my answer is, he made the Super Soaker by accident.

CRAFT CHALLENGE (SHAKA-LAKA-BOOM)

by Ali Imam, 4th Grade

The engineer said, "I'm going to drop it and knock it down!" So he knocked it down and it fell on three people.

Student Samples for *Whoosh!*

CRAFT CHALLENGE (WASN'T-WASN'T-WAS PATTERN)

by Ali Imam, 4th Grade

It wasn't easy. It wasn't fun. But I was finally ready to try dunking in the pool with my friends.

CRAFT CHALLENGE (WASN'T-WASN'T-WAS PATTERN)

by Donghwa Lee, 9th Grade

It wasn't quick. It wasn't planned. But the plan to destroy the iron fence worked with the BOOM.

TRUISM

by Syd Wright, 6th Grade

Perseverance leads to success. If you work at something for long enough, you will get it.

21 Caves

by Nell Cross Beckerman and illustrated by Kalen Chock

Summary: This book takes the reader on a journey through several of the different kinds of caves around the world and introduces us to globally well-known caves.

Why We Love It: Most striking is the mixture of texts. For each featured cave, there is a lyrical piece, followed by a page of facts about the cave.

Topics: caves, ecosystems, speleology, spelunkers, limestone, rock formations, stalactites, stalagmites, crystals, fossils, underwater cave systems, bats, cave paintings, bioluminescence, lava, volcanic rock

Big Ideas: exploration, curiosity, wonders of the earth, discovery

Back Matter:

- Author's note
- Illustrator's note
- Cave rules
- List of spelunking equipment
- "More Fun Facts About Caves!"

LESSON STEPS:

1 QUICK WRITE.

What is something ordinary that you see every day? Where do you think it comes from?

Write about this for 3 minutes and then set it aside.

2 READ.

Read the picture book *Caves* by Nell Cross Beckerman and discuss the story. Discuss parts of the story that stick out to you or that you connect with. What writer's craft moves do you notice the author using? Notice the parts of the story.

Caves
by Nell Cross Beckerman and illustrated by Kalen Chock

3 SHARE THE STRUCTURE.

Show the students the structure found in the picture book. Reread the story, looking for chunks together and watching for how the author moves from one part to the other.

> **All About a Place**

| Poetic impression of the place | Factual details about it (Reporter's Formula: *who*, *what*, *where*, *when*, *how*, and *why*) | One thing that happened there |

4 INVITATION TO WRITE.

Here are several ways you can get students to write.

- Have students use the text structure to write a kernel essay summary of the story. (Give them between 5 and 10 minutes to do this.)

- Have the students use the text structure to write their own piece in a kernel essay. (Give them between 5 and 10 minutes to do this.)

- See what students come up with. (Give them around 10 minutes.) Here are some possibilities:

  o A page of thoughts in their quick write

  o Examples of the author's craft moves

  o A text structure

Whatever they choose to write, let them know that they can change anything they need to and make it their own.

5 SHARE.

Invite students to try their writing on someone else's ears. This is a crucial step! The sharing is just as important as the writing.

Want to Go Deeper?
Try these options.

OPTION 1: CRAFT CHALLENGE

- **Noun + Verb Pitchfork:** This author uses a noun + verb pitchfork pattern where she combines several two-word phrases with a noun and verb in a row. Here's an example from the story:

  *"In the humid, hot swamp, **gators swim, turtles plop, snakes skim, water rushes**."*

  Look through your piece to see where you can use a noun + verb pitchfork. After you write, try it out on someone's ears to see how it sounds in your writing.

OPTION 2: ANALYZE

1. **Start with a big idea.**

   - If you want students to find the big ideas themselves, try asking, "What big ideas do you see in this story that tell you what it's really about?"

   - If students need a nudge, try using some of the big ideas from the list in this lesson's introduction and have students provide evidence from the story to support their answers. Ask, "How is this story about [the big idea]? How does the author explore [the big idea]? Where in the story do you see that?"

2. **Turn the big idea into a truism (thematic statement).**

   Once you have identified the big ideas, use one of them to create truisms for this story. Here are a few (found in the story) to get you started:

   - *It's important to be willing to have adventures.*

   - *There are still things to discover about this world.*

   Have students write and share their own truisms.

   Ask them to prove their truisms by providing evidence from the text. They might imagine a listener saying, "Oh yeah? How do you know? How is that true in the story?"

Want to Go Deeper?
Try these options.

OPTION 3:
READING RESPONSE

Students can compose short or extended responses to demonstrate understanding by answering any of these questions. Look in the appendix to find a list titled "Basic Reading Response Text Structures" and a list of "Useful Essay Question Stems for Nonfiction Texts."

Questions for Reading Response

- Explain how two of the caves are similar to each other.
- Explain a discovery made in one of the caves.
- Explain the role of water in the formation of a cave.
- Explain some ways that caves have been used throughout time.
- Explain why people are not allowed in Bracken Cave.

OPTION 4:
EXTENSION IDEAS

- Dig into the back matter:
    o Use the author's note and the "More Fun Facts About Caves!" piece as short nonfiction texts to read, discuss, create and answer questions, and write.
- Research the history of one of the caves.
    o Create an infographic about that cave.
    o Create a poem based on your research.
- If possible, explore caves in your area.
- If there isn't a cave in your area, consider taking a virtual tour.
- Do further research on caves using caves.org (home of the National Speleological Society).
- Use the text structure "All About a Place" to write about a place(s) that you have researched.
- Consider pairing this book with the book *All Thirteen: The Incredible Cave Rescue of the Thai Boys' Soccer Team* by Christina Soontornvat.
- Build a cave in your classroom for students to explore, read in, or create cave art.

QUICK WRITE

by Arthur McWhorter, Kindergarten

Fossils: They come from little creatures from a long, long time ago.

QUICK WRITE

by James Mancuso, 4th Grade

When I'm at camp, I see foxes pass by our cabin. I hear everyone playing basketball, pickle ball, carpet ball, and gaga ball. I hear the bell for breakfast when it's time to eat. I love my camp.

QUICK WRITE

by Skylar Buxton, 5th Grade

Every day when I go outside, I see these weird, fluffy caterpillars all over the place. I know they aren't from butterfly eggs, so what if they are from moth eggs? I think this because I have never seen a caterpillar be fluffy.

KERNEL ESSAY (USING "ALL ABOUT A PLACE")

by Arthur McWhorter, Kindergarten

My favorite place is our neighbor's house because my friends live there. I feel great when I'm there because I'm having fun. We play.

KERNEL ESSAY (USING "ALL ABOUT A PLACE")

by Lawson Frankland, 4th Grade

The Botanical Gardens is a place with beautiful, awesome, wondering sculptures that glow in the night sky. It has plants, sculptures, trails, and many more amazing things. Many people at many ages would like to visit it. You and your family would have a great time. One thing that happened there is that there was a crowd of over 90 people there!

KERNEL ESSAY (USING "ALL ABOUT A PLACE")

by Ashley Perez, 9th Grade

The track silences the mind as much as an empty room. In 1970, the track and football field was named after Leo Aguilar. Leo Aguilar was a young boy who died of a neck injury.

TRUISM

by Ryan Bolner, 3rd Grade

It is important to respect nature.

CRAFT CHALLENGE (NOUN + VERB PITCHFORK)

by Summer Buxton, 5th Grade

Inside the cave, water drips, crystals shine, salamanders hide and bats fly.

CRAFT CHALLENGE (NOUN + VERB PITCHFORK)

by Harper Schneider, 5th Grade

In the cold West Virginia weather, snow falls, horns honk, sheep bleat, children laugh.

CRAFT CHALLENGE (NOUN + VERB PITCHFORK)

by Lilliana Garcia, 5th Grade

In the forest, trees sway, flowers dance, birds sing, and the rocks crackle under my feet.

READING RESPONSE (USING THE TEXT STRUCTURE "RACE")

by Hudson Lopez, 6th Grade

Q: Explain why people are not allowed in Bracken Cave.

A: People are not allowed in Bracken Cave because conservationists work to protect the bats that enter the cave. They build a gate to keep people out. In the story, on pages 21-22, it says, "Bat conservationists work to protect bats from people by building gates at some entrances, letting bats enter and exit, but keeping people out." This means conservationists want to keep all the bats safe from people that may be looking to destroy their amazing homes.

22 I Am Made of Mountains: An Ode to National Parks—the Landscapes of Us

by Alexandra S. D. Hinrichs and illustrated by Vivian Mineker

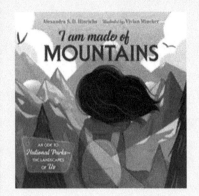

Summary: This is a book about several national parks, organized by rhyming couplets followed by short bursts of information (infoshots).

Why We Love It: Kayla loves national parks! She loves them so much that her classroom tables are named after them, her students do a big project on them each year, and it is on her family bucket list to visit each one. Not only does this book do a great job of quickly informing the reader of several different parks, but it also provides some great back matter for deeper reading.

Topics: national parks, geography, the United States, nature, landforms, landscapes, weather, wildlife, plants, animals, forests, oceans

Big Ideas: exploration, nature's beauty, appreciating nature, travel

Back Matter:

- "National Parks in the United States"
- "What Kids Across the US Love About the National Parks They've Visited!"
- Selected sources
- National park map (in the end papers)

LESSON STEPS:

1 QUICK WRITE.
(Choose One):

- What is a place you know a lot about? Describe it.
- If you could visit a place, where would it be, and why? Why should others visit it, too?
- Have you ever been to a state park or a national park? Describe it.

Write about this for 3 minutes and then set it aside.

2 READ.

Read the picture book *I Am Made of Mountains: An Ode to National Parks—the Landscapes of Us* by Alexandra S. D. Hinrichs and discuss the story. Discuss parts of the story that stick out to you or that you connect with. What writer's craft moves do you notice the author using? Notice the parts of the story.

I Am Made of Mountains: An Ode to National Parks—the Landscapes of Us
by Alexandra S. D. Hinrichs and illustrated by Vivian Mineker

3 SHARE THE STRUCTURE.

Show the students the structure found in the picture book. Reread the story, looking for chunks together and watching for how the author moves from one part to the other.

A Place Personified			
I [the place] am made of _____.	I [the place] do/have/am _____.	Infoshot (Facts and information about the place)	Repeat steps as often as necessary.

4 INVITATION TO WRITE.

Here are several ways you can get students to write.

- Have students use the text structure to write a kernel essay summary of the story. (Give them between 5 and 10 minutes to do this.)

- Have the students use the text structure to write their own piece in a kernel essay. (Give them between 5 and 10 minutes to do this.)

- See what students come up with. (Give them around 10 minutes.) Here are some possibilities:

  o A page of thoughts in their quick write

  o Examples of the author's craft moves

  o A text structure

Whatever they choose to write, let them know that they can change anything they need to and make it their own.

5 SHARE.

Invite students to try their writing on someone else's ears. This is a crucial step! The sharing is just as important as the writing.

Want to Go Deeper?

Try these options.

OPTION 1: CRAFT CHALLENGE

- **Personification:** This author uses personification to describe each park. Personification is giving nonhuman objects human capabilities. Here is an example from the story:

  "I am made of mountains. Whole worlds rest on my shoulders. I risk a peek and cannot speak, filled up with sky and boulders."

  Look through your piece to see where you can use personification. After you write, try it out on someone's ears to see how it sounds in your writing.

- **Rhyming Couplets:** In this story, the author uses two lines that rhyme, which is called a rhyming couplet and is a tool we usually see in poetry. Here's an example from the story:

  *"I am made of forest, turning golden by the **season**.*

  *I wander without plans, not needing any **reason**."*

  Look through your piece to see where you can use some rhyming couplets. After you write, try it out on someone's ears to see how it sounds in your writing.

OPTION 2: ANALYZE

1. **Start with a big idea.**

   - If you want students to find the big ideas themselves, try asking, "What big ideas do you see in this story that tell you what it's really about?"

   - If students need a nudge, try using some of the big ideas from the list in this lesson's introduction and have students provide evidence from the story to support their answers. Ask, "How is this story about [the big idea]? How does the author explore [the big idea]? Where in the story do you see that?"

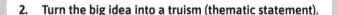

2. **Turn the big idea into a truism (thematic statement).**

   Once you have identified the big ideas, use one of them to create truisms for this story. Here are a few (found in the story) to get you started:

   - *There is so much beauty to be explored.*

   - *It is important to care for nature.*

   - *People should explore their own countries.*

   Have students write and share their own truisms.

   Ask them to prove their truisms by providing evidence from the text. They might imagine a listener saying, "Oh yeah? How do you know? How is that true in the story?"

Want to Go Deeper?
Try these options.

OPTION 3: READING RESPONSE

Students can compose short or extended responses to demonstrate understanding by answering any of these questions. Look in the appendix to find a list titled "Basic Reading Response Text Structures" and a list of "Useful Essay Question Stems for Nonfiction Texts."

Questions for Reading Response

- Compare and contrast two of the parks.

- What is the author's purpose in writing this book?

- Explain some ways people might benefit from visiting a national park.

- How does the description of [a national park] affect the reader's understanding of [glaciers, mountains, geysers, etc.]?

- Read "Troubled Beginnings" under "National Parks in the United States" in the back matter. How does this affect the reader's understanding of national parks?

- What is the most important thing people can learn from visiting national parks?

OPTION 4: EXTENSION IDEAS

- Dig into the back matter:
  - Use the "National Parks in the United States" piece as a short nonfiction text to read, discuss, create and answer questions, and write.
  - Use the selected sources to jump-start research about one of the national parks.

- Research about another park or place:
  - Create an infographic about your research.
  - Create a poem based on your research.
  - Use the text structure "A Place Personified" to write about that place.
  - Create your own book (like this one) with your research (or a class book with your combined research).

- Watch one of the national park videos from the official national park website (each park has its own; see https://www.nps.gov/findapark/index.htm) to learn more about a particular park.

- Use the map in the end papers to find each park that you read about or parks near you.

- Make a timeline that shows when each park became official.

- Contact a local park ranger to come speak about the local park, nature, and wildlife. Possibly combine this talk with a field trip to a local park.

QUICK WRITE

by Arthur McWhorter, Kindergarten

I saw a bird flying in the air and it was super pretty. I saw it at the park near my house. I saw a lizard camouflaged on a tree.

QUICK WRITE

by Holden Dewar, 7th Grade

I have been to a couple state parks. I will describe Goose Island State Park. Like its name suggests, the park is found on Goose Island, right outside Rockport, Texas, near Corpus Christi. It is very marshy on the water.

QUICK WRITE

by Alex Chen, 7th Grade

I would like to visit San Francisco because of the many places I would like to see. First of all, I've never been to any other state than Texas since I was three. So, I would like to see what the other states also have to offer. Secondly, my dad's college, UC Berkeley, is also there, so I would like to visit the college with my dad and see where his old classes were. I also want to visit the Golden Gate Bridge because I want to see how long it really is and see if it was actually golden before. Lastly, I would like to visit the giant sequoias of San Francisco a little far away, since I really want to see the sheer size of these trees. I also haven't known anybody that has been to these giant trees, so I can say I have visited them.

KERNEL ESSAY (USING "A PLACE PERSONIFIED")

by Holden Dewar, 7th Grade

I, Yosemite, am the best of the national parks. Not to brag, but I am made of limestone. I have gorges, plateaus, climbing areas, and rivers. Here's a fun fact: have you seen the movie *Free Solo*? It was filmed here.

KERNEL ESSAY (USING "A PLACE PERSONIFIED")

by Hazel Gonzalez, 4th Grade

I, the Gonzalez house, am made of wood. I have a door, a roof, carpet upstairs, and a floor downstairs. I can be found on Google maps. I am Hazel's favorite house.

KERNEL ESSAY (USING "A PLACE PERSONIFIED")

by Alex Chen, 7th Grade

I, the Golden Gate Bridge, am made of rusted, red metal.

I, the Golden Gate Bridge, have many cars on me and will always provide transport until the end.

The Golden Gate Bridge was constructed in 1937 and has the longest bridge span with a span of 1.7 miles, or about 2,737 meters.

KERNEL ESSAY (USING "A PLACE PERSONIFIED")

by Yuxuan Li, 7th Grade

Regent's Park

I am made of greenery.

I am covered in grass, blooming flowers, and lush trees in the spring.

Regent's Park (officially "The Regent's Park") is one of the Royal Parks of London. Covering over 5,000 acres of historic parkland, the parks provide beautiful green spaces right in the heart of the capital where you can escape the rush of Central London.

Highgate Cemetery

I am made of graves.

I hold the memories of the deceased for evermore.

Highgate Cemetery is a place of burial in north London, England, designed by architect Stephen Geary. Highgate Cemetery is notable both for some of the people buried there as well as for its de facto status as a nature reserve.

Tower of London

I am made of history.

I have many pale towers that loom over the city.

The Tower of London is a historic castle on the north bank of the River Thames in central London, England. It was founded toward the end of 1066 as part of the Norman Conquest.

London Underground

I am made of trains.

I have many tunnels running under all of London, holding the city together.

The London Underground is a rapid transit system serving Greater London and some parts of the adjacent home counties of Buckinghamshire, Essex, and Hertfordshire in England. The Underground has its origins in the Metropolitan Railway, opening on 10 January 1863 as the world's first underground passenger railway.

Trafalgar Square

I am made of people.

I stand in the middle of London, red buses running through me.

Trafalgar Square is a public square that features some of London's top attractions, from galleries and historic buildings to statues and monuments.

Student Samples for
I Am Made of Mountains

Trafalgar Square is in Westminster, in central London. It's surrounded by the National Gallery to the north; St. Martins-in-the-Fields Church and The Strand to the east; Whitehall to the south; and Admiralty Arch and The Mall to the southwest.

A: The author's purpose is to spread awareness of national parks and entice more people to come. There is wilderness, landscape, and treasures of each place, which shows that each national park has its own special quality.

READING RESPONSE (USING THE TEXT STRUCTURE "RACE")

by Berlin Growcock, 3rd Grade

Q: What is the author's purpose in writing this book?

Over and Under the Rainforest

by Kate Messner and illustrated by Christopher Silas Neal

Summary: *Over and Under the Rainforest* takes the reader on a walk through the rainforest, exploring the foliage and witnessing the wildlife that live there.

Why We Love It: We love the whole *Over and Under* series by Kate Messner. We love the gentle walk through the area and the observations made along the way. It is a great way to "visit" a place and spark curiosity for further study.

Topics: rainforests, rainforest canopy, hiking, trees, rivers, flora and fauna, ecosystem, wildlife (oropendolas, toucans, agoutis, long-nosed bats, crocodiles, emerald basilisks, poison dart frogs, capuchin monkeys, leaf-cutter ants, long-snouted anteaters, blue morpho butterflies, sloths, parrot snakes, eyelash palm pit vipers, howler monkeys, orb spiders, jaguars, squirrel cuckoos, woodpeckers, motmots), Costa Rica

Big Ideas: exploration, exploring nature, discovery, the wonder of nature, being in the wild, appreciating nature, outdoor adventure, the natural world

Back Matter:

- Author's note
- "About the Animals"
- Further reading
- Sources

LESSON STEPS:

1 QUICK WRITE.
(CHOOSE ONE):

- Have you ever explored the outdoors? Where did you go? What was it like?
- Have you ever spent time watching an animal or a bug? What did you notice?
- How many different creatures live in your neighborhood? Make a list.
- Can you imagine living in a place with a lot of wild animals? What would that be like?

Write about this for 3 minutes and then set it aside.

2 READ.

Read the picture book *Over and Under the Rainforest* by Kate Messner and discuss the story. Discuss parts of the story that stick out to you or that you connect with. What writer's craft moves do you notice the author using? Notice the parts of the story.

23 over and Under the Rainforest
by Kate Messner and illustrated by Christopher Silas Neal

3 SHARE THE STRUCTURE.

Show the students the structure found in the picture book. Reread the story, looking for chunks together and watching for how the author moves from one part to the other.

Birdwalk

Where we are going	One thing we see (with details)	Another thing we see (with details)	Another thing we see (with details)	How we know when it's time to finish

4 INVITATION TO WRITE.

Here are several ways you can get students to write.

- Have students use the text structure to write a kernel essay summary of the story. (Give them between 5 and 10 minutes to do this.)

- Have the students use the text structure to write their own piece in a kernel essay. (Give them between 5 and 10 minutes to do this.)

- See what students come up with. (Give them around 10 minutes.) Here are some possibilities:
  - A page of thoughts in their quick write
  - Examples of the author's craft moves
  - A text structure

Whatever they choose to write, let them know that they can change anything they need to and make it their own.

5 SHARE.

Invite students to try their writing on someone else's ears. This is a crucial step! The sharing is just as important as the writing.

Want to Go Deeper?
Try These Options.

OPTION 1: CRAFT CHALLENGE

- **Alliteration:** In this story, the author uses alliteration, which is the repetition of the beginning sounds of words that are near each other. Here are some examples from the story.

  *"Into the rainforest we hike, through **slivers** of **sunlight** and dripping-wet leaves."*

  *"**Chatters** and **chirps** and a howling roar."*

  *"Toucans croak and **bicker** over **breakfast**."*

  Look through your piece to see where you can use alliteration. After you write, try it out on someone's ears to see how it sounds in your writing.

- **Strong Verbs:** In this story, the author uses strong verbs, which are action words like *eat, run,* and *play*. Strong verbs make your writing clear and paint the best picture possible for your reader. Here are some examples from the story:

  *"Up in the trees, oropendolas **gurgle** in low-swinging nests. Toucans **croak** and **bicker** over breakfast."*

  Look through your piece to see where you can use some strong verbs. After you write, try it out on someone's ears to see how it sounds in your writing.

- **Hyphenated Adjectives:** This author uses several hyphenated adjectives. Adjectives are words that describe nouns, and hyphenated adjectives are two words that are glued together with a hyphen. Here are some examples from the story:

  *"Into the rainforest we hike, through slivers of sunlight and **dripping-wet** leaves."*

  *"The afternoon rain begins with a patter—a **pitter-soft** drumming on the leaves up above."*

  *"A **long-snouted** anteater snuffles along, sniffing for a meal of his own."*

  Look through your piece and see where you can use some hyphenated adjectives. Try it out on someone's ears to see how it sounds in your writing.

- **Directional Echoes:** All throughout the text, this author uses what we like to call directional echoes, where she describes two different directions like north and south, up and down, or left and right. Here is an example from the story:

  *"**Up in the trees**, long-nosed bats sleep away the daylight, all in a row. **Down on the bank**, sleepy crocodiles bask in the sun."*

  Look through your piece and see where you can use some directional echoes. Try it out on someone's ears to see how it sounds in your writing.

OPTION 2: ANALYZE

1. **Start with a big idea.**

   - If you want students to find the big ideas themselves, try asking, "What big ideas do you see in this story that tell you what it's really about?"

   - If students need a nudge, try using some of the big ideas from the list in this lesson's introduction and have students provide evidence from the story to support their answers. Ask, "How is this story about [the big idea]? How does the author explore [the big idea]? Where in the story do you see that?"

2. **Turn the big idea into a truism (thematic statement).**

   Once you have identified the big ideas, use one of them to create truisms for this story. Here are a few (found in the story) to get you started:

   - *In this world, there are so many places to explore.*

   - *Many different kinds of creatures can live near each other.*

   - *People have to look out for potential dangers, anywhere they go.*

   Have students write and share their own truisms.

   Ask them to prove their truisms by providing evidence from the text. They might imagine a listener saying, "Oh yeah? How do you know? How is that true in the story?"

Want to Go Deeper?
Try these options.

OPTION 3: READING RESPONSE

Students can compose short or extended responses to demonstrate understanding by answering any of these questions. Look in the appendix to find a list titled "Basic Reading Response Text Structures" and a list of "Useful Essay Question Stems for Nonfiction Texts."

Questions for Reading Response

- Explain what happens in the story (retell).
- Explain why the author used the title *Over and Under the Rainforest*.
- Explain why the author wrote this book.
- Leaving the rainforest at night is important because it shows what?
- What is the effect of the author's use of description?

OPTION 4: EXTENSION IDEAS

- Dig into the back matter:
  o Use the author's note and the "About the Animals" piece as short nonfiction texts to read, discuss, create and answer questions, and write.
- Research more about the animals in the book and/or the rainforest.
  o Create an infographic about the topic.
  o Create a poem based on your research.
  o Use the text structure to write about your research (or another topic).
  o Watch the YouTube video "Rainforests for Kids | Learn All About the Two Types of Rainforests," available at https://www.youtube.com/watch?v=sEQMEllUyks.
- Assign an animal (from the book/rainforest) for each student to research and then put on an informative play in which students dress up and speak as their animal.
- Read some of the other books in the *Over and Under series*. They are all fantastic!

QUICK WRITE

by Jackson Guenther, 5th Grade

My sister and I once were playing outside in our yard. It was a sunny day, but fairly chilly. Then I noticed a leaf crawling around on the ground. As I inspected it closer, I realized that the leaf was being carried by two ants. And then I saw that there were lots of moving leaves. I followed the trail and came across a huge ant mound. I've visited that mound a lot now and I'm entranced every time.

QUICK WRITE

by Payton West, 6th Grade

I think living in a place with a lot of wild animals would be cool, but also scary. It takes a lot of courage to see a wild crocodile or lion because THEY COULD KILL YOU!!

CRAFT CHALLENGE (HYPHENATED ADJECTIVES)

by Harper Hsieh, 4th Grade

Spring has **bitter-sweet** rain.

CRAFT CHALLENGE (HYPHENATED ADJECTIVES)

by Jackson Guenther, 5th Grade

The **dusty-tall** ant mound wall was an obelisk in a barren plain.

CRAFT CHALLENGE (HYPHENATED ADJECTIVES)

by Zachary Oblitas, 9th Grade

I looked out the **half-opened** window.

I stumbled across the famous **short-stumped** tree.

CRAFT CHALLENGE (DIRECTIONAL ECHOES)

by Jackson Guenther, 5th Grade

Down at **the bottom of** the valley, the water pools up, forming a river. **And at the very top** lie the headwaters, feeding the entire river all the way down the river, becoming a tributary.

CRAFT CHALLENGE (DIRECTIONAL ECHOES)

by Zachary Oblitas, 9th Grade

North of the small village, **by the mountains**, there was a giant, dormant volcano.

CRAFT CHALLENGE (DIRECTIONAL ECHOES)

by Maanasa Nichanametla, 9th Grade

Left of the sky, darkness flooding into the light. **On the right,** the gorgeous pops of red and orange light fighting to stay alive.

KERNEL ESSAY (USING "BIRDWALK")

by Harper Hsieh, 4th Grade

I go to Big Sky, Montana, every year. I see fresh snow falling from the sky. I go skiing there. I see skiers racing down the slopes. I see lifts with people about to ski. I know our time is ending because we have to return to our own skies.

KERNEL ESSAY (USING "BIRDWALK")

by Jackson Guenther, 5th Grade

At the ranch, up the creek and across a riverbed of rocks, there is a sight to see. A series of plateaus, a staircase for giants, is a glorious waterfall with sunlight refracting throughout the water like a prism, casting miniature rainbow adding color to the lush green environment. The foliage in that area makes the rest of the ranch look like the Sahara Desert. The basking falls collect in pools, spilling over to form a triangle, looking like the formation of pins when you go bowling. As the sun sets, I mourn, for I've sat an hour there, watching, and I could've spent another. But I will come back.

KERNEL ESSAY (USING "BIRDWALK")

by Corbett Hanzel, 5th Grade

Me and Sam were driving around the vast web of roads at the ranch. I saw an armadillo. He looked to be a juvenile. For some reason, he just sat there like a lump of wood. We made another turn onto the road we dump animal corpses on. One of the dead deer was plopped in the center of the road. Its flesh was rotting away, making the whole road stink. The sun started setting and you could see stars in the sky. We realized dinner was probably ready, so we headed back to the house.

KERNEL ESSAY (USING "BIRDWALK")

by Maanasa Nichanametla, 9th Grade

In New Hampshire, my cousins and I hiked up a beautiful mountain with rocky slides, branch-filled biking paths, and beautiful viewed areas.

When hiking up, I came across these beautiful bushes along our path with big glowing blueberries ready to pluck. When plopped in our mouths, we were surprised from the sweetness of the fruit.

When going up the rocky slant part of the mountain, with every step taken, you can find a footprint engraved into the stone, almost like a fossil that could be you one day.

When you get to the top of the gorgeous mountain, the view you get is spectacular. The trees fanned out. People small as ants. Cities towering. But most importantly, you are risen over everyone.

When seen on TV, these natural figures seem cool and all, but when looked at with your own eyes, it's heaven that can't be described. The fresh air and beautiful structures—it's an experience nothing can prepare you for.

The Brilliant Deep: Rebuilding the World's Coral Reefs

by Kate Messner and illustrated by Matthew Forsythe

Summary: As a young boy, Ken Nedimyer was interested in the ocean, and while diving, he discovered that the coral in the area was dying. When he got older, he conducted experiments, which led to his important work regrowing the coral reefs today.

Why We Love It: Many of us have believed that the coral reefs are dying and cannot be saved. However, this story offers hope and shows us that maybe they can. And as usual, it starts with just one person.

Topics: coral reefs, conservation, environmental science, scientists, coral reef restoration, Ken Nedimyer, Coral Restoration Foundation, pioneers, oceans, sea life, Florida Keys, scuba, diving, rock farms, coral colonies, experiments, climate change

Big Ideas: wonder of nature, human ingenuity, caring for the earth, problem solving, observation, regrowth, hope, volunteering, making a difference, reversing climate change

Back Matter:

- "What Happened to the Coral Reefs?"
- "How Can Kids Help?"
- "Read More"
- "Explore Online"
- "Coral Reef Vocabulary"

LESSON STEPS:

1 QUICK WRITE.
(CHOOSE ONE):

- Have you ever taken care of something that was broken, sick, or falling apart? What happened?

- What is something that you are interested in—something that you are curious about and would like to study?

- What problem in our world do you think needs solving? What would you do?

Write about this for 3 minutes and then set it aside.

2 READ.

Read the picture book *The Brilliant Deep: Rebuilding the World's Coral Reefs* by Kate Messner and discuss the story. Discuss parts of the story that stick out to you or that you connect with. What writer's craft moves do you notice the author using? Notice the parts of the story.

24 The Brilliant Deep: Rebuilding the World's Coral Reefs

by Kate Messner and illustrated by Matthew Forsythe

3 SHARE THE STRUCTURE.

Show the students the structure found in the picture book. Reread the story, looking for chunks together and watching for how the author moves from one part to the other.

Saving Something You Love

What someone was interested in	How that interest grew	A problem that the person noticed	What that person figured out	How their idea worked out

4 INVITATION TO WRITE.

Here are several ways you can get students to write.

- Have students use the text structure to write a kernel essay summary of the story. (Give them between 5 and 10 minutes to do this.)

- Have the students use the text structure to write their own piece in a kernel essay. (Give them between 5 and 10 minutes to do this.)

- See what students come up with. (Give them around 10 minutes.) Here are some possibilities:

  - A page of thoughts in their quick write
  - Examples of the author's craft moves
  - A text structure

Whatever they choose to write, let them know that they can change anything they need to and make it their own.

5 SHARE.

Invite students to try their writing on someone else's ears. This is a crucial step! The sharing is just as important as the writing.

Want to Go Deeper?
Try These Options.

OPTION 1: CRAFT CHALLENGE

- **Anaphork (Anaphora + Pitchfork):** This author uses the rhetorical device anaphora and adds a pitchfork. In other words, she repeats a word or phrase at the beginning of a sentence (anaphora) and does this three times (like a pitchfork). Kayla's students named this an "anaphork." Authors and speakers do this to create rhythm, to stir emotion, or to emphasize or bring focus to something. Here is an example from the story:

  *"**Some** become food. **Some** are washed into the deep sea. **Some** drift in the currents until they come to rest, not too deep, on the ocean floor."*

  Look through your piece and see where you can use an anaphork. It is a great way to combine two sentences and add some sentence variety to your writing. Try it out on someone's ears to see how it sounds in your writing.

- **Metaphor:** In this story, the author uses a metaphor, which is a figure of speech that describes something by saying it is something else—like a simile, but without *like* or *as*. Here's an example from the story:

  *"The sea urchins had started to die. **They were the gardeners** of the reef, **tiny groundskeepers** who control the algae."*

  Look through your piece to see where you can use a metaphor. After you write, try it out on someone's ears to see how it sounds in your writing.

- **Echo Ending:** This author uses an echo ending (the beginning and the end of the story are the same or similar). Here are the words from the story:

  "It starts with one."

  Look at the beginning and end of your story and see if you can use something similar in both places. Maybe try a line of dialogue, or something that happens, or even the description of an image. Try it out on someone's ears to see how it sounds in your writing.

OPTION 2: ANALYZE

1. **Start with a big idea.**

   - If you want students to find the big ideas themselves, try asking, "What big ideas do you see in this story that tell you what it's really about?"

   - If students need a nudge, try using some of the big ideas from the list in this lesson's introduction and have students provide evidence from the story to support their answers. Ask, "How is this story about [the big idea]? How does the author explore [the big idea]? Where in the story do you see that?"

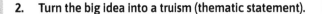

2. **Turn the big idea into a truism (thematic statement).**

   Once you have identified the big ideas, use one of them to create truisms for this story. Here are a few (found in the story) to get you started:

   - *All it takes is one idea to change the world.*

   - *"Anything might be possible if you set your mind to it."*

   - *It's important not to give up hope too fast.*

   Have students write and share their own truisms.

   Ask them to prove their truisms by providing evidence from the text. They might imagine a listener saying, "Oh yeah? How do you know? How is that true in the story?"

Want to Go Deeper?
Try these options.

OPTION 3: READING RESPONSE

Students can compose short or extended responses to demonstrate understanding by answering any of these questions. Look in the appendix to find a list titled "Basic Reading Response Text Structures" and a list of "Useful Essay Question Stems for Nonfiction Texts."

Questions for Reading Response

- Explain how sea urchins are beneficial to the coral reefs.

- Explain the benefits of rebuilding the coral reefs.

- Explain the relationship between the rocks and the coral reefs.

- Explain what the author means by the line, "It starts with one."

- Explain the importance of Ken's childhood interest in the story.

OPTION 4: EXTENSION IDEAS

- Dig into the back matter:
  - Use "What Happened to the Coral Reefs?" and "How Can Kids Help?" as short nonfiction texts to read, discuss, create and answer questions, and write.
  - Consider helping to save the coral reefs by donating to the Coral Restoration Foundation.
- If you have one near you, take a field trip to an aquarium.
- Invite an environmental scientist, scuba diver, or oceanographer to come to your school to talk about what they do.
- Research more about coral, ocean life, the Coral Restoration Foundation, Ken Nedimyer's work, or other environmental scientists.
  - Watch the YouTube video "CNN: CNN Hero, Ken Nedimyer Bringing Life Back to Coral Reefs," available at https://www.youtube.com/watch?v=VWcjoj0_5Yc.
  - Create an infographic about the topic.
  - Create a poem based on your research.
  - Use the text structure to write about your research (or another topic).

KERNEL ESSAY (+ CRAFT CHALLENGES: ANAPHORK AND AN ECHO ENDING)

by John Kothmann, 5th Grade

A cowboy always gets back on his horse. My family loves the rodeo, and we annually took a trip to San Angelo, Texas, to watch the rodeo with my whole extended family. When I was seven, the rodeo grew on me and before I knew it, I was cheering on every eight-second ride. I loved every aspect of the rodeo. **Some** fell off. **Some** stayed on. **Some** got right back on. One year, though, we noticed there was no carnival and then we were told the rodeo was taking budget cuts and they would lose the rodeo next year! A bullet felt like it hit me as I processed the news, and I knew I had to do something. After that night's show, I knew that whatever I could do, I should do. I talked to my grandpa, the man who has had perfect rodeo attendance 20 years straight, and we devised a plan to raise money for the rodeo. We decided to put QR codes all around the city that took you to a website to donate money. After a month, we saw we had raised more than $200,000! The next day we were excited to go to the head of the rodeo's office and present him with the money. Not only did we raise enough money, but there was enough left for a small stadium renovation! My family and I continue to go to the rodeo. A cowboy always gets back on his horse.

KERNEL ESSAY (+ CRAFT CHALLENGES: ANAPHORK AND AN ECHO ENDING)

by Jackson Guenther, 5th Grade

I love Legos. They inspire creativity, problem solving, ingenuity, and structural engineering. As a kid, I got my first Lego set at the age of five, and to me, it was 24 karat gold. And I only loved them more when I went to the malls to check out Lego stores. They had everything. They had gigantic star destroyers. They had beautifully made paintings. And they had a wall. A wall, a gigantic wall made completely of Legos, only holding even more Lego sets. By age ten, my room was its own Lego store. I had entire desks and shelves dedicated to Legos. I had beautifully made paintings. I had gigantic star destroyers. I had Legos. But my mom said I couldn't get any more Legos. She said I couldn't get any more until I cleaned my room. But I wanted Legos, and my room was full of the shiny, plastic bricks. But then I had an idea. I needed more Lego storage, so I would build storage out of Legos. So, I began to begin a project and that project was my life to me. When I finished, I went to my mom, overjoyed, and told her. She gave me a Lego box, and I started building. I love Legos.

Student Samples for
The Brilliant Deep

KERNEL ESSAY (USING "SAVING SOMETHING YOU LOVE")

by **Whit Wright, 8th Grade**

I was interested in the sport of wiffleball. My interest grew as I began to watch a YouTube channel that made videos of wiffleball. I wanted to play at my house, but I noticed that I didn't have a proper strike zone. I figured out that with a long sheet of paper, a cardboard box, and some duct tape, I could make my own. After this invention, my brothers and I were able to play countless hours of wiffleball in the backyard.

CRAFT CHALLENGE (METAPHOR)

by **Whit Wright, 8th Grade**

I was a racecar. I flew around the bases and I was about to reach home base. I dove for home and I had officially hit my first home run ever.

CRAFT CHALLENGE (METAPHOR)

by **Kari Kepler, 8th Grade**

Some people are the duct tape to friend groups. They keep it together.

CRAFT CHALLENGE (ANAPHORK)

by **Whit Wright, 8th Grade**

Most want to be famous. Most want to be extremely rich. Most want to be the coolest and most athletic person on the face of the earth.

CRAFT CHALLENGE (ANAPHORK)

by **Hrishik Trivedi, 9th Grade**

World problems can be solved. **World** peace can be solved. **World** hunger can be solved.

READING RESPONSE (USING THE TEXT STRUCTURE "RACE")

by **Noah Hoberman, 3rd Grade**

Q: Explain the benefits of rebuilding the coral reefs.

A: One of the benefits of saving the coral reef is the fish will come back. In the story, it states the fish start to disappear after the reefs started to die. On page 13, it says that Ken noticed there weren't as many fish. This shows that if the coral reefs start to die, the fish will disappear. Some fish will even die.

The Floating Field: How a Group of Thai Boys Built Their Own Soccer Field

by Scott Riley and illustrated by Nguyen Quang and Kim Lien

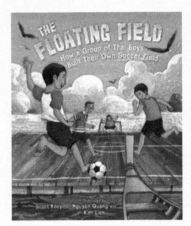

Summary: Prasit and his friends live in Thailand in a floating community, where all of the buildings are on stilts, and they play soccer during the brief times when the tide is out. The boys build a floating platform as a soccer field and eventually compete with other teams.

Why We Love It: A floating soccer field just sounds impossible, yet these boys made it work, using scraps and tenacity. We love most that it really happened.

Topics: Thailand, Koh Panyee, village life, island life, high tide, low tide, full moon, sandbar, buildings on stilts, soccer, sports, 1986 World Cup, soccer teams, engineering, STEM, history

Big Ideas: overcoming obstacles, overcoming the odds, working together, resourcefulness, ingenuity, solving a problem, creative solutions, determination, grit, passion, teamwork, community, going after your dreams, forging new ground, blazing a new path

Back Matter:

- Author's note
- "Prasit's Perspective"
- "Words You Might Hear on the Floating Field"
- Bibliography
- Further reading

LESSON STEPS:

1 QUICK WRITE.
(CHOOSE ONE):

- What is your favorite sport? Why do you like it?

- Have you ever been told that you couldn't do something? (Maybe you were told you were too small, or too weak, or too unskilled to do something. Maybe you didn't have the right materials.) What did you do about it?

- Do you know the story of how something was invented? What is it?

- Have you ever had an obstacle stand in your way when you wanted to do something? What was it? What did you do about it?

Write about this for 3 minutes and then set it aside.

2 READ.

Read the picture book *The Floating Field: How a Group of Thai Boys Built Their Own Soccer Field* by Scott Riley and discuss the story. Discuss parts of the story that stick out to you or that you connect with. What writer's craft moves do you notice the author using? Notice the parts of the story.

25 The Floating Field: How a Group of Thai Boys Built Their Own Soccer Field

by Scott Riley and illustrated by Nguyen Quang and Kim Lien

3 SHARE THE STRUCTURE.

Show the students the structure found in the picture book. Reread the story, looking for chunks together and watching for how the author moves from one part to the other.

An Inventor and the Invention					
Who the person was	What sparked the idea for the invention	The process: What happened first?	The process: What happened next?	The process: What happened last?	How it was received or How it changed things

4 INVITATION TO WRITE.

Here are several ways you can get students to write.

- Have students use the text structure to write a kernel essay summary of the story. (Give them between 5 and 10 minutes to do this.)

- Have the students use the text structure to write their own piece in a kernel essay. (Give them between 5 and 10 minutes to do this.)

- See what students come up with. (Give them around 10 minutes.) Here are some possibilities:

    o A page of thoughts in their quick write

    o Examples of the author's craft moves

    o A text structure

Whatever they choose to write, let them know that they can change anything they need to and make it their own.

5 SHARE.

Invite students to try their writing on someone else's ears. This is a crucial step! The sharing is just as important as the writing.

Want to Go Deeper?
Try These Options.

OPTION 1: CRAFT CHALLENGE

- **Two-Word Sentences:** All a sentence really needs is a subject and a predicate, which is what allows for two-word sentences. This author uses a few right next to each other, so it's basically like a pitchfork. Here are the examples from the story:

  "Hammers flew. Nails bent. Boards split."

  Look through your piece to see where you can use a few two-word sentences. After you write, try it out on someone's ears to see how it sounds in your writing.

- **Pitchforked Participial Phrases:** In this story, the author uses pitchforked participial phrases. A participle is a verb that ends with -*ing* or -*ed* but is serving the function of an adjective (a describing word), such as *toasted buns* or *dripping with butter* (which is actually a participial phrase). Here is an example from the story:

  *"Within minutes, sheets of rain came pouring down, **drenching uniforms, filling cleats, and flooding the field.**"*

  Look through your piece and see where you can try some pitchforked participial phrases. Try it out on someone's ears to see how it sounds in your writing.

- **Directional Echoes:** This author uses what we like to call directional echoes, where he describes two different directions like north and south, up and down, or left and right. Here is an example from the story:

  *"**Above them**, the full moon had set and the sun was rising. **Below them**, the tides were already shifting."*

  Look through your piece and see where you can use some directional echoes. Try it out on someone's ears to see how it sounds in your writing.

OPTION 2: ANALYZE

1. **Start with a big idea.**

   - If you want students to find the big ideas themselves, try asking, "What big ideas do you see in this story that tell you what it's really about?"

   - If students need a nudge, try using some of the big ideas from the list in this lesson's introduction and have students provide evidence from the story to support their answers. Ask, "How is this story about [the big idea]? How does the author explore [the big idea]? Where in the story do you see that?"

2. **Turn the big idea into a truism (thematic statement).**

   Once you have identified the big ideas, use one of them to create truisms for this story. Here are a few (found in the story) to get you started:

   - *"What's most important is that anything is possible."*

   - *"As a community or team, you can overcome incredibly impossible odds."*

   - *Play is an important part of every childhood.*

   Have students write and share their own truisms.

   Ask them to prove their truisms by providing evidence from the text. They might imagine a listener saying, "Oh yeah? How do you know? How is that true in the story?"

Want to Go Deeper?
Try these options.

OPTION 3: READING RESPONSE

Students can compose short or extended responses to demonstrate understanding by answering any of these questions. Look in the appendix to find a list titled "Basic Reading Response Text Structures" and a list of "Useful Essay Question Stems for Nonfiction Texts."

Questions for Reading Response

- What challenge do Prasit and his friends face?
- Why are the tides important in the lives of the boys?
- How do the actions of the boys support the theme that anything is possible?
- What is meant by the phrase "a town built on stilts"?
- What causes the boys to realize they should take off their shoes during the important game?
- How does the author show that the community supports the boys?

OPTION 4: EXTENSION IDEAS

- Dig into the back matter:
  - Use the author's note and the "Prasit's Perspective" piece as short nonfiction texts to read, discuss, create and answer questions, and write.
- Research more about soccer, Thailand, Koh Panyee, or other soccer fields (or sports arenas) in unexpected places.
  - Create an infographic about the topic.
  - Create a poem based on your research.
  - Use the text structure to write about your research (or another topic).
  - Watch the YouTube video "TMB Panyee FC Short Film" (spoken in Thai with subtitles in English), available at https://www.youtube.com/watch?v=jU4oA3kkAWU.
  - Try playing soccer (or another sport) in a nontraditional place or way.

QUICK WRITE

by Sejan Nagi, 4th Grade

My favorite sport is swimming because that sport makes your body move for exercise. It is also great doing laps around the pool for exercise.

QUICK WRITE

by Hemanshu Viswanathan, 9th Grade

I have had an obstacle before of believing in myself. People had always told me to do it, but it was not that easy. One day, my dad said that part of believing in yourself is to get in that moment and forget what is happening outside of the thing that is happening. This happened while we were going to a soccer game, and I played one of my best games ever.

KERNEL ESSAY RETELL (USING "AN INVENTOR AND THE INVENTION")

by Whit Wright, 8th Grade

The book *The Floating Field* was a story of a boy named Prasit and his friends. Whenever they could, the boys would head to the sandbar and play soccer until one day, after the waves covered the sandbar, Prasit suggested to build their own soccer field. Finally, they got to play their first match on the floating field. This changed everything because the boys were able to play soccer every day for however long they wanted. In the end, they became good enough to compete in a tournament.

KERNEL ESSAY (USING "AN INVENTOR AND THE INVENTION")

by Celena Weng, 9th Grade

Since Albert Camus was a philosopher, he had many types of thought which he put in his writing. Camus wrote about how he considered suicide as a truly serious problem, but people still do it. Camus provided answers as to how to live, accept, and celebrate the feelings of absurdity. Camus gave three direct answers: revolt, freedom, and lastly passion. Many people criticized his ideas because they were "too depressive."

CRAFT CHALLENGE (DIRECTIONAL ECHOES)

by Sejan Nagi, 4th Grade

Above them, they saw the sun shining. **Below them,** they saw the bright green grass.

CRAFT CHALLENGE (DIRECTIONAL ECHOES)

by Celena Weng, 9th Grade

On my left, there are people chattering and laughing away. **On my right,** it's dead silent, the tension so dense it could drown everyone in this room.

READING RESPONSE (USING THE TEXT STRUCTURE "RACE")

by Whit Wright, 8th Grade

Q: How does the author show that the community supports the boys?

A: The author shows that the community supports the boys by showing how dedicated the village is to the team. Two examples of this are when the people stop to cheer for the team's miniature game, and when the village provides jerseys and other soccer gear for the team's tournament. These examples show that the people of the town truly care about the boys' success.

The Secret Kingdom: Nek Chand, a Changing India, and a Hidden World of Art

by Barb Rosenstock and illustrated by Claire A. Nivola

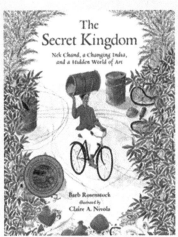

Summary: Accustomed to village life and forced to move to the new city of Chandigarh because of the partition of India and Pakistan, Nek Chand finds himself longing for home. While working his new job as a government road inspector, he finds materials left over from the recent demolition and construction of the new city. Nek uses these found items to create his own secret garden and keeps it hidden until his treasure is discovered and then threatened.

Why We Love It: This is a beautiful story of creating one's own place and using discarded materials to craft something magical. We love the imagination and creativity, but also the way the community came together to save Nek's work.

Topics: Nek Chand, India, the partition of India and Pakistan, art, folk art, recycling, nature, secret gardens, art gardens, sculptures, mosaics, the Rock Garden of Chandigarh, reusing trash, governments, gardens, village life, city life, reconstruction, building

Big Ideas: creativity, imagination, ingenuity, beautifying your environment, trash to treasure, perseverance, working hard, grit, overcoming obstacles, change, progress, going against the grain, breaking the rules, activism, speaking up for others, sharing your gift with others

Back Matter:

- Author's note
- Bibliography

LESSON STEPS:

1 QUICK WRITE.
(CHOOSE ONE):

- Have you ever picked up a common, everyday object and turned it into something else?

- Do you ever think about what happens to trash when we throw it out? What can you imagine might be the best thing to happen to it?

- Have you ever created a secret place (like a fort, or a hiding place, or a tent) that only you knew about? What was it like being inside that place? Describe it.

Write about this for 3 minutes and then set it aside.

2 READ.

Read the picture book *The Secret Kingdom: Nek Chand, a Changing India, and a Hidden World of Art* by Barb Rosenstock and discuss the story. Discuss parts of the story that stick out to you or that you connect with. What writer's craft moves do you notice the author using? Notice the parts of the story.

26 The Secret Kingdom: Nek Chand, a Changing India, and a Hidden World of Art

by Barb Rosenstock and illustrated by Claire A. Nivola

3 SHARE THE STRUCTURE.

Show the students the structure found in the picture book. Reread the story, looking for chunks together and watching for how the author moves from one part to the other.

A Problem Solver's Journey

The person's background and what brought them to the situation	What they noticed that gave them an idea	How the new idea started to take shape	A new problem that popped up and how it was solved	The result and who all benefitted

4 INVITATION TO WRITE.

Here are several ways you can get students to write.

- Have students use the text structure to write a kernel essay summary of the story. (Give them between 5 and 10 minutes to do this.)

- Have the students use the text structure to write their own piece in a kernel essay. (Give them between 5 and 10 minutes to do this.)

- See what students come up with. (Give them around 10 minutes.) Here are some possibilities:

   - A page of thoughts in their quick write
   - Examples of the author's craft moves
   - A text structure

Whatever they choose to write, let them know that they can change anything they need to and make it their own.

5 SHARE.

Invite students to try their writing on someone else's ears. This is a crucial step! The sharing is just as important as the writing.

Want to Go Deeper?

Try These Options.

OPTION 1: CRAFT CHALLENGE

- **Microscope Sentence:** This author uses a type of sentence that we call a microscope sentence, which is a sentence that zooms out, then zooms in, and then focuses on someone or something. Here's an example from the story:

  "On the continent of Asia, near the mighty Himalayas, in the Punjab region of long ago, sat the tiny village of Berian Kalan, the place Nek Chand Saini called home."

  Look through your piece to see where you can use a microscope sentence. After you write, try it out on someone's ears to see how it sounds in your writing.

- **Anaphora + Participles:** This author uses anaphora (the repetition of the first words in a sentence or phrase) and pairs it with participles (verbs that end with *-ed* or *-ing*, used as an adjective). Here are some examples from the story:

  "***Where were*** *the* **curving paths** *and* **flowing streams**? ***Where were*** *the* **singing men**, *the* **swaying women**?"

  Look through your piece to see where you can try anaphora, or participles, or both. After you write, try it out on someone's ears to see how it sounds in your writing.

OPTION 2: ANALYZE

1. **Start with a big idea.**

   - If you want students to find the big ideas themselves, try asking, "What big ideas do you see in this story that tell you what it's really about?"

   - If students need a nudge, try using some of the big ideas from the list in this lesson's introduction and have students provide evidence from the story to support their answers. Ask, "How is this story about [the big idea]? How does the author explore [the big idea]? Where in the story do you see that?"

2. **Turn the big idea into a truism (thematic statement).**

   Once you have identified the big ideas, use one of them to create truisms for this story. Here are a few (found in the story) to get you started:

   - *Beauty can be found in the discarded.*

   - *Our passions, when shared with others, can take on a life of their own.*

   - *The secret places we make are special.*

   - *Broken rules might not always need to be punished.*

   Have students write and share their own truisms.

   Ask them to prove their truisms by providing evidence from the text. They might imagine a listener saying, "Oh yeah? How do you know? How is that true in the story?"

Want to Go Deeper?
Try these options.

OPTION 3: READING RESPONSE

Students can compose short or extended responses to demonstrate understanding by answering any of these questions. Look in the appendix to find a list titled "Basic Reading Response Text Structures" and a list of "Useful Essay Question Stems for Nonfiction Texts."

Questions for Reading Response

- Explain how Nek shows determination throughout the story.
- Compare Nek's early life in the village to his later life in the city.
- What happened in the story? (Retell.)
- Explain the importance of the secret kingdom to the people of Chandigarh.
- Explain why the government wanted to demolish Nek's secret kingdom.

OPTION 4: EXTENSION IDEAS

- Dig into the back matter:
  - Use the author's note as a short nonfiction text to read, discuss, create and answer questions, and write.
- Research more about Nek Chand, the Rock Garden of Chandigarh, the partition of India and Pakistan, other folk artists, or art created from trash/discarded items:
  - Create an infographic about your research.
  - Create a poem based on your research.
  - Use the text structure to write about your research.
- Watch the YouTube video "Rock Garden Chandigarh Official (English)," available at https://www.youtube.com/watch?v=X-cCr2H1I30.
- Create individual mosaics and then put them together to create a larger project to display on a wall.
- Consider pairing this book with the middle-grade epistolary novel *The Night Diary* by Veera Hiranandani.
- Help preserve and protect Nek Chand's Rock Garden in Chandigarh by writing letters:
  - Visit www.nekchand.org.
  - The Nek Chand Foundation, P.O. Box 44, Watford, WD25 8LN, United Kingdom

QUICK WRITE

by CD Vardiman, 7th Grade

Back when I was around seven, my favorite thing to do was to take the sheets off my bed and shove them under my desk and crawl in with my dog and my iPad and pretend I was in a fort and my dog was my noble steed.

QUICK WRITE

by Tripp Walker, 5th Grade

Once when I was eight, I found a peculiar acorn with a hollow inside, so it looked like a spaceship in a way. I was in a park with a jungle gym. I pretended that there was a person in this "natural spaceship" and they had to navigate through a future city to get to the getaway vehicle, my car.

QUICK WRITE

by Alex Chen, 7th Grade

I think that trash usually goes to a landfill and is usually left there rotting. Not a good story for a piece of trash, right? Well, it can go to a company that could actually recycle the trash and make new goods for it, so it's used again and again, not left rotting in the landfills or somewhere else in a similar place. I think that would be the best thing happening to a small, singular piece of trash.

KERNEL ESSAY (USING "A PROBLEM SOLVER'S JOURNEY")

by Tripp Walker, 5th Grade

Kevin was from Boston visiting a camp while his parents visited their friends in California. At the camp he noticed that there was an old mini golf course covered with old debris and leaves. He thought, "Let's clean it up." He noticed other people were also sad that they couldn't play mini golf. So, he gathered them together to help clean it up. After they were finished, they realized why it kept getting dirty; the river had formed a natural path to the course. So, Kevin and the others got together and made a makeshift dam out of ropes. After people realized the courses were functional, mini golf became the most popular attraction there.

KERNEL ESSAY RETELL (USING "A PROBLEM SOLVER'S JOURNEY")

by Alex Chen, 7th Grade

On the continent of Asia, in the south, in British-controlled India, and around the Himalayas, in the Punjab region was a small town. In the town, there was a kid named Nek. He was always told at least one story when the seasons came in. They told him a story during harvest, during spring, during the monsoon, and during the holidays. They kept telling him

stories about the seasons and eventually his head couldn't take any more stories anymore. So in order to express his stories, he built a small secret kingdom with these stories about the village that he was in. He kept building, and building, and building until the partition came in. His family was forced to move to another town.

What Nek notices is that the city is the exact opposite of the village that he was in. It was boring. Where were the colors? Where were the interesting, curved roads? Where were the singing men? Where were the happy children?

So, he goes to some government-controlled land and starts to build. He builds arches, he builds fields, he builds actual colorful buildings, he builds singing people, and he builds happy children. Just like before, he built, he expanded, and he built, and he expanded until his secret kingdom was many acres in length and width.

That was when his kingdom wasn't a secret anymore. Government-controlled police members eventually found his kingdom and wanted to tear down the kingdom apart and arrest Nek. They didn't want interesting roads and singing people. They wanted boring gray parking lots and cars that were just hunks of metal.

But the word spread of this mysterious kingdom and many people started seeing this kingdom, looking at its true beauty. Then once the government said they wanted to tear down this kingdom, they weren't so happy with that and said that Nek shouldn't be arrested, and the kingdom should stay. So after thousands of people protested to keep this kingdom alive, the government decided not to tear it down.

Now, Nek kept building for years until he died a few years ago. His legacy of the rock garden still moves on in time.

TRUISM

by Jackson Guenther, 5th Grade
Making the world a better place requires action and determination.

TRUISM

by Marvelous Bukari, 7th Grade
Hard work has many rewards.

READING RESPONSE (USING THE TEXT STRUCTURE "QA12345")

by Jackson Guenther, 5th Grade
Q: Explain how Nek shows determination throughout the story.

A: Nek shows determination throughout the story by making his own paradise. As a kid, he made his own little city with all the aspects of his beloved stories. This means that instead of wanting things to change, he goes and changes them himself. As an adult, he built another metropolis, but this time, it was on a much larger scale. This means that his ethics were the same growing up, which makes him a man of character. Nek shows determination throughout the story by creating his own paradise that he shared with the world.

27 A Garden in Your Belly: Meet the Microbes in Your Gut

by Masha D'yans

Summary: This book takes the reader on a colorful trip through the gut. The author transforms a complex system into something readers can visualize.

Why We Love It: These beautiful illustrations coupled with the simple metaphors of a river and creatures keep the reader engaged. We love how the inner workings of the gut become clear to us. Gut health can make the difference between good health and illness, and it's important that our students grow up knowing that what happens in the gut is more than just disgusting waste.

Topics: gut health, human body, stomach, intestines, microbiome, microorganisms, microbes, taking care of one's body, healthy food, junk food, digestion, mood

Big Ideas: health, your incredible body, taking care of yourself, going outside, nourishment, cause and effect

Back Matter:

- "What Is a Microbiome?"
- Glossary
- "Amazing Gut Facts"

LESSON STEPS:

1 QUICK WRITE.
(Choose One):

- Can you think of a time you had a really upset stomach? What do you think caused it?
- Look at your hands, your feet, or your belly. Talk about what you think goes on inside your skin.

Write about this for 3 minutes and then set it aside.

2 READ.

Read the picture book *A Garden in Your Belly: Meet the Microbes in Your Gut* by Masha D'yans and discuss the story. Discuss parts of the story that stick out to you or that you connect with. What writer's craft moves do you notice the author using? Notice the parts of the story.

A Garden in Your Belly: Meet the Microbes in Your Gut

by Masha D'yans

3 SHARE THE STRUCTURE.

Show the students the structure found in the picture book. Reread the story, looking for chunks together and watching for how the author moves from one part to the other.

Zooming In on a System					
In _____ [place] is _____ [a system].	How that system was built	Parts of the system and what each part does (This part does this . . .)	If this happens, this problem occurs	If this happens, this good thing occurs	That's why . . .

4 INVITATION TO WRITE.

Here are several ways you can get students to write.

- Have students use the text structure to write a kernel essay summary of the story. (Give them between 5 and 10 minutes to do this.)

- Have the students use the text structure to write their own piece in a kernel essay. (Give them between 5 and 10 minutes to do this.)

- See what students come up with. (Give them around 10 minutes.) Here are some possibilities:

  o A page of thoughts in their quick write

  o Examples of the author's craft moves

  o A text structure

Whatever they choose to write, let them know that they can change anything they need to and make it their own.

5 SHARE.

Invite students to try their writing on someone else's ears. This is a crucial step! The sharing is just as important as the writing.

Want to Go Deeper?
Try these options.

OPTION 1: CRAFT CHALLENGE

- **Prepositional Phrase Catalog:** In this story, the author creates a list, which is a rhetorical device called a catalog, and in this case, the list happens to consist of prepositional phrases. Here's the example from the story:

  *"You get new microbes **from your dog, from your best friend, from the ground underfoot, from food, and even from this book!**"*

  Look through your piece to see where you can use a prepositional phrase catalog. After you write, try it out on someone's ears to see how it sounds in your writing.

- **Metaphor:** In this story, the author uses a metaphor, which is a figure of speech that describes something by saying it is something else—like a simile, but without *like* or *as*. Here's an example from the story:

  "Inside you flows a great river . . . it nourishes a garden in your belly full of life and wonder."

  Look through your piece to see where you can use a metaphor. After you write, try it out on someone's ears to see how it sounds in your writing.

OPTION 2: ANALYZE

1. **Start with a big idea.**

   - If you want students to find the big ideas themselves, try asking, "What big ideas do you see in this story that tell you what it's really about?"

   - If students need a nudge, try using some of the big ideas from the list in this lesson's introduction and have students provide evidence from the story to support their answers. Ask, "How is this story about [the big idea]? How does the author explore [the big idea]? Where in the story do you see that?"

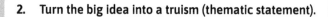

2. **Turn the big idea into a truism (thematic statement).**

   Once you have identified the big ideas, use one of them to create truisms for this story. Here are a few (found in the story) to get you started:

   - *If we want our body to take care of us, we need to take care of it.*

   - *In a system, each part is important.*

   - *It's surprising what can make us healthy.*

   Have students write and share their own truisms.

   Ask them to prove their truisms by providing evidence from the text. They might imagine a listener saying, "Oh yeah? How do you know? How is that true in the story?"

Want to Go Deeper?
Try these options.

OPTION 3: READING RESPONSE

Students can compose short or extended responses to demonstrate understanding by answering any of these questions. Look in the appendix to find a list titled "Basic Reading Response Text Structures" and a list of "Useful Essay Question Stems for Nonfiction Texts."

Questions for Reading Response

- Explain how healthy foods benefit microorganisms.
- Explain the effects that unhealthy foods have on your body's "river."
- How is your body's microbiome like a garden?
- Explain what happens when you get too hungry.
- Explain how food can affect your mood.
- Explain how outdoor experiences benefit your gut health.

OPTION 4: EXTENSION IDEAS

- Dig into the back matter:
  - Use the "What Is a Microbiome?" and "Amazing Gut Facts" pieces as short nonfiction texts to read, discuss, create and answer questions, and write.
- Research more about systems in the body (or any system, really):
  - Create an infographic about your research.
  - Create a poem based on your research.
  - Use the text structure "Zooming In on a System" to write about your research.

QUICK WRITE

by Jackson Silva, 4th Grade

One time I had a real upset stomach. I had a headache, and I felt like I would throw up. The thing that caused it was that I didn't drink enough water.

QUICK WRITE

by Hop Dorris, 5th Grade

When I had an upset stomach, I was at a fancy restaurant. I got back to my house and my stomach hurt so bad. I knew I should have never ordered that lava cake, even though my dad told me not to over and over and over again. But I couldn't resist the mushy, perfectly brown lava cake.

QUICK WRITE

by Sahana Kallur, 9th Grade

The dirt, the fresh air, the left-over moisturizer from my skin care routine. My skin takes it all. Soap and water running down toward my feet and my stomach. The love and warmth or a hug from my grandmother who I only see once a year. My skin takes it all. My trauma, my hardships, the anxiety-filled middle school days. My skin took it all in and got thicker, but also resilient and delicate.

KERNEL ESSAY (USING "ZOOMING IN ON A SYSTEM")

by Hop Dorris, 5th Grade

In Texas, there is a ShareLunker program. This started in 1996 to breed bigger bass. So, if you catch a bass over 13 pounds, you could call a game warden and they would have a tag for the fish and take it to a hatchery. Then they will put it in a 50-gallon tank with a male or a female and they will soon breed more gigantic bass. If it doesn't work out, they will probably put it with a different fish and hope they make babies. If they breed, big bass will start showing up. That's why someone created the ShareLunker program.

KERNEL ESSAY (USING "ZOOMING IN ON A SYSTEM")

by Deeksha Dhamotharan, 9th Grade

In school, there is my friend group. We met each other over the years. We shared classes and talk. Each person is their own part. Anika is the therapist friend; Sarah is there to be silly. Kureha and Victoria are there to provide snacks; Guraman, Theo, and I are there to yap about our interests. If we fight, there's a lot of awkward tension between us. If someone achieves something, we celebrate. That's why I love my friends.

CRAFT CHALLENGE (PREPOSITIONAL PHRASE CATALOG)

by Lorelei Mueller, 5th Grade

You get sick from your friend, from the table, from the computer, from your dog, and even your pillow.

CRAFT CHALLENGE (METAPHOR)

by Maanasa Nichanametla, 9th Grade

Muscles are the pillows that comfort your bones. They create a cozy home for your body to live in.

TRUISM

by Andres Longoria, 6th Grade

It is important to eat well and be healthy overall.

TRUISM

by Richard "Cash" Corrigan, 6th Grade

If you take care of things in a good way, then they will take care of you back.

READING RESPONSE (USING THE TEXT STRUCTURE "RACE")

by Andres Longoria, 6th Grade

Q: How is your body's microbiome like a garden?

A: Your body's microbiome is like a garden because when you are first born, you collect microbials or "sprouts." You get new microbes or "sprouts" from food as you grow. On page five, it states, "You got the first seeds when you were born. You collect more microbial sprouts by breathing, touching, eating, and playing." On page six, it says, "You get new microbes from your dog, from your best friend, from the ground underfoot, from food, and even from this book." This evidence means that you get new microbials and microbes as you grow, as you eat, and even just breathing. It is like a garden because everything grows and produces energy, just like plants in a garden.

READING RESPONSE (USING THE TEXT STRUCTURE "RACE")

by Richard "Cash" Corrigan, 6th Grade

Q: Explain how healthy foods benefit microorganisms.

A: Healthy foods can benefit microorganisms and your body. They can help your body become stronger like your brain cells, your muscle cells, and blood cells. Also, if you keep your microorganisms healthy, you have a better chance of fighting off bad bacteria and illnesses.

In the text it states that eating healthy can impact your health in a very good way because it helps you perform in a better way. It makes your mind stronger and your ability to do things sharper.

I think that this is true because if a person wants to perform well in school or in athletics, if they eat healthy it will help their body to function well, but if they eat things that will make their body feel bloated or weak, they cannot perform as well as they would if they ate healthy.

Blue: A History of the Color as Deep as the Sea and as Wide as the Sky

by Nana Ekua Brew-Hammond and illustrated by Daniel Minter

Summary: For many years, the color blue was difficult to reproduce, so it was mainly available only to the wealthy. The author digs into the history of the color blue and how it eventually became attainable to everyone.

Why We Love It: We had no idea that the color blue had such a storied past. This book not only enlightened us, but built in us a curiosity and a desire to research more.

Topics: colors, blue, the history of color, slavery, myths, farming, textiles, royalty, idioms

Big Ideas: history, deception, difficult past, journey, suffering, discovery, invention

Back Matter:

- Selected sources
- Author's note
- "Blue Facts"
- "Want to Explore More?"

LESSON STEPS:

1 QUICK WRITE.

What is something ordinary that you see every day? Where do you think it comes from?

Write about this for 3 minutes and then set it aside.

2 READ.

Read the picture book *Blue* by Nana Ekua Brew-Hammond and discuss the story. Discuss parts of the story that stick out to you or that you connect with. What writer's craft moves do you notice the author using? Notice the parts of the story.

Blue: A History of the Color as Deep as the Sea and as Wide as the Sky

by Nana Ekua Brew-Hammond and illustrated by Daniel Minter

3 SHARE THE STRUCTURE.

Show the students the structure found in the picture book. Reread the story, looking for chunks together and watching for how the author moves from one part to the other.

Origin Story

Have you ever wondered where _____ comes from?	Timeline: Ways it was used and/or found in the past	How it is found, made, and/or used now

4 INVITATION TO WRITE.

Here are several ways you can get students to write.

- Have students use the text structure to write a kernel essay summary of the story. (Give them between 5 and 10 minutes to do this.)

- Have the students use the text structure to write their own piece in a kernel essay. (Give them between 5 and 10 minutes to do this.)

- See what students come up with. (Give them around 10 minutes.) Here are some possibilities:
  - A page of thoughts in their quick write
  - Examples of the author's craft moves
  - A text structure

Whatever they choose to write, let them know that they can change anything they need to and make it their own.

5 SHARE.

Invite students to try their writing on someone else's ears. This is a crucial step! The sharing is just as important as the writing.

Want to Go Deeper?
Try These Options.

OPTION 1: CRAFT CHALLENGE

- **Parallel Paradox:** This author uses a rhetorical device called a parallel paradox. A paradox is a statement that seems to contradict itself, or seems to go against itself, but may contain a basic or underlying truth when examined more closely—for example, "Less is more," or "You have to fight fire with fire." When the paradox repeats the same pattern, it's called a parallel paradox. Here's an example from the story:

  *"**It's in** the sky, **but you can't** touch it. **It's in** the sea, **but when you** cup it, it disappears."*

  Look through your piece to see where you can use a parallel paradox or mimic this sentence pattern: It's _____, but you can't _____. After you write, try it out on someone's ears to see how it sounds in your writing.

OPTION 2: ANALYZE

1. **Start with a big idea.**

   - If you want students to find the big ideas themselves, try asking, "What big ideas do you see in this story that tell you what it's really about?"

   - If students need a nudge, try using some of the big ideas from the list in this lesson's introduction and have students provide evidence from the story to support their answers. Ask, "How is this story about [the big idea]? How does the author explore [the big idea]? Where in the story do you see that?"

2. **Turn the big idea into a truism (thematic statement).**

   Once you have identified the big ideas, use one of them to create truisms for this story. Here are a few (found in the story) to get you started:

   - *Sometimes, the things we love have painful pasts.*

   - *When we take the time to learn something's history, we might appreciate it more.*

   Have students write and share their own truisms.

   Ask them to prove their truisms by providing evidence from the text. They might imagine a listener saying, "Oh yeah? How do you know? How is that true in the story?"

Want to Go Deeper?
Try these options.

OPTION 3: READING RESPONSE

Students can compose short or extended responses to demonstrate understanding by answering any of these questions. Look in the appendix to find a list titled "Basic Reading Response Text Structures" and a list of "Useful Essay Question Stems for Nonfiction Texts."

Questions for Reading Response

- What does the color blue represent in the book?
- How does the availability of blue change throughout the book?
- The author includes a description of getting blue from the snail shell to show _____.
- Why was blue so valuable at the beginning?
- Explain the reason why the scientist spent so long looking for a way to manufacture blue.

OPTION 4: EXTENSION IDEAS

- Dig into the back matter:
  - Use the author's note or the "Want to Explore More?" piece as short nonfiction texts to read, discuss, create and answer questions, and write.
  - Use the selected sources to jump-start research about this part of history.
- Research the history of a color:
  - Create an infographic about that color.
  - Create a poem based on your research.
- Research/collect idioms that involve colors.
- Use the text structure "Origin Story" to write about how something got its start.
- Make a timeline of the history of blue.

Student Samples from *Blue*

QUICK WRITE

by Fiona Bell, 4th Grade

Every day I see and use pencils. Pencils are mostly wooden, but mechanical pencils are made from plastic. A metal head is on the top of a wooden pencil. A rubber eraser is sitting on the top of the metal crown. Pencils are made in factories where hundreds to thousands are produced every day.

QUICK WRITE

by Sarah Drexler, 4th Grade

Have you ever wondered where sweaters come from? I have always wondered where sweaters come from. Back then, sweaters were used for warmth, so then the wearer didn't get colds. They are made by wool and the wool comes from the sheep. Then they clean it and put it in the big wheel. Have you ever watched Sleeping Beauty? The wheel that she goes to sleep by is the wheel they use. Next it turns into yarn and then they knit it. They are now used for fashion.

QUICK WRITE

by Emerson Thomas, 5th Grade

Every day when I get back home, I see my dog, Daisy, waiting impatiently at the door. The sight of my blonde dog had become a monstrous view. I have no idea what she is waiting for. Maybe my mom or my dad or even just simply, company.

QUICK WRITE

by Poppy Alston, 5th Grade

Something ordinary that I see every day is the plants when I come to school. I think they come from the ground because the gardeners planted the seeds there. The plants are so pretty and all different colors.

KERNEL ESSAY (WRITTEN BEFORE DOING RESEARCH USING "ORIGIN STORY")

by Emerson Thomas, 5th Grade

Water, soil, and grass. I bet you know where they all come from, but what about oil? Back then, oil was mainly used for battle ships or planes. Oil was dug up from the earth using drills. Now, oil is dug up with oil rigs. Recently, oil has been used for cruise ships, yachts, and other boats. Also, oil is very expensive and used in gasoline.

CRAFT CHALLENGE (PARALLEL PARADOX)

by Poppy Alston, 5th Grade

It's planted, but it's not growing.

CRAFT CHALLENGE (PARALLEL PARADOX)

by Fiona Bell, 4th Grade

It's cold, but it can burn you.

Branches of Hope: The 9/11 Survivor Tree

by Ann Magee and illustrated by Nicole Wong

Summary: *Branches of Hope* tells the poignant story of a tree that survived the 9/11 attacks on the Twin Towers. The tree was then taken away so that it might heal and continue to grow, and a decade later, it was returned to its original home where it still grows today.

Why We Love It: For younger readers, this book serves as a gentle bridge into the topic of the terrorist attacks on 9/11. We also love the dual narrative: The text and main illustrations tell the public story of the events, while the inset illustrations show a personal family experience that mirrors it.

Topics: 9/11, trees, 9/11 Survivor Tree, 9/11 memorial, New York, terrorist attacks, Ground Zero, Twin Towers, first responders, seasons

Big Ideas: survival, memorials, hope, life after destruction, resilience, the healing power of nature, devastation, rebuilding, hope amidst hardship, recovery, how nature depends on people, community, coming together through tragedy, working together

Back Matter:

- "More About the Survivor Tree's Journey"
- "A Note From the Author"
- Selected bibliography

LESSON STEPS:

1 QUICK WRITE.
(Choose One):

- Think of a time when it felt like everything was going wrong and then one thing went right. What happened?

- Think of a time you helped something survive. It might be a plant, an animal, or a person. What happened?

- Think about a time when something big happened and it affected a lot of people. It might have been a natural disaster, a power outage, or an eclipse. What happened?

Write about this for 3 minutes and then set it aside.

2 READ.

Read the picture book *Branches of Hope: The 9/11 Survivor Tree* by Ann Magee and discuss the story. Discuss parts of the story that stick out to you or that you connect with. What writer's craft moves do you notice the author using? Notice the parts of the story.

Branches of Hope: The 9/11 Survivor Tree
by Ann Magee and illustrated by Nicole Wong

3 SHARE THE STRUCTURE.

Show the students the structure found in the picture book. Reread the story, looking for chunks together and watching for how the author moves from one part to the other.

A Memory

Where were you, and what were you doing?	What happened first?	What happened next?	What happened next?	What happened last?

4 INVITATION TO WRITE.

Here are several ways you can get students to write.

- Have students use the text structure to write a kernel essay summary of the story. (Give them between 5 and 10 minutes to do this.)

- Have the students use the text structure to write their own piece in a kernel essay. (Give them between 5 and 10 minutes to do this.)

- See what students come up with. (Give them around 10 minutes.) Here are some possibilities:

  o A page of thoughts in their quick write

  o Examples of the author's craft moves

  o A text structure

Whatever they choose to write, let them know that they can change anything they need to and make it their own.

5 SHARE.

Invite students to try their writing on someone else's ears. This is a crucial step! The sharing is just as important as the writing.

Want to Go Deeper?
Try these options.

OPTION 1: CRAFT CHALLENGE

- **Personification:** This author uses personification when describing the tree's actions. Personification is giving nonhuman objects human capabilities. Here is an example from the story:

  "Buried in darkness, the tree reached up, longing for the light."

  Look through your piece to see where you can use personification. After you write, try it out on someone's ears to see how it sounds in your writing.

- **Sensory Details:** This author uses sensory details to describe the sounds and sights in the story. Sensory details are details that describe what one might hear, see, taste, touch, and smell. Here's an example from the story:

  "The sky roared and exploded. Fire rained down, down, down. Sidewalks rumbled. Buildings crumbled."

  Look through your piece to see where you can use sensory details. After you write, try it out on someone's ears to see how it sounds in your writing.

OPTION 2: ANALYZE

1. **Start with a big idea.**

   - If you want students to find the big ideas themselves, try asking, "What big ideas do you see in this story that tell you what it's really about?"

   - If students need a nudge, try using some of the big ideas from the list in this lesson's introduction and have students provide evidence from the story to support their answers. Ask, "How is this story about [the big idea]? How does the author explore [the big idea]? Where in the story do you see that?"

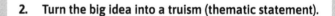

2. **Turn the big idea into a truism (thematic statement).**

   Once you have identified the big ideas, use one of them to create truisms for this story. Here are a few (found in the story) to get you started:

   - *Even a small survival story has the incredible power to bring hope.*

   - *People are resilient.*

   - *Scars help us remember, but they don't have to be the end.*

   - *Scars can tell a story.*

   Have students write and share their own truisms.

   Ask them to prove their truisms by providing evidence from the text. They might imagine a listener saying, "Oh yeah? How do you know? How is that true in the story?"

Want to Go Deeper?
Try these options.

OPTION 3:
READING RESPONSE

Students can compose short or extended responses to demonstrate understanding by answering any of these questions. Look in the appendix to find a list titled "Basic Reading Response Text Structures" and a list of "Useful Essay Question Stems for Nonfiction Texts."

Questions for Reading Response

- What does the tree represent in the story?

- Explain how the passage of time is shown in the story.

- Describe the changes that the tree went through.

- Explain whether or not it was worth the energy, time, and effort to save the tree.

- Explain how the tree and the people benefitted each other.

OPTION 4:
EXTENSION IDEAS

- Dig into the back matter:
  - Use the "More About the Survivor Tree's Journey" and "A Note From the Author" pieces as short nonfiction texts to read, discuss, create and answer questions, and write.
  - Use the selected bibliography to conduct further research.
- Research more about 9/11:
  - Create an infographic about your research.
  - Create a poem based on your research.
- Write letters to first responders to thank them for their work.
- Plant trees as a class.
- Research another event in history (or use the quick write) and use the text structure "A Memory" to write about that event.

QUICK WRITE

by **Leila Kirkpatrick, 3rd Grade**

Four or five years ago, people got COVID. At first, it wasn't that bad, but then it got worse, and people had to shut down schools, airports, stores, churches, and football stadiums. Some people got very sick and they had to wear masks and stay six feet apart.

READING RESPONSE (USING THE TEXT STRUCTURE "RACE")

by **Sydney Hines, 12th Grade**

Q: Explain how the passage of time is shown in the story.

A: The passage of time in the story is spread out in areas of growth and seasons. The tree begins the story basking in warmth. Then after experiencing the darkness of 9/11, the tree is taken away and sleeps during the winter. The author describes both the tree's growth through seasons and New York City's growth in rebuilding after 9/11. The tree grows taller as families return to normal day-to-day activities. As each season passes, more changes happen to both the tree and society.

KERNEL ESSAY (USING "A MEMORY") + CRAFT CHALLENGE (SENSORY DETAILS)

by **Zinnia Briseño, 5th Grade**

I was on the field playing flag football. I pulled someone's belt. Later I tried pulling it again. They said, "No!" and stepped back, right into me. My thumb popped and cracked as the pain ran through my hand.

KERNEL ESSAY (USING "A MEMORY")

by **Hannah Gagliano, 4th Grade**

I was in my garage on my gymnastics bar. Me and my babysitter saw a lizard struggling to live. We put it in a container. We brought it outside. We put it in a tree and gave it water.

CRAFT CHALLENGE (PERSONIFICATION)

by **Zinnia Briseño, 5th Grade**

The little seedling crawled out of the soil searching for the light up ahead.

CRAFT CHALLENGE (SENSORY DETAILS)

by **Hannah Gagliano, 4th Grade**

When I pulled the slice of pizza, the stringy, gooey, yummy cheese pulled away from the plate.

Fire Shapes the World

by Joanna Cooke and illustrated by Cornelia Li and Diāna Renžina

Summary: This book traces the history of fire, including its prehistoric role in developing our natural habitats, and its interactions with people and nature throughout history.

Why We Love It: This book expands our perception of fire and makes us aware of so much more than its negative, destructive qualities, giving us a more balanced view of one of the four elements.

Topics: fire, wildfires, adaptation, plants, animals, campfires, earth's history, the environment

Big Ideas: destruction, creation, change, effects on our planet, survival, power, rebirth

Back Matter:

- Author's note
- Further reading
- Websites

LESSON STEPS:

1 QUICK WRITE.
(CHOOSE ONE):

- What do you think of when you think about fire?
- What are some things you know about fire?
- Is fire a good thing or a bad thing? Why do you think that?

Write about this for 3 minutes and then set it aside.

2 READ.

Read the picture book *Fire Shapes the World* by Joanna Cooke and discuss the story. Discuss parts of the story that stick out to you or that you connect with. What writer's craft moves do you notice the author using? Notice the parts of the story.

Fire Shapes the World
by Joanna Cooke and illustrated by
Cornelia Li and Diāna Renžina

3 SHARE THE STRUCTURE.

Show the students the structure found in the picture book. Reread the story, looking for chunks together and watching for how the author moves from one part to the other.

The Whole Story of Something				
What the thing is	Past: When (and/or how) it started	Past: After that it _____.	Present: Now it is _____ and _____.	Future: It is _____ and will be _____.

4 INVITATION TO WRITE.

Here are several ways you can get students to write.

- Have students use the text structure to write a kernel essay summary of the story. (Give them between 5 and 10 minutes to do this.)

- Have the students use the text structure to write their own piece in a kernel essay. (Give them between 5 and 10 minutes to do this.)

- See what students come up with. (Give them around 10 minutes.) Here are some possibilities:
  o A page of thoughts in their quick write
  o Examples of the author's craft moves
  o A text structure

Whatever they choose to write, let them know that they can change anything they need to and make it their own.

5 SHARE.

Invite students to try their writing on someone else's ears. This is a crucial step! The sharing is just as important as the writing.

Want to Go Deeper?
Try These Options.

OPTION 1: CRAFT CHALLENGE

- **Participles and Participial Phrases:** This author uses participles and participial phrases. A participle is a verb that ends with *-ed* or *-ing* and is used as an adjective. A participial phrase is a participle with a few more words tacked on to it. Here are some examples from the story:

    *"Deep in the wilderness, a fire smolders. It creeps in yellow and crimson bursts **flaring as the wind shifts**, **transforming the forest around it**."* (These are participial phrases.)

    *"The world kept changing—**drying** and **cooling**, **wetting** and **heating**—and fires kept burning."* (These are participles.)

  Look through your piece to see where you can use participles and/or participial phrases. After you write, try it out on someone's ears to see how it sounds in your writing.

- **Fragmented Metaphor:** In this story, the author uses a metaphor (a figure of speech that describes something by saying it is something else—like a simile, but without *like* or *as*) by using a list (or pitchfork!) of incomplete sentences, or fragments. Here's an example from the story:

    "Fire is also this: An opening pinecone. A seed released onto warm ash. A fireweed sprouting."

  Look through your piece to see where you can use a fragmented metaphor. After you write, try it out on someone's ears to see how it sounds in your writing.

OPTION 2: ANALYZE

1. **Start with a big idea.**

   - If you want students to find the big ideas themselves, try asking, "What big ideas do you see in this story that tell you what it's really about?"

   - If students need a nudge, try using some of the big ideas from the list in this lesson's introduction and have students provide evidence from the story to support their answers. Ask, "How is this story about [the big idea]? How does the author explore [the big idea]? Where in the story do you see that?"

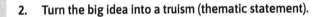

2. **Turn the big idea into a truism (thematic statement).**

   Once you have identified the big ideas, use one of them to create truisms for this story. Here are a few (found in the story) to get you started:

   - *Most people think that fire is destructive, but there's more to it than that.*

   - *Some things can have different uses in different situations.*

   - *Sometimes when something is destroyed, new things can come out of it.*

   Have students write and share their own truisms.

   Ask them to prove their truisms by providing evidence from the text. They might imagine a listener saying, "Oh yeah? How do you know? How is that true in the story?"

Want to Go Deeper?
Try these options.

OPTION 3: READING RESPONSE

Students can compose short or extended responses to demonstrate understanding by answering any of these questions. Look in the appendix to find a list titled "Basic Reading Response Text Structures" and a list of "Useful Essay Question Stems for Nonfiction Texts."

Questions for Reading Response

- Explain two benefits of fire.
- Is fire a good thing or a bad thing? Explain your opinion.
- Explain the relationship between fire and people long ago.
- Explain how animals have been affected by fires.
- Explain how fire can create new plant growth.
- What is the author's purpose in writing this book?

OPTION 4: EXTENSION IDEAS

- Dig into the back matter:
  - Use the author's note as a short nonfiction text to read, discuss, create and answer questions, and write.
  - Use the further reading and websites to jump-start research about fire.
- Research more about fire or another element (air, water, or earth):
  - Create an infographic about your research.
  - Create a poem based on your research.
  - Use the text structure "The Whole Story of Something" to write about that element.
- Contact a local park ranger to come speak about the effects of fire on the local nature and wildlife. Possibly combine this talk with a field trip to a local park.
- Contact someone to come speak about controlled burns.

Student Samples for *Fire Shapes the World*

QUICK WRITE

by Carlotta Febres, 4th Grade

I think fire is a good thing, but it can be bad too. Fire is very dangerous because it is very hot and can burn you. Fire also can give us light and heat.

KERNEL ESSAY (USING "THE WHOLE STORY OF SOMETHING")

by Leila Kirkpatrick, 3rd Grade

We had our house built in the country. Before our house was built, there were a lot of trees and land. When they started building our house, they cut down a lot of trees. Now that our house is built, we have a deck, chickens, and a pergola. Someday, I will maybe live in this house by myself.

CRAFT CHALLENGE (PARTICIPLES AND PARTICIPIAL PHRASES)

by Carlotta Febres, 4th Grade

The Hogwarts staircases won't stay put-moving and turning, coming and leaving-they will never stop moving.

CRAFT CHALLENGE (FRAGMENTED METAPHOR)

by Riley Walker, 4th Grade

iPhone is also this: an electric wonder. A device released into the world. Hand-held recreation.

TRUISM

by Eviana Reyes, 6th Grade

Even if things seem bad, there can be a good opportunity in anything.

READING RESPONSE (USING THE TEXT STRUCTURE "RACE")

by Eviana Reyes, 6th Grade

Q: What is the author's purpose in writing this book?

A: The author's purpose in writing this book is to show us that fire is not only a bad thing, but it can also be good. In the story it states that fire has both the power to destroy and the power to create. This shows that although fire can be destructive, it can also bring people together and make way for new things to come.

READING RESPONSE (USING THE TEXT STRUCTURE "RACE")

by Owen Jenné, 2nd Grade

Q: Explain the relationship between fire and people long ago.

A: The relationship between fire and people is they had a ritual with it and it was sacred. From pages 15 to 18, it explains how early people saw fire and the way they thought about it. This shows how people back then thought about fire and how it helped the land.

31 Fry Bread: A Native American Family Story
by Kevin Noble Maillard and illustrated
by Juana Martinez-Neal

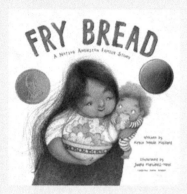

Summary: *Fry Bread* explores Native American culture and tradition while revealing that fry bread is much more than food. It is sound, color, time, history, nation, and so much more.

Why We Love It: Not only do we love the celebration of Native American culture, but we also love how the book is accessible to all types of learners. You might choose to read only the main text, which is a beautiful collection of lyrical metaphors. Or you might dip into the back matter, a wealth of informational text that fleshes out each of the "Fry bread is . . ." statements. It's almost a whole book in itself!

Topics: fry bread, Native American culture, Native American history, food, cooking, North American tribes, Indigenous peoples

Big Ideas: culture, community, family, friends, heritage, bringing people together, tradition, legacy, Native identity, passing down traditions, the cultural importance of food

Back Matter:

- "Kevin's Fry Bread" recipe
- Author's note

LESSON STEPS:

1 QUICK WRITE.
(Choose One):

- What is a food that your family makes? Describe it.

- Have you ever cooked something with your family or friends? What did you make? Who were you with? Describe the experience.

- What is something in your family or culture that you are proud of?

Write about this for 3 minutes and then set it aside.

2 READ.

Read the picture book *Fry Bread: A Native American Family Story* by Kevin Noble Maillard and discuss the story. Discuss parts of the story that stick out to you or that you connect with. What writer's craft moves do you notice the author using? Notice the parts of the story.

Fry Bread: A Native American Family Story

by Kevin Noble Maillard and illustrated
by Juana Martinez-Neal

3 SHARE THE STRUCTURE.

Show the students the structure found in the picture book. Reread the story, looking for chunks together and watching for how the author moves from one part to the other.

Extended Metaphors

_____ is _____. (Plus a pitchforked explanation)	_____ is _____. (Plus a pitchforked explanation)	_____ is _____. (Plus a pitchforked explanation)	_____ is _____. (Plus a pitchforked explanation)

4 INVITATION TO WRITE.

Here are several ways you can get students to write.

- Have students use the text structure to write a kernel essay summary of the story. (Give them between 5 and 10 minutes to do this.)

- Have the students use the text structure to write their own piece in a kernel essay. (Give them between 5 and 10 minutes to do this.)

- See what students come up with. (Give them around 10 minutes.) Here are some possibilities:

  o A page of thoughts in their quick write

  o Examples of the author's craft moves

  o A text structure

Whatever they choose to write, let them know that they can change anything they need to and make it their own.

5 SHARE.

Invite students to try their writing on someone else's ears. This is a crucial step! The sharing is just as important as the writing.

Want to Go Deeper?
Try these options.

OPTION 1: CRAFT CHALLENGE

- **Similes:** In this story, the author uses similes (comparisons using *like* or *as*). Here are some examples from the story:

  "Hands mold the dough

  Flat like a pancake

  Round like a ball

  Or puffy like Nana's soft pillow"

  Look through your piece to see where you can use some similes. After you write, try it out on someone's ears to see how it sounds in your writing.

- **Metaphors:** Throughout this story, the author uses metaphors to say what fry bread is. A metaphor is a figure of speech that describes something by saying it is something else—like a simile, but without *like* or *as*. Here are some examples from the story:

  "Fry bread is time."

  "Fry bread is history."

  "Fry bread is nation."

  Look through your piece to see where you can use some metaphors. After you write, try it out on someone's ears to see how it sounds in your writing.

OPTION 2: ANALYZE

1. **Start with a big idea.**

   - If you want students to find the big ideas themselves, try asking, "What big ideas do you see in this story that tell you what it's really about?"

   - If students need a nudge, try using some of the big ideas from the list in this lesson's introduction and have students provide evidence from the story to support their answers. Ask, "How is this story about [the big idea]? How does the author explore [the big idea]? Where in the story do you see that?"

2. **Turn the big idea into a truism (thematic statement).**

   Once you have identified the big ideas, use one of them to create truisms for this story. Here are a few (found in the story) to get you started:

   - *Sometimes food is more than nourishment; it can be culture or tradition or identity.*

   - *Sharing our food with each other is sharing pieces of ourselves.*

   - *Food can bring families together.*

   Have students write and share their own truisms.

   Ask them to prove their truisms by providing evidence from the text. They might imagine a listener saying, "Oh yeah? How do you know? How is that true in the story?"

Want to Go Deeper?
Try these options.

OPTION 3: READING RESPONSE

Students can compose short or extended responses to demonstrate understanding by answering any of these questions. Look in the appendix to find a list titled "Basic Reading Response Text Structures" and a list of "Useful Essay Question Stems for Nonfiction Texts."

Questions for Reading Response

- What does the author mean by "Fry bread is _____"? (Choose one of the words.)
- Explain how fry bread might bring people together.
- Explain why this author might have written this book.
- How does the author show that there are different ways to make fry bread?
- How was fry bread invented?

OPTION 4: EXTENSION IDEAS

- Dig into the back matter:
  - Use the "Kevin's Fry Bread" recipe and the author's note as short nonfiction texts to read, discuss, create and answer questions, and write.
- Research more about Native American culture, food, and history:
  - Create an infographic about your research.
  - Create a poem based on your research.
- Make fry bread together as a class.
- Have a bread tasting to sample breads from different cultures (such as naan, pita, matzo, tortillas, sopapillas, etc.).
- Use the text structure "Extended Metaphors" to write an informative piece, a poem, a thank-you note, or a story.

Student Samples for *Fry Bread*

QUICK WRITE

by Harper Hsieh, 4th Grade

My favorite food that I make with family is crab noodle soup. Crab noodle soup is the rich crab juice as the soup, with crab pieces. The noodles are famous Chinese noodles. After we assemble the basics, we add other rich vegetables.

QUICK WRITE

by Elena Valladares, 5th Grade

Something in my family's culture that I'm proud of is the traditions. Every family has its own traditions, but we have some fun ones in the Hispanic culture. Every Dia de los Muertos we set up an offrenda. An offrenda is a way you can remember loved ones who have passed. It's very sweet getting together and talking about each and every person on the offrenda.

Another tradition we do is we get Rosca de Reyes every Three Kings Day. Whoever finds the baby Jesus will get a tamale party on February 2nd.

These are just a few of the traditions my family celebrates. It's important to celebrate traditions with family because it's a nice way to celebrate your family's history.

QUICK WRITE

by Laylah Szymaszek, 6th Grade

My family always makes the same breakfast on Christmas morning: biscuits and gravy. It's something that we have done every year for as long as I can remember. Every year without fail, we open presents, make homemade gravy, cook the biscuits, and eat breakfast together. It's something I love and will continue to do for the rest of my life.

QUICK WRITE

by Mercedes Mabel Holmes, 6th Grade

I have cooked a cake for my older sister when it was her 21st birthday. I cooked it with my mom and younger sibling. We had so much fun taking turns pouring the ingredients into the bowl and mixing it all together. It was a moment I will never forget.

QUICK WRITE

by Ruha Komaragiri, 9th Grade

Something in my culture that I am proud of is our traditional clothing style. Unlike many other cultures, our dresses themselves are statement pieces. They are covered in beautiful embroidery that ranges from flowers to animals or anything you can think of. These dresses are filled with vibrant colors and patterns. These dresses are like no other.

KERNEL ESSAY (USING "EXTENDED METAPHORS")

by Elena Valladares, 5th Grade

War is hatred. Everyone is against everyone. Hatred causes war.

War is pain. Pain is what people feel in the crossfire.

War is trauma. War leaves physical and mental scars from traumatic experiences. Traumatic events can never be erased.

War is fear. War is scary for those in danger. Fear is everywhere during war time.

KERNEL ESSAY (USING "EXTENDED METAPHORS")

by Harper Hsieh, 4th Grade

Volleyball is time. Volleyball takes time to get good and takes time to practice.

Volleyball is life. Volleyball takes up part of your life so you can enjoy yourself.

Volleyball is excitement. Volleyball can get exciting when you win.

Volleyball is joy. Volleyball gives you joy to just play with your friends.

KERNEL ESSAY (USING "EXTENDED METAPHORS")

by Zachary Aboukhamis, 6th Grade

Kousas are friends. My grandma makes amazing Kousa with love. Her homemade savory sauce is what always hits the spot.

Kousas are family. Kousa is cooked to perfection. The natural hard outer layer of the squash turns into a butter-like texture. My grandma makes it once a month. My mom also makes them. It's extraordinarily hard to compare.

Kousas are cousins. When I was ten, my cousins and I learned how to make it together. It's easy to make! You put your rice and meat filling inside the empty squash. You then put it into the oven.

Kousas are grandma. Whenever I taste a kousa, it's like floating into heaven. With the tomato-like sauce, it makes it extravagant!

KERNEL ESSAY (USING "EXTENDED METAPHORS")

by Aashna Bhandari, 6th Grade

Pav Bhaji is my culture. It is a thick potato gravy that you eat with bread such as burger buns or Hawaiian rolls. This is a dish originated from Maharashtra, India, and is typically eaten with your hands. You can also add onions and tomatoes with it.

Pav Bhaji is my family. My brother is in college now, but when we were little, when he was home, we would eat it. Sometimes before school, our mom would ask us what we wanted for dinner. This dish would be the first thing we would ask for.

Pav Bhaji is my comfort. When I am sick, my mom immediately makes Pav Bhaji. This always makes me feel better. It's just the warmness of the gravy with

the crispy rolls and onions. All of this together is the perfect combination for you to feel immediately better.

Pav Bhaji is my *memories*. I have so many good memories of coming home after a long day of school and my mom surprising me with Pav Bhaji and everything being better. Then we would all sit down and talk about our day and then sometimes we would watch a movie after.

KERNEL ESSAY (USING "EXTENDED METAPHORS")

by Jinyoung Park, 9th Grade

Friendship is a bowl of soup. It makes your heart warm. You need to be careful and approach slowly.

Friendship is a candle. It will guide you out from the darkest time. You can always blow it out, but it can also be lit again.

Friendship is stories. All the memories you have make your friendship.

TRUISM

by William Brockwell, 7th Grade

Even though people try to break tradition, it stays with us like a shadow because tradition shapes us into who we are.

READING RESPONSE (USING THE TEXT STRUCTURE "THE EFFECT OF AN AUTHOR'S CHOICE")

by William Brockwell, 7th Grade

Q: Explain how fry bread might bring people together.

A: The author uses sensory images to show that fry bread is often made with a group of people. The author shows us this when we see more than one person on each page, and those people are often working to complete a common goal: making fry bread. Another way this book shows bringing people together and family is how the people interact. The elders are often educating the young. These two examples convey a strong feeling of people coming together. I think the idea to take away from this book is that family and tradition are what makes us who we are.

Fungi Grow

by Maria Gianferrari and illustrated by Diana Sudyka

Summary: *Fungi Grow* takes the reader above ground, below ground, and all through the places where fungi grow while introducing an astounding variety of mushrooms.

Why We Love It: This book is rich with information and is beautifully illustrated, with labels naming each fungus. We love how the book is accessible to all types of learners: You can read only the big text, you can add in the infoshots on each page for a greater understanding, and you can add the rich back matter for an even deeper experience. Whichever way you choose, you are bound to learn something new.

Topics: plants, mushrooms, fungi, spores, the growing process, mycelium, roots, trees, forests, life cycles, mycology, nature, ecosystems

Big Ideas: growth, new life, appreciating nature, symbiosis in nature

Back Matter:

- "Warning!"
- Glossary
- "How Fungi Heal and Help"
- "Fun Fungi Facts"
- "Fungi Life Cycle" (infographic)
- Sources
- "Further Reading for Kids"
- Additional resources
- Blogs and websites

LESSON STEPS:

1 QUICK WRITE.
(CHOOSE ONE):

- Do you like mushrooms on your pizza, or do you pick them off?

- Have you ever walked outside and seen mushrooms growing in the grass? How do you imagine they grew there?

- Have you ever planted something and watched it grow? What was that like?

- What is something in nature you find interesting?

Write about this for 3 minutes and then set it aside.

2 READ.

Read the picture book *Fungi Grow* by Maria Gianferrari and discuss the story. Discuss parts of the story that stick out to you or that you connect with. What writer's craft moves do you notice the author using? Notice the parts of the story.

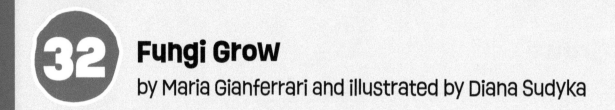

32 **Fungi Grow**

by Maria Gianferrari and illustrated by Diana Sudyka

3 SHARE THE STRUCTURE.

Show the students the structure found in the picture book. Reread the story, looking for chunks together and watching for how the author moves from one part to the other.

How Something Grows

The first stage: How it begins	The next stage: How it develops	The last stage: How it finishes	Some interesting facts about it

4 INVITATION TO WRITE.

Here are several ways you can get students to write.

- Have students use the text structure to write a kernel essay summary of the story. (Give them between 5 and 10 minutes to do this.)

- Have the students use the text structure to write their own piece in a kernel essay. (Give them between 5 and 10 minutes to do this.)

- See what students come up with. (Give them around 10 minutes.) Here are some possibilities:
  - A page of thoughts in their quick write
  - Examples of the author's craft moves
  - A text structure

Whatever they choose to write, let them know that they can change anything they need to and make it their own.

5 SHARE.

Invite students to try their writing on someone else's ears. This is a crucial step! The sharing is just as important as the writing.

Want to Go Deeper?
Try These Options.

OPTION 1: CRAFT CHALLENGE

- **Two-Word Sentences:** All a sentence really needs is a subject and a predicate, which is what allows for two-word sentences. This author uses a few throughout the book. Here are some examples from the story:

  "Fungi grow."

  "Mushrooms sprout."

  Look through your piece to see where you can use a few two-word sentences. After you write, try it out on someone's ears to see how it sounds in your writing.

- **Onomatopoeia:** This author uses sound words called onomatopoeias (words that imitate sounds, like *hiss* or *hiccup*). Here are some examples from the story:

  "Puff!"

  "Plop!"

  "Poof!"

  "Pee-ew!"

  Look through your piece to see where you can use some onomatopoeias. After you write, try it out on someone's ears to see how it sounds in your writing.

- **Pitchforked Verbs:** A pitchfork represents the act of taking one thing and branching it into a few more things. In this story, the author pitchforks some strong verbs. Here are some examples from the story:

  *"Mushrooms **branch, poke, splash, and swirl**. Mushrooms **bewitch, beguile, and multiply**."*

  Look through your piece to see where you can pitchfork some of your verbs. After you write, try it out on someone's ears to see how it sounds in your writing.

OPTION 2: ANALYZE

1. **Start with a big idea.**

   - If you want students to find the big ideas themselves, try asking, "What big ideas do you see in this story that tell you what it's really about?"

   - If students need a nudge, try using some of the big ideas from the list in this lesson's introduction and have students provide evidence from the story to support their answers. Ask, "How is this story about [the big idea]? How does the author explore [the big idea]? Where in the story do you see that?"

2. **Turn the big idea into a truism (thematic statement).**

   Once you have identified the big ideas, use one of them to create truisms for this story. Here are a few (found in the story) to get you started:

   - *It's surprising how living things connect with each other.*

   - *The invisible work of life is sometimes the most important.*

   - *Sometimes it is difficult to tell the difference between something that is healthy and something that is dangerous.*

   Have students write and share their own truisms.

   Ask them to prove their truisms by providing evidence from the text. They might imagine a listener saying, "Oh yeah? How do you know? How is that true in the story?"

Want to Go Deeper?
Try these options.

OPTION 3:
READING RESPONSE

Students can compose short or extended responses to demonstrate understanding by answering any of these questions. Look in the appendix to find a list titled "Basic Reading Response Text Structures" and a list of "Useful Essay Question Stems for Nonfiction Texts."

Questions for Reading Response

- Explain how the fungi help the trees.
- Explain some of the benefits of fungi.
- What does the author mean by the words "They flourish and thrive where plants can't"?
- Explain why the author added a warning at the end of the book.
- Explain the process by which fungi grow.

OPTION 4:
EXTENSION IDEAS

- Dig into the back matter:
  - Use "How Fungi Heal and Help," "Fun Fungi Facts," and "Fungi Life Cycle" (infographic) as short nonfiction texts to read, discuss, create and answer questions, and write.
  - Use the sources, "Further Reading for Kids," additional resources, and blogs and websites for further research.
- Research more about fungi (maybe assign each student their own fungus or dig into a few together):
  - Create an infographic about your research.
  - Create a poem based on your research.
  - Create a scrapbook out of your research.
- Read how Kitchen Pride Mushroom Farms prepares their soil for mushroom growth: https://www.kitchenpride.com/compost-sales.
- Contact a local gardener, botanist, and/or entomologist to talk about plants.
- Grow mushrooms as a class.
- Take a field trip to a mushroom farm (like this one: https://www.kitchenpride.com/), local garden center, botanical garden, or nursery to learn more about mushrooms and fungi.

Student Samples for
Fungi Grow

QUICK WRITE

by Khavir Patel, 4th Grade

When I see mushrooms, I imagine them as bad luck because they are super rare. I believe they are a message from the gods and relatives warning me. I imagine the energy of its life can cause impacts, powerful impacts. I believe they hold wisdom, but bad wisdom.

QUICK WRITE

by Brynnlea Cook, 6th Grade

One thing in nature that I find interesting is flowers. They are beautiful and can smell amazing. I still have so many questions about them. How do they have color on their petals? Why do some of them smell good? And how do they produce the smell?

QUICK WRITE

by Hanley Bahl, 6th Grade

Have you ever planted something and watched it grow? Well if not, here is what it is like. Planting something and watching it grow is like having a dog and giving it water and food. If you get lucky, you can watch it grow, but don't close your eyes, for the plant can be all grown up. It could grow so tall that you have to look up at [it], or it could turn into something amazing.

QUICK WRITE

by Leah Langner, 6th Grade

Do you like mushrooms on your pizza or do you like mushrooms at all? I think mushrooms are gross on pizza and worse by themselves. I would pick the mushrooms off the top. Mushrooms are too bland and weird textured for me.

KERNEL ESSAY (USING "HOW SOMETHING GROWS")

by Brynnlea Cook, 6th Grade

A sunflower begins as a seed in the ground. It starts to grow roots so that it can start sprouting, then it will grow a stem. It will grow a bud that will blossom eventually. It can take up to a month to form a bud. They need plenty of water and sunlight.

KERNEL ESSAY (USING "HOW SOMETHING GROWS")

by Corbett Hanzel, 5th Grade

Some pollen and a nut make a baby tree. The tree starts sprouting out of the nut. The tree grows roots to collect water and nutrients and leaves to collect energy and sugar. You can tell how old it is by counting the rings in the middle, after you cut it down.

CRAFT CHALLENGE (PITCHFORKED VERBS)

by Khavir Patel, 4th Grade

Lions eat, hunt, live, and scare. Lions jump, protect, and hide.

33 The Only Way to Make Bread
by Cristina Quintero and illustrated by Sarah Gonzales

Summary: There are many ways to make bread—many different ingredients, methods, and tools. *The Only Way to Make Bread* celebrates them all and reminds readers that the only way to make bread is the way you do it.

Why We Love It: We love the message of this book: "There is only one way to make [bread]: your way." We were instantly reminded of our own families' bread traditions and know that this book is a perfect catalyst for discussion, writing, and delicious classroom activities.

Topics: bread, making bread, how-tos (procedures), baking, ingredients, baking tools, food preparation, food literacy, recipes

Big Ideas: making things your way, making things together, diversity, culture building, traditions, different ways to do things, community, togetherness, spending time together

Back Matter:

- "Breads!" (infographic)
- Arepas recipe
- Pandesal recipe

LESSON STEPS:

1 QUICK WRITE.
(Choose One):

- Have you ever baked anything? What did you make? Describe the experience.
- Have you ever made food with your family? What did you make? Describe the experience.
- What kind of bread (or food) is your favorite to eat or to make? Why? Who do you eat or make it with?

Write about this for 3 minutes and then set it aside.

2 READ.

Read the picture book *The Only Way to Make Bread* by Cristina Quintero and discuss the story. Discuss parts of the story that stick out to you or that you connect with. What writer's craft moves do you notice the author using? Notice the parts of the story.

The Only Way to Make Bread
by Cristina Quintero and illustrated by Sarah Gonzales

3 SHARE THE STRUCTURE.

Show the students the structure found in the picture book. Reread the story, looking for chunks together and watching for how the author moves from one part to the other.

Steps for Doing Something: A How-To Structure (Plus a Truism)

When you _____, you need _____.	First, do this.	Then, do this.	Then, do this.	When you're done, do this.	That's why . . .

4 INVITATION TO WRITE.

Here are several ways you can get students to write.

- Have students use the text structure to write a kernel essay summary of the story. (Give them between 5 and 10 minutes to do this.)

- Have the students use the text structure to write their own piece in a kernel essay. (Give them between 5 and 10 minutes to do this.)

- See what students come up with. (Give them around 10 minutes.) Here are some possibilities:

  o A page of thoughts in their quick write

  o Examples of the author's craft moves

  o A text structure

Whatever they choose to write, let them know that they can change anything they need to and make it their own.

5 SHARE.

Invite students to try their writing on someone else's ears. This is a crucial step! The sharing is just as important as the writing.

Want to Go Deeper?
Try these options.

OPTION 1: CRAFT CHALLENGE

- **Anaphork (Anaphora + Pitchfork):** This author uses something we call an anaphork, a rhetorical device that combines anaphora—the repeating of a beginning word or phrase in successive phrases—and a pitchfork. Here's an example from the story:

  *"**Some doughs** like to bubble, **some doughs** are sticky and wet, **some doughs** stay small and **some** need time to double in size."*

  Look through your piece to see where you can try an anaphork. After you write, try it out on someone's ears to see how it sounds in your writing.

- **Similes:** This author uses similes to describe the bread dough. A simile is a comparison using *like* or *as*. Here are some examples from the story:

  *"Sometimes the dough is soft, loose and shaggy **like an old T-shirt**. Sometimes it's bouncy and firm **like fresh playdough**. Sometimes the dough is smooth and round **like the fullest moon**."*

  Look through your piece to see where you can use a simile or two. After you write, try it out on someone's ears to see how it sounds in your writing.

- **Pitchforked Contrasts:** This author uses a pitchfork of contrasts, which is a series of contrasting words (two opposite things next to two more opposite things). Here is an example from the story:

  *"Now for the very best part: When your bread is done, whether **spongy or dry**, **fluffy or flat**, you absolutely must find someone to share it with."*

  Look through your piece to see where you can use pitchforked contrasts. Try it out on someone's ears to see how it sounds in your writing.

OPTION 2: ANALYZE

1. **Start with a big idea.**

   - If you want students to find the big ideas themselves, try asking, "What big ideas do you see in this story that tell you what it's really about?"

   - If students need a nudge, try using some of the big ideas from the list in this lesson's introduction and have students provide evidence from the story to support their answers. Ask, "How is this story about [the big idea]? How does the author explore [the big idea]? Where in the story do you see that?"

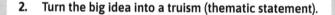

2. **Turn the big idea into a truism (thematic statement).**

   Once you have identified the big ideas, use one of them to create truisms for this story. Here are a few (found in the story) to get you started:

   - *"Bread must always be broken together."*

   - *The best things are made with love.*

   - *There are different ways of doing things, and there is value in each way.*

   - *Every culture has the same basic needs.*

   Have students write and share their own truisms.

   Ask them to prove their truisms by providing evidence from the text. They might imagine a listener saying, "Oh yeah? How do you know? How is that true in the story?"

Want to Go Deeper?
Try these options.

OPTION 3: READING RESPONSE

Students can compose short or extended responses to demonstrate understanding by answering any of these questions. Look in the appendix to find a list titled "Basic Reading Response Text Structures" and a list of "Useful Essay Question Stems for Nonfiction Texts."

Questions for Reading Response

- What effect does the title have on the reader?
- What is one reason the author presents the information in chronological order?
- Explain what bread symbolizes in the book.
- Using the back matter, compare and contrast the bread from two different cultures or countries. How are they alike or different?
- What is the most important step in making bread?

OPTION 4: EXTENSION IDEAS

- Dig into the back matter:
  - Use the "Breads!" infographic and recipes as short nonfiction texts to read, discuss, create and answer questions, and write.
  - Make one or both recipes in the back of the book.
- Research more about breads, foods, bakers, and family food traditions:
  - Create an infographic about the topic.
  - Create a poem based on your research.
  - Use the text structure to write about your research (or another topic).
  - Watch the YouTube video "Ever Wonder How Bread Is Made? Highlights Kids," available from https://www.youtube.com/watch?v=yzqsdUJbDOk.
- If you live near one, take a field trip to a bread factory or a bakery.
- Invite a baker to your school to talk about their work (and hopefully bring samples!).
- Have students gather bread recipes from home and put them together in a class cookbook.
- Make bread together as a class.
- Host a bread potluck and have everyone bring some bread from home (bought or made).
- For a unit on food and making things, consider pairing this book with one of the following:
  - *Fry Bread: A Native American Family Story* by Kevin Noble Maillard
  - *Tamales for Christmas* by Stephen Briseño
  - *Magic Ramen: The Story of Momofuku Ando* by Andrea Wang

QUICK WRITE

by **Abigail Alberta, 5th Grade**

My Nana and I love to make banana bread together. We use our special bowl and make sure the bananas are ready. First, we cream the butter and sugar. Next, we add the bananas, sour cream, and vanilla. We put the dry ingredients together in a separate bowl. Then, while the mixer is spinning, we slowly dump in the dry ingredients. Then we pour the mix in the pan and bake it. Baking with my Nana makes me feel special. I love being able to share baking banana bread with my Nana.

QUICK WRITE

by **Kathryn Taylor, 6th Grade**

I have baked something before. It was a German chocolate cake for my dad's birthday. I thought it was very fun, even though I dropped an egg on my foot. In the end, I thought it was fun. I loved the taste of the cake, and my dad thought it was beautiful.

QUICK WRITE

by **Catherine Kindrai, 6th Grade**

Do you like chocolate chip cookies, because I love baking them. Baking the chocolate chip cookies was a fun experience. I got flour everywhere and I remember cleaning it up while the cookies baked. My parents tried them and gave me compliments on my baking skills.

KERNEL ESSAY (USING "STEPS FOR DOING SOMETHING")

by **Catherine Kindrai, 6th Grade**

When you do a cartwheel, you need practice. First, try a teeter totter. This is when you put one arm up and the opposite leg up and touch your hand to the ground. Then try a handstand. You do this by putting both hands on the ground then pushing your feet off the ground. Do a teeter totter, then into a handstand, then go back down. Work on your landing by doing a teeter totter a few more times. When you're done with the steps above, try to put it all together. It might take a few tries, but eventually you will be able to do a cartwheel.

KERNEL ESSAY (USING "STEPS FOR DOING SOMETHING")

by **Kathryn Taylor, 6th Grade**

When you paint, you need to do the following steps. First, you need to get a piece of paper, paint, a cup of water, a paper plate, and brushes. Then put paint on the plate, then get the paint brushes and paint the paper. And then clean off the brushes with the water and throw

Student Samples for
The Only Way to Make Bread

away the paper plate. When you're done, you can let the paper dry until the next day. Painting is a way to share yourself with the world.

KERNEL ESSAY (USING "STEPS FOR DOING SOMETHING")

by Brystol Johnson, 6th Grade

When you take up a horse (get them geared up), you need grooming supplies. First, get your horse, or the horse you're riding. Then brush their backs and pick their hooves. Then put on the saddle pad and saddle the horse. When you're done, put on the girth (strap that keeps the saddle in place) and bridle (steering system). All horses are different, and some may not like being groomed.

READING RESPONSE (USING THE TEXT STRUCTURE "FIGURING OUT THE READING")

by Catalina Caruso, 6th Grade

Q: What is the most important step in making bread?

A: I read the words, "You always want to make your bread with love," which told me that most importantly, your number one step is putting love and care into whatever you make. Then I read the words, "Bread must always be broken together," which told me that sharing is caring, and you put love into the bread to share it with your family, because family is always the most important. Then I knew that putting love, work, and care were the most important ingredients.

34 The Secret Code Inside You: All About Your DNA

by Rajani LaRocca, MD, and illustrated by Steven Salerno

Summary: Wrapped in poetic language is the easy-to-understand explanation of what makes you *you*. This book takes readers into the smallest parts of us and gives us insight into our DNA, cells, and chromosomes.

Why We Love It: We were captivated with this book from page 1. The rhyming lyrical prose pulls the reader right in and sneaks in the scientific facts in a way that just about anyone can understand. We also appreciate that this was written by a fabulous author who happens to be a doctor!

Topics: DNA, genetics, genes, the human body, cells, family traits, proteins, chromosomes, biology, double helix, STEM

Big Ideas: identity, uniqueness, personal choice, being one of a kind, parts of a whole, science

Back Matter:

- "DNA Facts"
- "Banana DNA Experiment"

LESSON STEPS:

① QUICK WRITE.
(Choose One):

- Who do you look the most like in your family? Describe what similarities you share.

- Who do you act the most like in your family? How are you similar?

- How are you alike or different from your family or the people with whom you live (actions, activities, hobbies, interests, habits)?

Write about this for 3 minutes and then set it aside.

② READ.

Read the picture book *The Secret Code Inside You: All About Your DNA* by Rajani LaRocca, MD, and discuss the story. Discuss parts of the story that stick out to you or that you connect with. What writer's craft moves do you notice the author using? Notice the parts of the story.

The Secret Code Inside You: All About Your DNA
by Rajani LaRocca, MD, and illustrated by Steven Salerno

3 SHARE THE STRUCTURE.

Show the students the structure found in the picture book. Reread the story, looking for chunks together and watching for how the author moves from one part to the other.

All About Something (With Infoshots)

Why aren't things a certain way?	Because _____.	_____ is _____ and does _____.	It causes _____.	It is made of _____, and it comes from _____.	It gives you _____.

4 INVITATION TO WRITE.

Here are several ways you can get students to write.

- Have students use the text structure to write a kernel essay summary of the story. (Give them between 5 and 10 minutes to do this.)
- Have the students use the text structure to write their own piece in a kernel essay. (Give them between 5 and 10 minutes to do this.)
- See what students come up with. (Give them around 10 minutes.) Here are some possibilities:
  - A page of thoughts in their quick write
  - Examples of the author's craft moves
  - A text structure

Whatever they choose to write, let them know that they can change anything they need to and make it their own.

5 SHARE.

Invite students to try their writing on someone else's ears. This is a crucial step! The sharing is just as important as the writing.

Want to Go Deeper?
Try these options.

OPTION 1: CRAFT CHALLENGE

- **Anaphork of Questions:** This author uses the rhetorical device anaphora and adds a pitchfork. In other words, she repeats a word or phrase at the beginning of a sentence (anaphora) and does this three times (like a pitchfork). Kayla's students named this an "anaphork." Authors and speakers do this to create rhythm, to stir emotion, or to emphasize or bring focus to something. This author created an anaphork of questions. Here's the example from the story:

    *"**Why** aren't you fuzzy like a dog, or buzzy like a bee? **Why** can't you eat ants with your nose, or breathe beneath the sea? **Why** aren't you finny like a fish, or grinny like a shark?"*

    Look through your piece to see where you can use an anaphork of questions. After you write, try it out on someone's ears to see how it sounds in your writing.

- **Rhyming Pattern:** This author has written the information in this book in the form of a poem, using a rhyming pattern in which just about every other line rhymes. Here is an example from the story:

    "It looks like twisted ladders,

    *or tiny, twirling **noodles**.*

    It makes us into people,

    *instead of into **poodles**."*

    Look through your piece to see where you can use a rhyming pattern. After you write, try it out on someone's ears to see how it sounds in your writing.

- **Polysyndeton + Catalog:** This author uses a rhetorical device called polysyndeton, which is the repeated use of coordinating conjunctions (instead of commas), to connect a catalog (a list) of items. Here is an example from the story:

    *"The code gives you amazing hands, but you choose how to play: **with trucks, or balls, or blocks, or dolls, with drums, or paints, or clay**."*

    Look through your piece to see where you can use polysyndeton or a catalog or both! Try it out on someone's ears to see how it sounds in your writing.

OPTION 2: ANALYZE

1. **Start with a big idea.**

    - If you want students to find the big ideas themselves, try asking, "What big ideas do you see in this story that tell you what it's really about?"

    - If students need a nudge, try using some of the big ideas from the list in this lesson's introduction and have students provide evidence from the story to support their answers. Ask, "How is this story about [the big idea]? How does the author explore [the big idea]? Where in the story do you see that?"

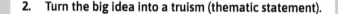

2. **Turn the big idea into a truism (thematic statement).**

    Once you have identified the big ideas, use one of them to create truisms for this story. Here are a few (found in the story) to get you started:

    - *Our genes may determine many things about our bodies, but who we become is up to us.*

    - *Everyone is different in some ways, and everyone is the same in some ways.*

    Have students write and share their own truisms.

    Ask them to prove their truisms by providing evidence from the text. They might imagine a listener saying, "Oh yeah? How do you know? How is that true in the story?"

Want to Go Deeper?
Try these options.

OPTION 3: READING RESPONSE

Students can compose short or extended responses to demonstrate understanding by answering any of these questions. Look in the appendix to find a list titled "Basic Reading Response Text Structures" and a list of "Useful Essay Question Stems for Nonfiction Texts."

Questions for Reading Response

- Explain why your DNA doesn't determine who you become.

- Explain what the author means by the line "Your code makes you uniquely you, but it's not all that matters."

- Explain why we aren't "Fuzzy like a dog, or buzzy like a bee."

- Explain the function of genes.

- Explain what your DNA determines and what it doesn't determine.

OPTION 4: EXTENSION IDEAS

- Dig into the back matter:
  - Use the "DNA Facts" and "Banana DNA Experiment" pieces as short nonfiction texts to read, discuss, create and answer questions, and write.
  - Do the banana DNA experiment together as a class.
- Research more about DNA, chromosomes, heredity, genetics, or other things about the human body:
  - Use the websites in the back matter for more research.
  - Create an infographic about the topic.
  - Create a poem based on your research.
  - Use the text structure to write about your research (or another topic).
  - Watch Rajani LaRocca, MD, talk about her book and how she became a doctor in a YouTube video, "Dr. Rajani Talks About the Science Behind THE SECRET CODE INSIDE OF YOU," available at https://www.youtube.com/watch?v=lGY-_-9y5Vc.
- For a unit on health and human bodies, consider pairing this book with one of the following:
  - *Your One and Only Heart* by Rajani LaRocca, MD
  - *A Garden in Your Belly: Meet the Microbes in Your Gut* by Masha D'yans

34 Student Samples for *The Secret Code Inside You: All About Your DNA*

QUICK WRITE

by Nicole Wong, 4th Grade

I act like my brother the most because we both love music, sing to music, and blast music in our rooms. We also love to hang out with friends.

QUICK WRITE

by Chloe Schildgen, 6th Grade

I'm different from my family because sometimes I dance funny when it gets around dark. I go to bed earlier than the rest of my family. I'm more energetic while my family likes to be chill and quiet.

QUICK WRITE

by Lydia Fuerstenberg, 6th Grade

I look nothing like my parents. They are brunettes and I am blonde.

QUICK WRITE

by Jocelyn Fecht, 6th Grade

Who I look like the most is my dad. He has big teeth and I have big teeth. He has blue, green, brown, and hazel eyes like me. And we both have freckles on our noses, too.

TRUISM

by Hodge Craig, 3rd Grade

It is important to make good choices.

CRAFT CHALLENGE (ANAPHORK OF QUESTIONS)

by Nicole Wong, 4th Grade

Why can't we fly like bats? **Why** do we hear through our ears? **Why** can't we walk on our hands?

READING RESPONSE (USING THE TEXT STRUCTURE "RACE")

by Hodge Craig, 3rd Grade

Q: Explain why your DNA doesn't determine who you become.

A: Your DNA doesn't determine who you become because your actions decide. In the story it says, "The code gives you an awesome brain, but you choose what you will be." This shows that your choices decide what you become.

Your One and Only Heart

by Rajani LaRocca, MD, and illustrated by Lauren Paige Conrad

Summary: *Your One and Only Heart* explores the physical human heart and all the jobs it does in the body with its contrasting qualities.

Why We Love It: Once again, Rajani LaRocca, MD, has captured us with her lyrical style and easy-to-access informational text. We have never thought of the heart this way and love learning about all the heart does.

Topics: the heart, the human body, the circulatory system, vital organs, anatomy, physiology, blood, the body's functions, muscles, arteries, STEM

Big Ideas: our wonderful bodies, uniqueness, contrasts, resilience, strength, parts of a whole, science

Back Matter:

- "More Heart Facts"
- "Outer Heart"
- "Inner Heart"

LESSON STEPS:

1 QUICK WRITE.
(CHOOSE ONE):

- Have you ever done an activity that made your heart beat really fast? What did you do?

- How many things is your body doing right now that you don't have to think about? List as many as you can.

- Have you ever thought about how hard your body works? What all does it do?

Write about this for 3 minutes and then set it aside.

2 READ.

Read the picture book *Your One and Only Heart* by Rajani LaRocca, MD, and discuss the story. Discuss parts of the story that stick out to you or that you connect with. What writer's craft moves do you notice the author using? Notice the parts of the story.

 **Your One and Only Heart**

by Rajani LaRocca, MD, and illustrated by Lauren Paige Conrad

3 SHARE THE STRUCTURE.

Show the students the structure found in the picture book. Reread the story, looking for chunks together and watching for how the author moves from one part to the other.

Extended Adjectives

_____ is _____. (And why)	_____ is _____. (And why)	_____ is _____. (And why)	_____ is _____. (And why)	Recap (everything that was said before)

4 INVITATION TO WRITE.

Here are several ways you can get students to write.

- Have students use the text structure to write a kernel essay summary of the story. (Give them between 5 and 10 minutes to do this.)

- Have the students use the text structure to write their own piece in a kernel essay. (Give them between 5 and 10 minutes to do this.)

- See what students come up with. (Give them around 10 minutes.) Here are some possibilities:
  - A page of thoughts in their quick write
  - Examples of the author's craft moves
  - A text structure

Whatever they choose to write, let them know that they can change anything they need to and make it their own.

5 SHARE.

Invite students to try their writing on someone else's ears. This is a crucial step! The sharing is just as important as the writing.

OPTION 1: CRAFT CHALLENGE

- **Parallel Paradox:** This author uses a rhetorical device called a paradox, which is a statement(s) that seems to contradict itself, or seems to go against itself, but may contain a basic or underlying truth when examined more closely—for example, "Less is more," or "You have to fight fire with fire." When the paradox repeats the same pattern, it's called a parallel paradox. Here are a few examples from the story:

  *"Your heart is **SIMPLE**.*

  *Your heart is **COMPLEX**.*

  *Your heart is **ENERGETIC**.*

  *Your heart is **RELAXED**."*

  Look through your piece to see where you can use a parallel paradox. After you write, try it out on someone's ears to see how it sounds in your writing.

- **Personification:** This author uses personification to describe the heart and the brain. Personification is giving nonhuman objects human capabilities. Here are a few examples from the story:

  *"When **it's excited**, it goes faster . . ."*

  *"**It's the captain** of Team Cardiovascular . . ."*

  *"Even the **brain gets to sleep**."*

  *"Your heart **is selfless**."*

  Look through your piece to see where you can use personification. After you write, try it out on someone's ears to see how it sounds in your writing.

- **Catalog of Gerunds:** This author uses a rhetorical device called a catalog, which is a list. In this story, the list is composed of gerunds, which are verbs that are acting like nouns. Here is the example from the story:

  *"In response to **moving***

  sitting

  thinking

  playing

  feeling

  ***sleeping**, your heart speeds up."*

  Look through your piece to see where you can use a catalog of gerunds. After you write, try it out on someone's ears to see how it sounds in your writing.

OPTION 2: ANALYZE

1. **Start with a big idea.**

   - If you want students to find the big ideas themselves, try asking, "What big ideas do you see in this story that tell you what it's really about?"

   - If students need a nudge, try using some of the big ideas from the list in this lesson's introduction and have students provide evidence from the story to support their answers. Ask, "How is this story about [the big idea]? How does the author explore [the big idea]? Where in the story do you see that?"

2. **Turn the big idea into a truism (thematic statement).**

   Once you have identified the big ideas, use one of them to create truisms for this story. Here are a few (found in the story) to get you started:

   - *Some things keep working even when we don't think about them.*

   - *Our bodies are amazing machines.*

   - *Every part of the whole has its own separate job to do.*

   Have students write and share their own truisms.

   Ask them to prove their truisms by providing evidence from the text. They might imagine a listener saying, "Oh yeah? How do you know? How is that true in the story?"

Want to Go Deeper?
Try these options.

OPTION 3: READING RESPONSE

Students can compose short or extended responses to demonstrate understanding by answering any of these questions. Look in the appendix to find a list titled "Basic Reading Response Text Structures" and a list of "Useful Essay Question Stems for Nonfiction Texts."

Questions for Reading Response

- Explain what the author means by "Your heart is selfless."
- Explain the importance of the heart being cooperative.
- Explain the importance of the consistent rhythm of your heart.
- What is one reason the author presents the information in contrasting order?
- Explain why it is important for the heart to relax.
- Do you think the heart is the most important organ in the body? Explain why or why not.

OPTION 4: EXTENSION IDEAS

- Dig into the back matter:
  - Use the "More Heart Facts," "Inner Heart," and "Outer Heart" pieces as short nonfiction texts to read, discuss, create and answer questions, and write.
- Research more about the heart, the circulatory system, or other systems in the human body:
  - Create an infographic about the topic.
  - Create a poem based on your research.
  - Use the text structure to write about your research (or another topic).
  - Watch the YouTube video, "The Human Heart for Kids" (by Learn Bright), available at https://www.youtube.com/watch?v=rnIUFrx0Djl.
- For a unit on health and human bodies, consider pairing this book with one of the following:
  - *The Secret Code Inside You: All About Your DNA* by Rajani LaRocca, MD
  - *A Garden in Your Belly: Meet the Microbes in Your Gut* by Masha D'yans

Student Samples for *Your One and Only Heart*

QUICK WRITE

by John Kothman, 5th Grade

Last year at summer camp, I had decided to do the trapeze at the ropes course. It was during our stampede time (a section of the afternoon reserved for doing WHATEVER we wanted) that I challenged myself to complete this daring feat. The trapeze is a large bar dangling from a tree that you need to jump and cling on to after jumping off the top of a tall telephone pole. I got suited up and began the trek up the pole. After shimmying my way up the pole, I took one last deep breath. I could see the narrow bar hanging around four feet away from me. I could feel the adrenaline rushing through me as I readied myself. I jumped. For a second it seemed as if time had stopped, and I looked out in front of me to see the bar. I stuck out my hand and . . . success! I looked down to see my counselors clapping and I could feel relief flush over my whole body.

QUICK WRITE

by Maggie Doll, 6th Grade

My heart is pumping blood. I'm writing. I am reading. My brain is giving directions. I'm thinking. My leg is moving.

QUICK WRITE

by Scarlett Earle, 5th Grade

When I promised my best friend that I was going on the Iron Rattler (a rollercoaster) with her, I regretted my choice instantly. My heart was jumping out of my chest when we were almost over the drop. At the end, I just started laughing.

KERNEL ESSAY (USING "EXTENDED ADJECTIVES")

by John Kothman, 5th Grade

Tennis is competitive. Each and every backhand volley and serve is a war for the point.

Tennis is tiring. Tennis drains all of your energy, but pays back in skills tenfold.

Tennis is fun. Every rally can teach you a lot, but also be exciting and fun.

Tennis is good for you. Tennis puts every muscle in your body under pressure and makes them bigger and stronger.

Tennis is a sport that is fun with a competitive edge. Tennis may help you grow, but also makes every muscle in your body ache.

Student Samples for *Your One and Only Heart*

KERNEL ESSAY (USING "EXTENDED ADJECTIVES")

by Fiona Bell, 4th Grade

Dogs are calm because they get sleepy. Dogs are energetic because they run around. Dogs are big because some dogs' genes make them grow to a certain size. Dogs are small because some of them grow to be a shorter size. Dogs are very fun to have around!

TRUISM

by Henry Ahl, 3rd Grade

You only get one heart, so it's important to treat it well.

CRAFT CHALLENGE (CATALOG OF GERUNDS)

by Fiona Bell, 4th Grade

I love playing, skiing, eating, singing, thinking, learning, doing, and creating.

READING RESPONSE (USING THE TEXT STRUCTURE "RACE")

by Henry Ahl, 3rd Grade

Q: Why is your heart important?

A: Your heart is important because it powers your whole body. One page 30, it says, "If the heart stops, everything else does, too." This shows the heart is very important.

Zap! Clap! Boom! The Story of a Thunderstorm

by Laura Purdie Salas and illustrated by Elly MacKay

Summary: *Zap! Clap! Boom! The Story of a Thunderstorm* takes readers through the event, from the calm beforehand, through the atmospheric changes, and into the clean and quiet after the storm has passed.

Why We Love It: This is nonfiction information delivered in a poem wrapped in a picture book! Not only would it be a great addition to a weather unit, but it is an example of how to convey research and information through a poem and artwork. The main text is just right for younger audiences, and the back matter deepens the learning for older readers.

Topics: weather, thunderstorms, clouds, rain, lighting, thunder, forces of nature, atmospheric elements, atmospheric change

Big Ideas: change, universal experiences, cycles

Back Matter:

- "The Science Behind Storms"
- Selected sources
- "For Further Exploration"

LESSON STEPS:

1 QUICK WRITE.
(CHOOSE ONE):

- Describe a storm you can remember.
- How do you feel about thunderstorms? Do you like them? Why or why not?
- What is the most unusual weather that you can remember? Describe that event.

Write about this for 3 minutes and then set it aside.

2 READ.

Read the picture book *Zap! Clap! Boom! The Story of a Thunderstorm* by Laura Purdie Salas and discuss the story. Discuss parts of the story that stick out to you or that you connect with. What writer's craft moves do you notice the author using? Notice the parts of the story.

36 zap! Clap! Boom! The Story of a Thunderstorm

by Laura Purdie Salas and illustrated by Elly MacKay

3 SHARE THE STRUCTURE.

Show the students the structure found in the picture book. Reread the story, looking for chunks together and watching for how the author moves from one part to the other.

A Weather Event			
What things are like before the event	What happens first (during the event)	What happens next (during the event)	What it feels like when the event is over

4 INVITATION TO WRITE.

Here are several ways you can get students to write.

- Have students use the text structure to write a kernel essay summary of the story. (Give them between 5 and 10 minutes to do this.)
- Have the students use the text structure to write their own piece in a kernel essay. (Give them between 5 and 10 minutes to do this.)
- See what students come up with. (Give them around 10 minutes.) Here are some possibilities:
  - A page of thoughts in their quick write
  - Examples of the author's craft moves
  - A text structure

Whatever they choose to write, let them know that they can change anything they need to and make it their own.

5 SHARE.

Invite students to try their writing on someone else's ears. This is a crucial step! The sharing is just as important as the writing.

Want to Go Deeper?
Try These Options.

OPTION 1: CRAFT CHALLENGE

- **Rhyming Pattern:** This author has written a poem to tell the story, using a rhyming pattern in which just about every other line rhymes. Here is an example from the story:

    "Sky is churning.

    *Breeze blows **stronger**.*

    Dry for now,

    *But not much **longer**."*

    Look through your piece to see where you can use a rhyming pattern. After you write, try it out on someone's ears to see how it sounds in your writing.

- **Onomatopoeia Refrain:** In this story, the author uses an onomatopoeia refrain. An onomatopoeia is a word that imitates the sound it makes, and a refrain is a line that is repeated on purpose. It is used throughout the story—she even uses it as her title! Here is an example from the story:

    "Zap! Clap! Boom!"

    Look through your piece to see where you can use an onomatopoeia refrain. After you write, try it out on someone's ears to see how it sounds in your writing.

- **Personification:** This author uses personification, which is giving nonhuman objects human capabilities. Here is an example from the story:

    "Rustling,

    murmuring

    rush begins

    *of **whispering leaves***

    *in **newborn***

    ***winds**."*

    Look through your piece to see where you can use personification. After you write, try it out on someone's ears to see how it sounds in your writing.

OPTION 2: ANALYZE

1. **Start with a big idea.**

    - If you want students to find the big ideas themselves, try asking, "What big ideas do you see in this story that tell you what it's really about?"

    - If students need a nudge, try using some of the big ideas from the list in this lesson's introduction and have students provide evidence from the story to support their answers. Ask, "How is this story about [the big idea]? How does the author explore [the big idea]? Where in the story do you see that?"

2. **Turn the big idea into a truism (thematic statement).**

    Once you have identified the big ideas, use one of them to create truisms for this story. Here are a few (found in the story) to get you started:

    - *Even though we expect things to happen, it's still surprising when they do.*

    - *Even the worst of times are usually temporary.*

     Have students write and share their own truisms.

    Ask them to prove their truisms by providing evidence from the text. They might imagine a listener saying, "Oh yeah? How do you know? How is that true in the story?"

Want to Go Deeper?
Try these options.

OPTION 3:
READING RESPONSE

Students can compose short or extended responses to demonstrate understanding by answering any of these questions. Look in the appendix to find a list titled "Basic Reading Response Text Structures" and a list of "Useful Essay Question Stems for Nonfiction Texts."

Questions for Reading Response

- Explain the signs that a storm is on its way.
- What is one reason the author presents the information in chronological order?
- Explain what happens in the story.
- Explain how the atmosphere is different before a storm and during a storm.
- Explain why the author uses so many onomatopoeias in the story.
- Read "The Science Behind Storms" in the back matter. Explain what happens before a thunderstorm.

OPTION 4:
EXTENSION IDEAS

- Dig into the back matter:
  - Use "The Science Behind Storms" as a short nonfiction text to read, discuss, create and answer questions, and write.
  - Use "For Further Exploration" to continue learning about storms.
- Chart the weather in your area over a period of time.
- Use this book to jump-start a unit on weather.
- Choose an extreme weather event, write a poem about it, and illustrate it.
- Research more about the weather:
  - Create an infographic about the topic.
  - Create a poem based on your research.

Student Samples for
Zap! Clap! Boom! The Story of a Thunderstorm

QUICK WRITE

by Hailey Cole, 5th Grade

I'm not a big fan of thunderstorms because every time I want to have a peaceful night . . . BOOM! No sleep! It's so annoying and it always starts in the middle of the night. I hate it.

QUICK WRITE

by McKinnley Mumm, 6th Grade

Dark, windy, cold, rainy night. I feel like thunderstorms can be relaxing. In my opinion, I like thunderstorms because they can be calming, relaxing, and peaceful. The most unusual weather that I can remember is a snowstorm in April. I had school that day and school ended up being canceled. It was really windy, and roads were covered in snow.

KERNEL ESSAY (USING "A WEATHER EVENT")

by Natalie Goings, 4th Grade

It was cold and windy. It had just rained, so there was ice all over some benches. When I came back outside, it was colder and windier. After the snow was gone, it was really nice to have power again.

KERNEL ESSAY (USING "A WEATHER EVENT")

by McKinnley Mumm, 6th Grade

Before the event, it was a regular night sky that was dark by 7:00. It was really windy. At first, it was just light snow falling down. As it fell to the ground, it melted. Then snow started to fall quickly and heavier. It started to stick to the ground. When it was over, it was cold. Wind blew the snow in the road and off the trees. I had to shovel, which was tiring.

CRAFT CHALLENGE (PERSONIFICATION)

by Hailey Cole, 5th Grade

Lightning strikes with a sound like the crack of a bone.

CRAFT CHALLENGE (PERSONIFICATION)

by Natalie Goings, 4th Grade

Night has its creepy whispers, lurking darkness, and worst of all, no one is awake to comfort you.

37 Bee Dance
by Rick Chrustowski

Summary: *Bee Dance* takes the reader on a forager bee's journey from the hive, to pollination, then back to the hive for its waggle dance of communication to the other bees.

Why We Love It: We love this simple explanation of the important work bees do. Coupled with beautiful illustrations, this book will be a fantastic addition to any unit on the planet, sustainability, nature, insects, animal lives, ecosystems, or even food production.

Topics: bees, honeybees, forager bees, honeybee behavior, beehives, hive behavior, pollination, honey, nature, insects

Big Ideas: communication, working together, teamwork, listening to others, following directions

Back Matter:

- "Why Do Honeybees Dance?"

LESSON STEPS:

1 QUICK WRITE.
(Choose One):

- Do you know how bees do their job? Explain what you know.

- Do you know how to do something really well? Explain how to do it step by step.

- Do you consider yourself more of a leader or a follower? Explain how you know.

Write about this for 3 minutes and then set it aside.

2 READ.

Read the picture book *Bee Dance* by Rick Chrustowski and discuss the story. Discuss parts of the story that stick out to you or that you connect with. What writer's craft moves do you notice the author using? Notice the parts of the story.

Bee Dance
by Rick Chrustowski

3 SHARE THE STRUCTURE.

Show the students the structure found in the picture book. Reread the story, looking for chunks together and watching for how the author moves from one part to the other.

Steps for Doing Something: A How-To Structure				
You know it's time to do something when _____.	First, do this.	Then, do this.	Then, do this.	When you're done, do this.

4 INVITATION TO WRITE.

Here are several ways you can get students to write.

- Have students use the text structure to write a kernel essay summary of the story. (Give them between 5 and 10 minutes to do this.)

- Have the students use the text structure to write their own piece in a kernel essay. (Give them between 5 and 10 minutes to do this.)

- See what students come up with. (Give them around 10 minutes.) Here are some possibilities:
  - A page of thoughts in their quick write
  - Examples of the author's craft moves
  - A text structure

Whatever they choose to write, let them know that they can change anything they need to and make it their own.

5 SHARE.

Invite students to try their writing on someone else's ears. This is a crucial step! The sharing is just as important as the writing.

Want to Go Deeper?
Try these options.

OPTION 1: CRAFT CHALLENGE

- **AAAWWUBBIS[1] Opener:** In this book, the author uses an AAAWWUBBIS opener: *After, Although, As, When, While, Until, Because, Before, If, Since.* When you start a sentence with an AAAWWUBBIS word, it requires a comma after the opening phrase or clause. Here is an example from the story:

  "**When** sunlight warms your honeybee wings**,** off you go on flower patrol."

  Look through your piece and see where you can use an AAAWWUBBIS opener. It is a great way to combine two sentences and add some sentence variety to your writing. Try it out on someone's ears to see how it sounds in your writing.

- **Imperative Pitchfork:** A pitchfork represents the act of taking one thing and branching it into a few more things. In this story, the author pitchforks imperative sentences, which give commands. Here is the example from the story:

  "**Do** the waggle dance, honeybee! **Make** a figure eight. **Twirl** in a circle. **Wag** your body up the middle run. Then **twirl** around the other side."

  Look through your piece to see where you can pitchfork some imperative sentences. After you write, try it out on someone's ears to see how it sounds in your writing.

OPTION 2: ANALYZE

1. **Start with a big idea.**

    - If you want students to find the big ideas themselves, try asking, "What big ideas do you see in this story that tell you what it's really about?"

    - If students need a nudge, try using some of the big ideas from the list in this lesson's introduction and have students provide evidence from the story to support their answers. Ask, "How is this story about [the big idea]? How does the author explore [the big idea]? Where in the story do you see that?"

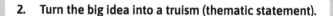

2. **Turn the big idea into a truism (thematic statement).**

    Once you have identified the big ideas, use one of them to create truisms for this story. Here are a few (found in the story) to get you started:

    - *Every creature has a special part to play in the world.*

    - *Sometimes teamwork is vital to nature.*

    - *Members of a community rely on each other in so many ways.*

    Have students write and share their own truisms.

    Ask them to prove their truisms by providing evidence from the text. They might imagine a listener saying, "Oh yeah? How do you know? How is that true in the story?"

---

[1]AAAWWUBBIS originated in Jeff Anderson's book *Mechanically Inclined* (2005). See Anderson, J. (2005). *Mechanically inclined: Building grammar, usage, and style into writer's workshop.* Taylor & Francis, p. 31.

Want to Go Deeper?
Try these options.

OPTION 3: READING RESPONSE

Students can compose short or extended responses to demonstrate understanding by answering any of these questions. Look in the appendix to find a list titled "Basic Reading Response Text Structures" and a list of "Useful Essay Question Stems for Nonfiction Texts."

Questions for Reading Response

- What is this story mainly about?
- Explain how flowers are beneficial to the bees.
- Explain why the bees do a dance.
- Explain the importance of communication in a bee's journey.
- Explain what happens in the story (retell).
- Explain whether bees are effective communicators.

OPTION 4: EXTENSION IDEAS

- Dig into the back matter:
  - Use "Why Do Honeybees Dance?" as a short nonfiction text to read, discuss, create and answer questions, and write.
- If you have one near you, take a field trip to a botanical garden.
- Invite a beekeeper to come to your school to demonstrate what they do.
- Research more about bees, pollination, or other insects:
  - Watch the YouTube video "How Do Bees Make Honey?" by Mystery Science, available at https://www.youtube.com/watch?v=cDlHHCGbMc4.
  - Create an infographic about the topic.
  - Create a poem based on your research.
  - Use the text structure to write about your research (or another topic).

QUICK WRITE

by Zachary Oblitas, 9th Grade

One thing that I know how to do really well is to make lemon sorbet on our little Ninja CREAMi machine. First, I squeeze the lemons according to the measurements, then I whisk together sugar, corn syrup, and hot water. After mixing, I pour the lemon juice into the mixture and freeze it overnight. Lastly, I put it into the machine, which transforms it into delicious lemon sorbet.

KERNEL ESSAY (USING "STEPS FOR DOING SOMETHING")

by Leila Kirkpatrick, 3rd Grade

You know it's time to make a sandwich when you're feeling hungry. First, you get meat, cheese, pickles, mayo, mustard, and bread. Then you take out the bread and put it on a plate. Then you put on the mayo and spread it and then put on the mustard and spread it. Then you put on the meat and the cheese and pickles. Lastly, you eat it.

CRAFT CHALLENGE (AAAWWUBBIS OPENER)

by Zachary Oblitas, 9th Grade

After the eclipse had ended, we all took off our special glasses.

CRAFT CHALLENGE (IMPERATIVE PITCHFORK)

by Mateo Nelson, 6th Grade

Grow up. Stop whining. Sit down. Get to work.

TRUISM

by Anish Muthuraman, 7th Grade

Sometimes in life, you should have a little fun along the way.

READING RESPONSE (USING THE TEXT STRUCTURE "RACE")

by Anish Muthuraman, 7th Grade

Q: What is this story mainly about?

A: This story is mostly about bees dancing while doing their job, making honey. I know this because the characters make figure eights and twirl around, see flowers bloom, and think about making honey. This shows bees are hard workers in the community, but also enjoy life and have fun with their friends.

Ivan: The Remarkable True Story of the Shopping Mall Gorilla

by Katherine Applegate and illustrated by Brian Karas

Summary: *Ivan* tells the true story of the famous gorilla. He was taken from his home in the Congo, kept in a cage at the B&I shopping mall for years, and then moved to Zoo Atlanta after many people objected to his treatment.

Why We Love It: While Ivan's story is a poignant one, it is also one of hope and coming together to make change for someone who couldn't speak for himself. We love learning more about everyone's favorite gorilla.

Topics: gorillas, *The One and Only Ivan,*[2] animal trapping, poaching, zoos, animal care, wild animals, Africa, nature, the mistreatment of animals, animal advocacy, habitats, treatment of animals in the wild

Big Ideas: loneliness, animal cruelty, caring for nature, activism, fighting for others, speaking up, taking action, respect for life

Back Matter:

- "About Ivan"
- "If You Want to Learn More"
- A note from Jodi Carrigan, Ivan's main keeper at Zoo Atlanta
- A painting by Ivan

LESSON STEPS:

1 QUICK WRITE.
(CHOOSE ONE):

- Have you ever been to a zoo? What do you remember about it? What animals did you see?

- Have you ever seen an animal that looked like it was really comfortable at the zoo? What kind of animal? How did you know it was comfortable?

- Have you ever seen an animal that looked like it was suffering in some way? How did it make you feel?

Write about this for 3 minutes and then set it aside.

2 READ.

Read the picture book *Ivan: The Remarkable True Story of the Shopping Mall Gorilla* by Katherine Applegate and discuss the story. Discuss parts of the story that stick out to you or that you connect with. What writer's craft moves do you notice the author using? Notice the parts of the story.

---

[2]Applegate, K. (Author), & Castelao, P. (Illustrator). (2012). *The one and only Ivan.* Harper.

38 Ivan: The Remarkable True Story of the Shopping Mall Gorilla

by Katherine Applegate and illustrated by Brian Karas

3 SHARE THE STRUCTURE.

Show the students the structure found in the picture book. Reread the story, looking for chunks together and watching for how the author moves from one part to the other.

A Memory Reflection

Where were you, and what were you doing?	What happened first?	What happened next?	What happened last?	How did you feel?

4 INVITATION TO WRITE.

Here are several ways you can get students to write.

- Have students use the text structure to write a kernel essay summary of the story. (Give them between 5 and 10 minutes to do this.)

- Have the students use the text structure to write their own piece in a kernel essay. (Give them between 5 and 10 minutes to do this.)

- See what students come up with. (Give them around 10 minutes.) Here are some possibilities:
  - A page of thoughts in their quick write
  - Examples of the author's craft moves
  - A text structure

Whatever they choose to write, let them know that they can change anything they need to and make it their own.

5 SHARE.

Invite students to try their writing on someone else's ears. This is a crucial step! The sharing is just as important as the writing.

Want to Go Deeper?
Try These Options.

OPTION 1: CRAFT CHALLENGE

- **Anadiplosis:** This author uses a rhetorical device called anadiplosis, which is when the last word or phrase in a clause, line, or sentence is repeated at the beginning of the next clause, line, or sentence. Here are some examples from the story:

  "The more the baby gorilla grew, the more he **played**. *The more he* **played**, *the more he learned."*

  "The one thing Ivan didn't need to learn was how to **eat**. *The more he* **ate**, *the more he* **grew**. *The more he* **grew**, *the less he could live a human life in a human house."*

  Look through your piece to see where you can use anadiplosis. After you write, try it out on someone's ears to see how it sounds in your writing.

- **Simile Pair:** In this story, the author uses a pair of similes right next to each other. A simile is a comparison using *like* or *as*. Here is the example from the story:

  "A man who owned a shopping mall had ordered and paid for them, **like** *a couple of pizzas,* **like** *a pair of shoes."*

  Look through your piece to see where you can use a simile pair. After you write, try it out on someone's ears to see how it sounds in your writing.

OPTION 2: ANALYZE

1. **Start with a big idea.**

   - If you want students to find the big ideas themselves, try asking, "What big ideas do you see in this story that tell you what it's really about?"

   - If students need a nudge, try using some of the big ideas from the list in this lesson's introduction and have students provide evidence from the story to support their answers. Ask, "How is this story about [the big idea]? How does the author explore [the big idea]? Where in the story do you see that?"

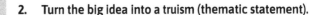

2. **Turn the big idea into a truism (thematic statement).**

   Once you have identified the big ideas, use one of them to create truisms for this story. Here are a few (found in the story) to get you started:

   - *Some injustice is easy to recognize.*

   - *Those who don't have a voice need others to speak up for them.*

   - *It takes people speaking up to make change.*

   Have students write and share their own truisms.

   Ask them to prove their truisms by providing evidence from the text. They might imagine a listener saying, "Oh yeah? How do you know? How is that true in the story?"

Want to Go Deeper?
Try these options.

OPTION 3: READING RESPONSE

Students can compose short or extended responses to demonstrate understanding by answering any of these questions. Look in the appendix to find a list titled "Basic Reading Response Text Structures" and a list of "Useful Essay Question Stems for Nonfiction Texts."

Questions for Reading Response

- Explain how the author's attitude is revealed by the line, "A man who owned a shopping mall had ordered and paid for them, like a couple of pizzas, like a pair of shoes."

- What happens in the story?

- Explain your opinion about whether animals should be removed from their natural habitats.

- Explain what caused a change in Ivan's living situation at the mall.

- Explain what the author means by the line, "In leafy calm, in gentle arms, a gorilla's life began again."

- Compare Ivan's behavior in the human home to his behavior in the cage at the mall.

OPTION 4: EXTENSION IDEAS

- Dig into the back matter:
  - Use the "About Ivan" piece and the note from Jodi Carrigan, Ivan's main keeper at Zoo Atlanta, as short nonfiction texts to read, discuss, create and answer questions, and write.
  - Use the ideas and resources listed in "If You Want to Learn More" for more research.
- If you have one near you, take a field trip to a zoo or an animal sanctuary.
- Research more about gorillas:
  - Create an infographic about the topic.
  - Create a poem based on your research.
  - Pretend that you are Ivan and write a letter to an important person in his life.
  - Watch the YouTube video "The Real-Life Story of Ivan the Gorilla," available at https://www.youtube.com/watch?v=yjdhcn0oI0M.

QUICK WRITE

by Arthur McWhorter, Kindergarten

The elephant was lying down and looked like it was asleep.

QUICK WRITE

by Zachary Oblitas, 9th Grade

Most of the times that I visit a zoo, I usually see one or more animals that look like they really just don't belong there. When I start to notice some of them, I think of how they would be a lot better off in the wild or in an animal sanctuary.

KERNEL ESSAY (USING "A MEMORY REFLECTION")

by Arthur McWhorter, Kindergarten

1. I was lying next to our dog.

2. I laid down first.

3. Then the dog laid down next to me.

4. We both fell asleep.

5. It felt great.

CRAFT CHALLENGE (SIMILE)

by Arthur McWhorter, Kindergarten

The elephant looked comfortable, just like my mom when she lays down.

CRAFT CHALLENGE (ANADIPLOSIS)

by Zachary Oblitas, 9th Grade

They decided to go on a movie marathon and watch TV. The more they watched TV, the more hungry they got. The more hungry they got, the less food there was.

READING RESPONSE (USING THE TEXT STRUCTURE "RACE"),

by Anish Muthuraman, 7th Grade

Q: Explain how the author's attitude is revealed by the line, "A man who owned a shopping mall had ordered and paid for them, like a couple of pizzas, like a pair of shoes."

A: This is a message to the reader that the owner treated the gorilla as a mere item. A mean, unworthy attitude is what is being shown by the example items. Ivan is compared to a pizza slice, or shoes, as the owner said. This means animals are worthless to some people.

READING RESPONSE (USING THE TEXT STRUCTURE "RACE") + TRUISM,

by Beau Smith, 3rd Grade

Q: Explain your opinion about whether animals should be removed from their natural habitats.

A: I think animals should not be removed from their natural habitats. My evidence from the text is, "Poachers with loud guns and cruel hands stole the little gorilla and another baby." This evidence makes me feel that way because the gorillas never got the chance to live the way they were supposed to live. **Things should stay where they belong.**

KERNEL ESSAY (USING "A MEMORY REFLECTION" + ANADIPLOSIS),

by Jackson Guenther, 5th Grade

The ball went up. The ball went down. I swung my racket, and the ball was served. The tennis court was like a football field, like an arena. The stadium seating was a mountain. The more effort, the more **practice**. The more **practice**, the more **skill**. The more **skill**, the more championships. One point was played. It went fast, like a lightning bolt. My serve aced my opponent, landing in the corner of his deuce box, a mile away from him. Fifteen to love. The ball went up. The ball went down. Another serve, this time on the odd side. He returned with a swift backhand. I was going to lose. It was 40 to 15. If you live, you **play**. If you **play**, you can **lose**. If you **lose**, you can learn. My mind gripped those and I hit the ball with an overhand. Game. I won four to three. I felt like a warrior, like a champion, like a first place winner.

Sergeant Reckless: The True Story of the Little Horse Who Became a Hero

by Patricia McCormick and illustrated by Iacopo Bruno

Summary: During the Korean War, U.S. Marines needed a horse to haul heavy ammunition. All they could find was a small, weak-looking horse named Reckless. They took a chance on her and started her training, which was hastened by her voracious appetite. Her performance under pressure earned her admiration and the rank of sergeant.

Why We Love It: We both fell in love with Sergeant Reckless as soon as we turned a few pages. We snickered as we read about her precociousness and her goat-like appetite. We had tears tugging at our eyes when we read about her bravery. And we were eager to share this story (and its beautiful illustrations!) with students as soon as we closed the last page.

Topics: horses, racehorses, pack horses, warhorses, military, military ranks, Marine Corps, soldiers, training animals, Korean War, history, combat, war, ammunition, Purple Heart

Big Ideas: serving your country, unlikely hero, underdog, taking a chance, bravery, wartime camaraderie, heroism, earning respect

Back Matter:

- Author's note
- Selected bibliography

LESSON STEPS:

1 QUICK WRITE.
(CHOOSE ONE):

- Have you ever felt (or been told) that you were too small, too weak, or too unskilled to do something? What did you do about it?

- Is there an animal you love? Who is it? Why do you love them?

- Think of someone (maybe someone in your family) who was an unexpected hero. Who is it? What did they do?

Write about this for 3 minutes and then set it aside.

2 READ.

Read the picture book *Sergeant Reckless: The True Story of the Little Horse Who Became a Hero* by Patricia McCormick and discuss the story. Discuss parts of the story that stick out to you or that you connect with. What writer's craft moves do you notice the author using? Notice the parts of the story.

Sergeant Reckless: The True Story of the Little Horse Who Became a Hero

by Patricia McCormick and illustrated by Iacopo Bruno

3 SHARE THE STRUCTURE.

Show the students the structure found in the picture book. Reread the story, looking for chunks together and watching for how the author moves from one part to the other.

A Memory (Plus a Truism)				
Where were you, and what were you doing?	What happened first?	What happened next?	What happened last?	Truism

4 INVITATION TO WRITE.

Here are several ways you can get students to write.

- Have students use the text structure to write a kernel essay summary of the story. (Give them between 5 and 10 minutes to do this.)

- Have the students use the text structure to write their own piece in a kernel essay. (Give them between 5 and 10 minutes to do this.)

- See what students come up with. (Give them around 10 minutes.) Here are some possibilities:
  - A page of thoughts in their quick write
  - Examples of the author's craft moves
  - A text structure

Whatever they choose to write, let them know that they can change anything they need to and make it their own.

5 SHARE.

Invite students to try their writing on someone else's ears. This is a crucial step! The sharing is just as important as the writing.

Want to Go Deeper?
Try These Options.

OPTION 1: CRAFT CHALLENGE

- **Renaming:** In this story, the author uses renaming, which is finding different words to say the same thing. Here's an example from the story.

    "One of the men held out a piece of bread. The mare gobbled it up. Then she devoured the rest of the loaf. . . . She licked the bowl clean."

    Instead of just saying, "She ate it," the author uses different words to describe the same eating.

    Look through your piece to see where you can use some renaming. After you write, try it out on someone's ears to see how it sounds in your writing.

- **Catalog of Fragments:** In this story, the author uses fragments (incomplete sentences) on purpose! In fact, she uses them to create a catalog, which is a list. Here is an example from the story:

    "An apple. Or a chocolate candy bar. Or a peanut butter sandwich. Even a can of beans. Whatever it was, Reckless ate it."

    Look through your piece to see where you can use a catalog of fragments. After you write, try it out on someone's ears to see how it sounds in your writing.

- **AAAWWUBBIS[3] Sandwich:** In this book, the author uses an AAAWWUBBIS sandwich. AAAWWUBBIS stands for *After, Although, As, When, While, Until, Because, Before, If, Since*. This author uses an AAAWWUBBIS phrase at the beginning of the sentence and at the end, so we call it an AAAWWUBBIS sandwich! Here is the example from the story:

    *"**After** she figured out which bunk belonged to the cook, she'd clip-clop into his tent at daybreak and lick his face **until** he woke up and served her breakfast."*

    Look through your piece and see where you can use an AAAWWUBBIS sandwich. It is a great way to combine two sentences and add some sentence variety to your writing. Try it out on someone's ears to see how it sounds in your writing.

OPTION 2: ANALYZE

1. **Start with a big idea.**

   - If you want students to find the big ideas themselves, try asking, "What big ideas do you see in this story that tell you what it's really about?"

   - If students need a nudge, try using some of the big ideas from the list in this lesson's introduction and have students provide evidence from the story to support their answers. Ask, "How is this story about [the big idea]? How does the author explore [the big idea]? Where in the story do you see that?"

2. **Turn the big idea into a truism (thematic statement).**

   Once you have identified the big ideas, use one of them to create truisms for this story. Here are a few (found in the story) to get you started:

   - *There can be an amazing bond between humans and animals.*

   - *Sometimes the ones we doubt surprise us with what they can do.*

   - *Sometimes bravery comes in small packages.*

   Have students write and share their own truisms.

   Ask them to prove their truisms by providing evidence from the text. They might imagine a listener saying, "Oh yeah? How do you know? How is that true in the story?"

---

[3]AAAWWUBBIS originated in Jeff Anderson's book *Mechanically Inclined* (2005). See Anderson, J. (2005). *Mechanically inclined: Building grammar, usage, and style into writer's workshop.* Taylor & Francis, p. 31.

Want to Go Deeper?
Try these options.

OPTION 3: READING RESPONSE

Students can compose short or extended responses to demonstrate understanding by answering any of these questions. Look in the appendix to find a list titled "Basic Reading Response Text Structures" and a list of "Useful Essay Question Stems for Nonfiction Texts."

Questions for Reading Response

- Explain what happens in the story (retell).
- Explain why the Marines doubted that Reckless could do the job.
- Explain what changed the Marines' mind about Reckless's ability to be a packhorse.
- Explain the role of food in this story.
- How does the setting influence the plot of the story?
- Explain why the Marines needed a horse for the Korean War.

OPTION 4: EXTENSION IDEAS

- Dig into the back matter:
  - Use the author's note as a short nonfiction text to read, discuss, create and answer questions, and write.
- Research more about Sergeant Reckless, the Korean War, the U.S. Marines, or other animal heroes:
  - Create an infographic about the topic.
  - Create a poem based on your research.
  - Use the text structure to write about your research (or another topic).
  - Watch the YouTube video "Sgt. Reckless," available at https://www.youtube.com/watch?v=w3PekI7QzcE.

Student Samples for *Sergeant Reckless*

QUICK WRITE

by Sahana Kallur, 9th Grade

I remember being laughed at when my goals were shared. Being the youngest person in the house is not easy and I felt as though I was too small and too weak to achieve big things. It made me become hard working and passionate about the things I love. I became determined to earn my goals and the things I most desired as well as earning the respect of others.

QUICK WRITE

by L Keyes, 10th Grade

Once my theatrical teacher labeled me as a violent person, publicly. That word stabbed me in the heart, bringing horrid pain, more than I would ever inflict onto another, although I recognized that such a comment could only be guided by her own hurt. Be the one to offer empathy and foster peace, not conflict.

CRAFT CHALLENGE (AAAWWUBBIS SANDWICH)

by L Keyes, 10th Grade

When you are talked down to, don't act negatively **until** you know why they did so.

CRAFT CHALLENGE (CATALOG OF FRAGMENTS)

by Sahana Kallur, 9th Grade

Sunsets on late night drives. Or camping. Or going to concerts. Even just waking up. Sunrises. Smores. One more month. Whatever it is, summer is almost here.

CRAFT CHALLENGE (CATALOG OF FRAGMENTS)

by Enrica Lu, 9th Grade

A flower. A carrot. A shovel. A cabbage. All the bugs. All found in my garden.

CRAFT CHALLENGE (CATALOG OF FRAGMENTS)

by L Keyes, 10th Grade

My hero is my mom. Or my dad. Or my teachers. However, they are all valuable to me.

TRUISM

by Holden Dewar, 7th Grade

In your most decisive battles, the smallest thing can change the outcome.

TRUISM

by Edward Galt Steves Dilley, 3rd Grade

If you work hard, good things will come.

READING RESPONSE (USING THE TEXT STRUCTURE "RACE")

by Merrit Nicewander, 6th Grade

Q: Explain why the Marines needed a horse for the Korean War.

A: The Marines needed a horse for the Korean War because they needed to carry lots of shells and ammunition up steep inclines. This is shown when the author says, "US marines were exhausted from hauling heavy ammunition uphill. . . . What if they could get a mule to carry the shells?" This means the Marines were wasting energy carrying ammunition when they could've easily found a horse to carry the shells.

READING RESPONSE (USING THE TEXT STRUCTURE "RACE")

by Brandt Barnes, 3rd Grade

Q: Explain the role of food in this story.

A: In the story, the food is important because it is a big part of Reckless's personality. She would eat anything she could get. This means whatever someone would put in front of her, she would eat and that would get her to do things for others.

Whale Fall: Exploring an Ocean-Floor Ecosystem

by Melissa Stewart and illustrated by Rob Dunlavey

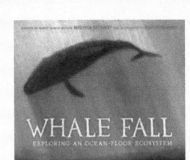

Summary: This book tracks what happens after a whale dies and falls to the bottom of the ocean floor and how much life is sustained after the death of the whale.

Why We Love It: We never had any idea about the undersea creatures whose lives are sustained by such an event. *Whale Fall* awakens curiosity about this part of our world. With each page turn, we found ourselves more fascinated, and we know that students will be, too.

Topics: whales, ocean life, life cycles, variety of species, symbiotic relationships, food chain

Big Ideas: new beginnings, end of life, community, interconnectedness, interdependence, hidden worlds

Back Matter:

- "More About Whale Falls"
- "More About Some Whale Fall Species" (pictures and information about each creature named in the book)
- Selected sources
- Further exploration (books, articles, photos, and videos)

LESSON STEPS:

1 QUICK WRITE.
(CHOOSE ONE):

- List: Think of things that end. How many can you list in the next 2 minutes?
- Write: Sometimes when something ends, it causes something else to begin. Think of something that, when it ends, causes a new thing to begin.

Write about this for 3 minutes and then set it aside.

2 READ.

Read the picture book *Whale Fall: Exploring an Ocean-Floor Ecosystem* by Melissa Stewart and discuss the story. Discuss parts of the story that stick out to you or that you connect with. What writer's craft moves do you notice the author using? Notice the parts of the story.

 **40** **Whale Fall: Exploring an Ocean-Floor Ecosystem**

by Melissa Stewart and illustrated by Rob Dunlavey

3 SHARE THE STRUCTURE.

Show the students the structure found in the picture book. Reread the story, looking for chunks together and watching for how the author moves from one part to the other.

An Ending That Causes a Cycle

When _____ ends	This cycle begins	First this happens	Then this happens	Then this happens

4 INVITATION TO WRITE.

Here are several ways you can get students to write.

- Have students use the text structure to write a kernel essay summary of the story. (Give them between 5 and 10 minutes to do this.)

- Have the students use the text structure to write their own piece in a kernel essay. (Give them between 5 and 10 minutes to do this.)

- See what students come up with. (Give them around 10 minutes.) Here are some possibilities:
  - A page of thoughts in their quick write
  - Examples of the author's craft moves
  - A text structure

Whatever they choose to write, let them know that they can change anything they need to and make it their own.

5 SHARE.

Invite students to try their writing on someone else's ears. This is a crucial step! The sharing is just as important as the writing.

Want to Go Deeper?
Try These Options.

OPTION 1: CRAFT CHALLENGE

- **Antithesis:** Antithesis is a rhetorical device that places two contrasting ideas side by side, usually through parallel structure. Here is an example from the story:

  *"**For the whale**, **it's the end** of a seventy-year life. But **for a little-known community** of deep sea denizens, **it's a new** beginning."*

Look through your piece to see where you can use antithesis. After you write, try it out on someone's ears to see how it sounds in your writing.

OPTION 2: ANALYZE

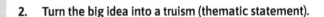

1. **Start with a big idea.**

   - If you want students to find the big ideas themselves, try asking, "What big ideas do you see in this story that tell you what it's really about?"

   - If students need a nudge, try using some of the big ideas from the list in this lesson's introduction and have students provide evidence from the story to support their answers. Ask, "How is this story about [the big idea]? How does the author explore [the big idea]? Where in the story do you see that?"

2. **Turn the big idea into a truism (thematic statement).**

   Once you have identified the big ideas, use one of them to create truisms for this story. Here are a few to get you started:

   - *Sometimes the end of something makes a way for a new beginning.*

   - *There are so many ways that members in a community rely on each other.*

 Have students write and share their own truisms.

Ask them to prove their truisms by providing evidence from the text. They might imagine a listener saying, "Oh yeah? How do you know? How is that true in the story?"

Want to Go Deeper?
Try these options.

OPTION 3:
READING RESPONSE

Students can compose short or extended responses to demonstrate understanding by answering any of these questions. Look in the appendix to find a list titled "Basic Reading Response Text Structures" and a list of "Useful Essay Question Stems for Nonfiction Texts."

Questions for Reading Response

- What is the author's purpose in writing this book?
- The sequence of events is important in the story because it shows what?
- What can the reader conclude from the events following the death of the whale?
- What does the word *community* suggest?
- Explain the benefits of the whale fall.

OPTION 4:
EXTENSION IDEAS

- Dig into the back matter:
  - Use the "More About Whale Falls" and "More About Some Whale Fall Species" pieces as short nonfiction texts to read, discuss, create and answer questions, and write.
  - Use the further resources to jump-start research about whales, sea creatures, and/or life cycles.
- Contrast underwater life cycles with the life cycles of creatures above ground.
- Choose another life-form from the book to research and create an infographic about it.
- Use the text structure to write about another cycle.

QUICK LIST

by Nicole Wong, 4th Grade

    Mushrooms

    Flowers

    Trees

    Plastic

    Glass

    Animals

    Humans

QUICK LIST

by L. Keyes, 10th Grade

    War

    Life

    Education

    Opportunities

QUICK WRITE

by L. Keyes, 10th Grade

Once war ends, people must change. The needs of healing begin. Cognitive reconstruction reshapes the education that had failed them. Future generations deserve harmony over their excuse of tranquility. Reconstruction is peace.

KERNEL ESSAY (USING "AN ENDING THAT CAUSES A CYCLE")

by Nicole Wong, 4th Grade

When the school year ends, summer begins. After summer ends, we become 5th graders. First, we find out our teachers. Then we get to know each other. Then we have a normal year.

KERNEL ESSAY (USING "AN ENDING THAT CAUSES A CYCLE")

by L. Keyes, 10th Grade

    When wars end,

    Reconstruction begins.

    People change,

    Then they rebuild from the ash,

    And reconciliation starts.

CRAFT CHALLENGE (ANTITHESIS)

by Nicole Wong, 4th Grade

For a flock of birds, it's the end of a 40-year life. But for a pack of wolves, it's a meal.

READING RESPONSE (USING THE TEXT STRUCTURE "RACE")

by Henry Ketabchi, 3rd Grade

Q: What is the author's purpose in writing this book?

A: The author's purpose in writing this book is showing how the whale's body repurposes after it dies. In the story, it states that the whale fall is a bountiful gift that can sustain life for another 50 years. This shows that the whale can feed and sustain life on the bottom of the ocean floor.

Winged Wonders: Solving the Monarch Migration Mystery

by Meeg Pincus and illustrated by Yas Imamura

Summary: Until 1976, many people wondered where the monarch butterflies went each year. Together, they discovered that the butterflies travel by the millions to roost in one particular oyamel grove in Mexico.

Why We Love It: So many of us have seen monarch butterflies that this book touches us all. We love learning how so many people helped solve the mystery.

Topics: monarch butterflies, migration, North America, Mexico, Canada, scientists, research, endangered animals

Big Ideas: curiosity, exploration, discovery, nature's beauty, appreciating nature, working together, teamwork, long-term study, finding answers, scientific discovery, helping nature, experimenting in the field

Back Matter:

- "More About the Monarch Migration Discovery"
- "How to Help Monarchs"

LESSON STEPS:

1 QUICK WRITE.
(Choose One):

- What is something that you are interested in—something that you are curious about and would like to study?

- What is your favorite insect? Describe it. What do you know about it?

- Have you ever watched a butterfly or a moth for very long? What did you notice?

- Have you ever tried to follow a butterfly? What do you think would happen if you did?

Write about this for 3 minutes and then set it aside.

2 READ.

Read the picture book *Winged Wonders: Solving the Monarch Migration Mystery* by Meeg Pincus and discuss the story. Discuss parts of the story that stick out to you or that you connect with. What writer's craft moves do you notice the author using? Notice the parts of the story.

Winged Wonders: Solving the Monarch Migration Mystery

by Meeg Pincus and illustrated by Yas Imamura

3 SHARE THE STRUCTURE.

Show the students the structure found in the picture book. Reread the story, looking for chunks together and watching for how the author moves from one part to the other.

Solving a Mystery				
The question	How _____ helped find the answer	How _____ helped find the answer	The answer they found	A new question

4 INVITATION TO WRITE.

Here are several ways you can get students to write.

- Have students use the text structure to write a kernel essay summary of the story. (Give them between 5 and 10 minutes to do this.)

- Have the students use the text structure to write their own piece in a kernel essay. (Give them between 5 and 10 minutes to do this.)

- See what students come up with. (Give them around 10 minutes.) Here are some possibilities:
  - A page of thoughts in their quick write
  - Examples of the author's craft moves
  - A text structure

Whatever they choose to write, let them know that they can change anything they need to and make it their own.

5 SHARE.

Invite students to try their writing on someone else's ears. This is a crucial step! The sharing is just as important as the writing.

Want to Go Deeper?
Try these options.

OPTION 1: CRAFT CHALLENGE

- **Anaphork of Questions:** This author uses the rhetorical device anaphora and adds a pitchfork. In other words, she repeats a word or phrase at the beginning of a sentence (anaphora) and does this three times (like a pitchfork). Kayla's students named this an "anaphork." Authors and speakers do this to create rhythm, to stir emotion, or to emphasize or bring focus to something. This author created an anaphork of questions. Here's an example from the story:

  > "So, **who** solved the age-old mystery? **Who** tracked these winged wonders from one end of the continent to the other? **Who** found their secret roosting place, a marvel of nature?"

  Look through your piece to see where you can use an anaphork of questions. After you write, try it out on someone's ears to see how it sounds in your writing.

- **Character Anaphork:** This author uses the rhetorical device anaphora and adds a pitchfork. In other words, she repeats a word or phrase at the beginning of a sentence (anaphora) and does this three times (like a pitchfork). Kayla's students named this an "anaphork." Authors and speakers do this to create rhythm, to stir emotion, or to emphasize or bring focus to something. This author names a person and then lists actions they did using an anaphork. Here's the example from the story:

  > "Was it Fred, the Canadian scientist,
  >
  > who spent . . . ,
  >
  > who drove . . . ,
  >
  > who tagged . . . ?"

  Look through your piece to see where you can use a character anaphork. After you write, try it out on someone's ears to see how it sounds in your writing.

OPTION 2: ANALYZE

1. **Start with a big idea.**

   - If you want students to find the big ideas themselves, try asking, "What big ideas do you see in this story that tell you what it's really about?"

   - If students need a nudge, try using some of the big ideas from the list in this lesson's introduction and have students provide evidence from the story to support their answers. Ask, "How is this story about [the big idea]? How does the author explore [the big idea]? Where in the story do you see that?"

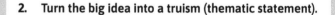

2. **Turn the big idea into a truism (thematic statement).**

   Once you have identified the big ideas, use one of them to create truisms for this story. Here are a few (found in the story) to get you started:

   - *The earth still has so many mysteries.*

   - *When people work together to solve a problem, even tiny contributions matter.*

   - *Some puzzles have lots of pieces, and it might take a lot of people to solve such a puzzle.*

   Have students write and share their own truisms.

   Ask them to prove their truisms by providing evidence from the text. They might imagine a listener saying, "Oh yeah? How do you know? How is that true in the story?"

Want to Go Deeper?
Try these options.

OPTION 3: READING RESPONSE

Students can compose short or extended responses to demonstrate understanding by answering any of these questions. Look in the appendix to find a list titled "Basic Reading Response Text Structures" and a list of "Useful Essay Question Stems for Nonfiction Texts."

Questions for Reading Response

- Explain how one of the people/groups contributed to finding the answer.
- Explain where the butterflies go.
- Explain the importance of teamwork in this story.
- Explain how Jim and his students benefitted Fred and his research.
- Explain how the characters are curious in this story.
- Explain how we know that monarch butterflies are in danger.

OPTION 4: EXTENSION IDEAS

- Dig into the back matter:
  - Use "More About the Monarch Migration Discovery" and "How to Help Monarchs" as short nonfiction texts to read, discuss, create and answer questions, and write.
  - Look at "How to Help Monarchs" for a list of other great extension ideas.
- Research more about monarch butterflies, migration, and/or other animals that migrate:
  - Create an infographic about your research.
  - Create a poem based on your research.
- Contact a local gardener, botanist, and/or entomologist to talk about plants that help monarch butterflies.
- Plant a butterfly garden together.
- Raise butterflies and release them.
- Make a list of questions to answer through research together.
- Take a field trip to a local garden center, botanical garden, or nursery to learn more about monarch butterflies and the plants that attract them.
- Watch the Nat Geo Kids video "Monarch Butterfly: Amazing Animals," available on YouTube at https://www.youtube.com/watch?v=1b87rwtXGzA.

QUICK WRITE

by Phoenix B., 10th Grade

Whenever I see a moth, whether it be clinging onto a streetlight or even onto a light source in my own home, I take time to really notice it; observe this spotted thing's behavior. "It saw the light and abandoned all other goals in order to reach it," I'd gather from my observations. To be a moth chasing a light. Just imagine, clinging to whatever light you find and forcing yourself to move on to another, after the previous one either fades away or goes out without warning. To be a moth chasing a light.

KERNEL ESSAY (USING "SOLVING A MYSTERY")

by Ruha Komaragiri, 9th Grade

How do the northern lights work? Kristian Birkeland built a device called "Terrella" to help better understand the northern lights. Sydney Chapman used mathematical models to help better understand the northern lights. Northern lights occur when charged particles from the sun hit or collide into the earth's atmosphere, making the colorful lights we see in the sky.

KERNEL ESSAY (USING "SOLVING A MYSTERY")

by L. Keyes, 10th Grade

Is history truly history? Philosophy focuses on the introspective factors of life. History is introspective. Psychology takes introspection and turns it into interpretation to understand the world around us. Therefore, history is how our ancestors perceived the world. How do we perceive and interpret events?

CRAFT CHALLENGE (CHARACTER ANAPHORK)

by L. Keyes, 10th Grade

The tapestry of time named history, where silence stands witness, where it holds the key to the past, where that key becomes a compass for our future.

CRAFT CHALLENGE (ANAPHORK OF QUESTIONS)

by L. Keyes, 10th Grade

Who sets the boundaries of discovery? Who is aware of the path of enlightenment? Who keeps these secrets?

READING RESPONSE (USING THE TEXT STRUCTURE "RACE")

by Tobias Smyth, 6th Grade

Q: Explain the importance of teamwork in this story.

A: All the people working together helped discover where the butterflies migrate. Along the way, all of them—the scientists, the citizen scientists, the regular folks—played a part in this discovery. This means that working together is why they were able to achieve their goal of finding where the butterflies went each year.

READING RESPONSE (USING THE TEXT STRUCTURE "FIGURING OUT THE READING") + TRUISM

by Catarina Caruso, 6th Grade

Q: Explain how one of the people/groups contributed to finding the answer.

A: I read the words, "All of them," which told me that every scientist worked together in different ways to help solve the question they were all wondering. Then I read the words, "Each person in small ways or large helped," which told me that even if you help either a little or a lot, you will contribute, and it is a team effort. Then I know that the message of this book is that **anything is possible when we work together as a team.**

Appendix

CONTENTS

Visit the companion website at
https://companion.corwin.com/courses/TS-nonfictionpicturebooks
for downloadable versions of the appendix resources.

Glossary of Terms

AAAWWUBBIS*	A sentence starting with an AAAWWUBBIS word—*After, Although, As, When, While, Until, Because, Before, If, Since*—requires a comma after the opening clause or phrase. It is basically a fun way of saying a complex sentence beginning with a subordinating conjunction.
AAAWWUBBIS* Sandwich	AAAWWUBBIS stands for *After, Although, As, When, While, Until, Because, Before, If, Since*. When an author uses an AAAWWUBBIS phrase at the beginning of the sentence and at the end, we call it an AAAWWUBBIS sandwich. Here's an example from *Sergeant Reckless* (Lesson 39): "**After** she figured out which bunk belonged to the cook, she'd clip-clop into his tent at daybreak and lick his face **until** he woke up and served her breakfast."
Anadiplosis	A rhetorical device in which the last word or phrase in a clause, line, or sentence is repeated at the beginning of the next clause, line, or sentence.
Anaphork	A combination of the rhetorical device anaphora—the repeating of a word or phrase in successive phrases—and a pitchfork. Kayla's students named this an anaphork.
Anaphork With an Antithetwist	A combination of the rhetorical devices anaphora (or an anaphork—anaphora + pitchfork) and antithesis. However, after the word is repeated in the anaphork, the author surprises us with a twist by using the rhetorical device antithesis (when two contrasting ideas are intentionally put next to each other, usually through a parallel structure twist that plays on the repetition). We call this an antithetwist. Here is the example from the story *Emmanuel's Dream* (Lesson 2) where we first discovered this pattern: "In Ghana, West Africa, a baby was born: **Two** bright eyes blinked in the light, **two** healthy lungs let out a powerful cry, **two** tiny fists opened and closed, **but only one** strong leg kicked."
Antithesis	A rhetorical device that intentionally places two contrasting ideas next to each other, usually through parallel structure.
Ba-Da-Bing	 A sentence that traditionally tells where your feet were (*ba*), what you saw (*da*), and what you thought (*bing*). This pattern is a great way to help writers put the readers into the shoes of characters or into the writers' own perspectives. There are many variations—sentence patterns that help writers provide details to readers.

*The name AAAWWUBBIS was first invented by teacher-author Jeff Anderson. See Anderson, J. (2005). *Mechanically inclined: Building grammar, usage, and style into writer's workshop.* Taylor & Francis, p. 31.

Beg-to-Differ Sentence Pattern	A sentence that follows this pattern: Some people _____. Others _____. But I _____. Here's an example from *One Plastic Bag* (Lesson 12) where we first discovered this pattern: "**Some people** in the village laugh at us. **Others** call us 'dirty.' **But I** believe what we are doing is good."
Catalog	A rhetorical device that is an intentional list of people, places, things, and ideas (nouns).
Craft Challenge	With each lesson, we provide students with at least one craft challenge, which takes a unique craft move that an author has used in a book and breaks it down for students to try to apply.
Different–Different–Alike Pattern	A sentence that follows this pattern: They didn't _____ [how they were different]. They didn't _____ [how they were different]. But they _____ [how they were the same]. Here's an example from *Martin & Anne* (Lesson 10) where we first discovered this pattern: "**They never** met. **They didn't** speak the same language. **But their** hearts beat with the same hope."
Directional Echoes	A description of two different directions like north and south, up and down, or left and right. Here's an example from *Over and Under the Rainforest* (Lesson 23) where we first discovered this pattern: "**Up in the trees**, long-nosed bats sleep away the daylight, all in a row. **Down on the bank**, sleepy crocodiles bask in the sun."
Echo Ending	When an author starts and ends a story with the same wording, phrasing, or ideas—like an echo!
Epistrophe	A writer employing this rhetorical device ends a series of sentences with the exact same word or phrase.
Geographic Pitchfork	A list (or pitchfork) of people, including their geography (the places they are from). We call that a geographic pitchfork. Here is the example from *The Boo-Boos That Changed the World* (Lesson 17) where we first discovered this pattern: "From boisterous hot-dog vendors in Brooklyn, fancy French winemakers, tired taxi drivers in Denmark, and English bobbies on bicycles to daredevil skateboarders in Saskatchewan, king-crab fisherman in Alaska, sweaty Ugandan soccer players, and applauding audiences at the Bolshoi Theatre in Moscow . . ."

Hypophora	A rhetorical device in which a writer asks a question and then immediately provides an answer for that question. Here are some examples from *The Crayon Man* (Lesson 19):
	"How could they make better, stronger crayons? Melted paraffin wax? Perhaps!" *"Would children like them? Children did!"*
Isn't/Is Simile	A simile is a comparison using *like* or *as*. An isn't/is simile follows this pattern: _____ isn't _____. It is _____, just like _____ [simile]. Here is an example from *Finding My Dance* (Lesson 3) where we first discovered this pattern: *"I was learning that dance **isn't** just one thing—**it is** fluid and evolves, **just as** a caterpillar becomes a butterfly."*
Kernel Essay	 The writing that comes as a result of following a text structure. The kernel essay is a highly organized set of sentences that a writer produces following the prompts of a text structure. It can be expanded into a longer paragraph, an essay, or even something bigger like a book! (See also "What Is a Kernel Essay?" in this book's introduction, page 10–11).
Microscope Sentence	A sentence that zooms out, then zooms in, and then focuses closely on someone or something. Here's an example from *The Crayon Man* (Lesson 19): *"In a small stone mill in Pennsylvania, in a top-secret lab, Edwin's team experimented."*

More-Than Metaphor	A metaphor is a comparison of two different things, without using *like* or *as* A more-than metaphor follows this pattern: _____ is more than _____ [this metaphor]. It is _____ [this stronger metaphor]. Here is the example from *The Boy Who Harnessed the Wind* (Lesson 18) where we first discovered this pattern: *"This windmill was **more than** a machine. It was **a weapon** to fight hunger."*
Myth Explosion	A sentence that lists myths or untruths that might have been spread about something and dispels them in the same sentence. Here's the example from the story *Joan Procter, Dragon Doctor* (Lesson 7), where we first noticed this pattern: *"The reports of Komodo dragons were greatly exaggerated: They could grow to ten feet, **not thirty**. They ran fast, **but not as fast as a motorcar**. They could be fierce, **but they were mostly gentle**."*
Onomatopoeia Refrain	An onomatopoeia is a word that imitates the sound it makes, and a refrain is a line that is repeated on purpose. Here is an example from *Zap! Clap! Boom!* (Lesson 36) where we first discovered this pattern: *"Zap! Clap! Boom!"*
Parallel Paradox	A paradox is a rhetorical device that seems to contradict itself, or seems to go against itself, but may contain a basic or underlying truth when examined more closely—for example, "Less is more," or "You have to fight fire with fire." When the paradox repeats the same pattern, it's called a parallel paradox. Here's an example from *Blue* (Lesson 28): *"**It's in** the sky, **but you can't** touch it. **It's in** the sea, **but when you** cup it, it disappears."*
Pitchfork	 A sentence (or series of sentences) that takes one thing and branches it off into three or more (as pictured for *stood*). Similar to the rule of three, this pattern is usually in sentence form. It takes something from being vague to being crystal clear.

	There are several variations that can be found throughout the book: • Alliterative Pitchfork, Lessons 7 and 11 • Anaphork, Lessons 1, 2, 5, 8, 9, 15, 24, and 33 • Anaphork of Questions, Lessons 34 and 41 • Anaphork With an Antithetwist, Lesson 2 • Character Anaphork, Lesson 41 • Geographic Pitchfork, Lesson 17
	• Imperative Pitchfork, Lesson 37 • Noun + Verb Pitchfork Pattern, Lessons 1 and 21 • Pitchforked Contrasts, Lesson 33 • Pitchforked Description, Lessons 14 and 16 • Pitchforked Metaphor, Lesson 14 • Pitchforked Participial Phrases, Lesson 25 • Pitchforked Verbs, Lessons 20 and 32
Polysyndeton	A rhetorical device that repeats the use of coordinating conjunctions (instead of commas) to connect items.
Refrain	A line that is repeated on purpose throughout a nonfiction picture book (or other text).
Renaming	Using different words to say the same thing. Here's an example from *Sergeant Reckless* (Lesson 39) in which the author uses different ways to say the horse ate something: "One of the men held out a piece of bread. **The mare gobbled it up**. Then **she devoured the rest of the loaf**. . . . She **licked the bowl clean**."
Shaka-Laka-Boom	 SHAKA-LAKA-BOOM WHAT SOMEONE SAID — WHAT SOMEONE DID — WHAT IMMEDIATELY HAPPENED A type of ba-da-bing sentence. This kind of sentence tells what you said (*shaka*), what you did (*laka*), and what immediately happened (*boom*). Here is an example from *Whoosh!* (Lesson 20): "'Sure,' Lonnie said. 'Wanna see?' [**shaka**] Lonnie worked the pump [**laka**], which squeezed air into a chamber [**boom**]. When he pulled the trigger [**laka**], the air escaped [**boom**], forcing water out with a WHOOSH! [**boom**]."

Text Structure	**Becoming Visible** | How I felt invisible (or left out)	What happened that started to change things	How things got better
---	---	---	 A text structure is the plan, or path, that a writer uses to "track movement of the mind." In other words, the structure will allow a reader to glimpse what the writer knows and how they know it. It can be created intentionally by a writer or gleaned from reading. For simplicity, we place these steps into sequenced, horizontal boxes, resembling stepping stones (as shown for the "Becoming Visible" text structure).
Translanguaging	The mixing in of other languages in all kinds of ways.
Truism	3. SO NOW VASHTI KNOWS THAT TO GET GOOD AT SOMETHING, YOU HAVE TO PRACTICE A LOT. A truism is a message or a truth about life that applies to nearly everyone. Truisms do not describe, and they do not command. Other words for *truism* are *theme, thematic statement, message, main point, life lesson,* and *thesis statement.*
Varied Refrain	A refrain is a line that is repeated throughout the book. Usually, a refrain uses the same words every time; however, in a varied refrain, the author may choose to start the refrain the same but change the ending a little each time. Here are some examples from *Tamales for Christmas* (Lesson 16) where we first discovered this pattern: *"With masa in one hand, corn husks in the other, **Grandma's just getting started**."* *"With masa in one hand, corn husks in the other, **Grandma is tenacious**."* *"With masa in one hand, corn husks in the other, **Grandma's just warming up.**"*
Wasn't–Wasn't–Was Pattern	A sentence that follows this pattern: It wasn't _____. It wasn't _____. But _____. Here's an example from *Whoosh!* (Lesson 20) where we first discovered this pattern: *"**It wasn't** easy. **It wasn't** obvious. **But** Lonnie found a solution."*
When–What Pattern	A pattern in which the author tells when something happened and then what happened. Here's an example from *Magic Ramen* (Lesson 9) where we first discovered this pattern: *"Day after day, Ando experimented.* *Night after night, he failed.* *Month after month, he kept trying.* *Nothing worked."* The author repeats this pattern: _____ after _____, noun/pronoun + verb.

Ways to Write a Response to *Any* Text

We've Read a Text. Now What?

OK, so you've read something with your students (a picture book, a nonfiction article, a short story, a novel, a poem, etc.). How can you take their learning deeper? How can you assess their comprehension? How can you get them to analyze? Here are a few options.

NAME	WHAT IS IT?	WHAT'S THE MAGIC HERE?	WHERE CAN I FIND IT?	EXAMPLE
Basic Response	A process—huge for self-regulation—for students to respond to what they read without giving them a question.	Basic responses produce higher-level discussion and writing about what students have read.	Bernabei, G., & Hover, J. (2022). *Text structures from fables*. Corwin. (Lesson 1) Briseño, S., Briseño, K., & Bernabei, G. (2023). *Text structures from picture books*. Corwin. Introduction to this book (page 8 and Appendix 8 page 325)	**Basic Reading Response Text Structures** *[Form: Story of My Thinking; Character Feelings; Making a Connection; Summary; The Effect of an Author's Choice]* Source: Bernabei & Hover (2022).
11-Minute Essay	A quick process—useful for teaching truisms—to produce an essay.	It creates high success. In a short time, students learn to quickly produce coherent thoughts connecting a theme to multiple sources. These mental gymnastics build stamina.	Bernabei, G. (2005). *Reviving the essay*. Discover Writing Press. (Lesson 5) Bernabei, G., & Reimer, J. (2013). *Fun-size academic writing*. Corwin. (Lesson 56) Bernabei, G. (2010). *Lightning in a bottle: Visual prompts for insights* [CD]. Trail of Breadcrumbs. Lane, B., & Bernabei, G. (2001). *Why we must run with scissors*. Discover Writing Press. (Lesson 23) Trail of Breadcrumbs YouTube channel (www.youtube.com/c/trailofbreadcrumbs/videos)	*One surefire STAAR structure* *truism — one example # — another example # — truism*

NAME	WHAT IS IT?	WHAT'S THE MAGIC HERE?	WHERE CAN I FIND IT?	EXAMPLE
One Special Sentence	A quick (sneaky) way for students to show, in one sentence, deep understanding of what they read.	These are fast and easy to write (and grade) without sacrificing depth and understanding.	**Ba-Da-Bing** Bernabei, G. (2005). *Reviving the essay.* Discover Writing Press. Bernabei, G. (2015). *Grammar keepers.* Corwin. (Lesson 78) Bernabei, G., & Hover, J. (2022). *Text structures and fables.* Corwin. (Lesson 8) Bernabei, G., Hover, J., & Candler, C. (2009). *Crunchtime.* Heinemann. (Chapter 3) Briseño, S., Briseño, K., & Bernabei, G. (2023). *Text structures from picture books.* Corwin. **Pitchfork** Bernabei, G. (2015). *Grammar keepers.* Corwin. (Chapter 6) Bernabei, G., & Reimer, J. (2013). *Fun-size academic writing.* Corwin. (Lesson 35: "Using Enumeration to Add Detail") **Shaka-Laka-Boom** Briseño, S., Briseño, K., & Bernabei, G. (2023). *Text structures from picture books.* Corwin.	

NAME	WHAT IS IT?	WHAT'S THE MAGIC HERE?	WHERE CAN I FIND IT?	EXAMPLE
Q and A	A process—huge for self-regulation—for students to write questions, choose a text structure, and then write their answer.	Q and A converts their natural processes into test-taking strategies.	Bernabei, G., & Hover, J. (2022). *Text structures and fables*. Corwin. (Lesson 4 and 5) Briseño, S., Briseño, K., & Bernabei, G. (2023). *Text structures from picture books*. Corwin. ("Introducing Your Students to Reading Response" lesson) Introduction to this book (page 8) and Appendix 8 (page 322)	 Source: Briseño, S., Briseño, K. & Bernabei, G. (2023) and Bernabei & Hover (2022).
Theme Chart	A brainstorming tool—useful for teaching truisms—that takes students from summary to theme.	The theme chart makes the abstract theme really concrete and visible for students. It makes analysis bite sized.	Briseño, S., Briseño, K., & Bernabei, G. (2023). *Text structures from picture books*. Corwin. (Lessons 16, 23, and 40, and the online companion)	 Source: Briseño, S., Briseño, K. & Bernabei, G. (2023).
Three-Things Response	A template for students to write multifaceted responses to an experience.	Three-things responses train students to have multiple angles of looking at something.	Bernabei, G., & Hover, J. (2022). *Text structures and fables*. Corwin. (Lesson 9) TrailofBreadcrumbs.net	 online resources 🔖 Available for download at https://companion.corwin.com/courses/TS-nonfictionpicturebooks.

NAME	WHAT IS IT?	WHAT'S THE MAGIC HERE?	WHERE CAN I FIND IT?	EXAMPLE
Truism	A life lesson.	Truisms help students recognize and apply theme in a concrete way.	Bernabei, G. (2010). *Lightning in a bottle: Visual prompts for insights* [CD]. Trail of Breadcrumbs. Bernabei, G., Hover, J., & Candler, C. (2009). *Crunchtime*. Heinemann. (Chapter 3) Bernabei, G., & Reimer, J. (2018). *Text structures from fairy tales*. Corwin. (Appendix) Briseño, S., Briseño, K., & Bernabei, G. (2023). *Text Structures from picture books*. Corwin. ("Introducing Your Students to Truisms" lesson) Trail of Breadcrumbs YouTube channel (www.youtube.com/c/trailofbreadcrumbs/videos) TrailofBreadcrumbs.net	The Truism Tree Available for download at https://companion.corwin.com/courses/TS-nonfictionpicturebooks.
Truism Braid	A magical process for tying multiple texts to a theme or to an answer to a question.	The truism braid unlocks depth of understanding the students already have. It also produces really high scores!	Trail of Breadcrumbs YouTube channel (www.youtube.com/c/trailofbreadcrumbs/videos) Bernabei, G., & Reimer, J. (2018). *Text structures from fairy tales*. Corwin. (Appendix) Briseño, S., Briseño, K., & Bernabei, G. (2023). *Text structures from picture books*. Corwin. (Online companion)	 Source: Briseño, S., Briseño, K. & Bernabei, G. (2023).

RESPONSE TO READING

READ
Read something together as a class or have students read their own books.

RESPOND
-Text Structures
-Ba-da-Bing
-Theme Chart
-Truism Braid
-Pre-made questions
-Create your own questions (question stems)

SHARE
Have students share their responses.

CHART
Chart their responses to create a bank of sentence starters, text structures, craft moves, etc.

For the Love of Back Matter

Teachers are always looking for well-written, short nonfiction texts, but they can be so hard to find. Did you know that the back matter of nonfiction picture books—even many fictional picture books—has just what we've all been looking for?

The back matter starts where the story finishes. It might include any of the following:

- Author's notes
- Additional facts and information
- Recipes
- Lists
- Infographics
- Timelines
- Maps
- Glossaries
- Lists of resources for further learning
- Selected bibliographies
- Photos, art, extras

How can we use it? Here are a few ideas:

1. Read a short passage from the back matter and create questions to answer and/or discuss, writing prompts, and so on.

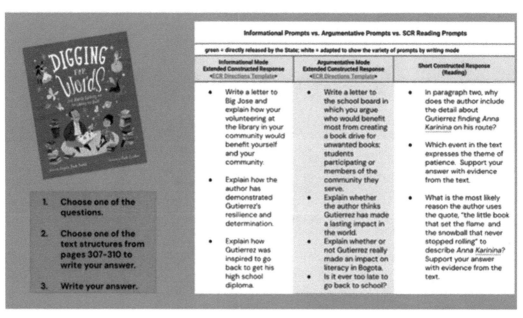

Source: Questions created by Orange Grove ISD Teachers.

2. Use the additional resources to inspire further research.

3. Use the back matter as a mentor text for research projects.

4. Do a crossover question (a question that involves more than one text) with the picture book and the back matter passage.

BACK MATTER TREASURE HUNT

NAME: _____   NAME: _____

BACK MATTER
TREASURE HUNT

With a partner, look through the backmatter of
your book and answer these quesitons.

How is the back matter laid out?	What is the most surprising text feature? What do you like about it?	What text features can you find?
Do you see anything that makes you curious?	Is there something in the back matter that is even more interesting to you than in the book?	What is something surprising that you learned from reading the back matter?
What one question could you ask about the text in the back matter?	Is there an illustration in the back matter that you find appealing? Why?	Which part of the back matter do you automatically want to skip? Why?
What is something that you want to share that you learned from the back matter?		What is one surprising word in the back matter?

online resources Available for download at https://companion.corwin.com/courses/TS-nonfictionpicturebooks.

5. Have the students do a treasure hunt with a partner to dig through the back matter.

Questions for the Teacher to Think About

• Is there a part of the back matter that seems like a text from a standardized test? Could you use any parts of this as a reading passage?

• What questions could you ask about any of the text in the back matter?

• Does any of this show students how to do research?

• Could you use this as a model for research or research projects?

• With what texts or videos could this be paired?

Now that you know how amazingly useful back matter can be, dig into some of the texts from this book.

Expanding Kernel Essays With Voices and Infoshots

What's the Classroom Problem?

I (Kayla) got this text from my friend Grace the other day:

"Would you be willing to point me to some resources I can use to help my students pop the kernel essay? They are good at using the text structure, but then half of them are stuck and think they are finished after that."

Writing a kernel essay using a text structure takes so much of the difficulty and guesswork out of writing. When we share, so many students are eager to add things to what they originally wrote—they are already revising and "popping" their kernel essays. It's easy for some students to turn each sentence into one or more paragraphs. But what about the ones who don't know what to do?

So, What's the Solution?

Enter expanding, or "popping," kernel essays with voices and infoshots.

By using the following lesson, you can write a whole essay in just about the same amount of time it takes to write a kernel essay. Really!

Lesson Steps

Moving From Quick List to Kernel Essay

1. To do this lesson, you will want to model the process on the board first, so make a quick list of specific memories with your students (moments involving animals, moments involving food, moments involving gifts, embarrassing moments, etc.).

2. Write a kernel essay with your students. Try using the memory structure to tell a personal story.

THE MEMORY STRUCTURE				
Where were you? (You may also wish to include what you were doing and/or who you were with.)	What happened first?	What happened next?	What happened last?	What did you realize? (This is a good place for a truism.)

Here's an example our friend Tim Martindell wrote:

"Puff the Green Cat"

1. My friends Jon and Lisa and I were riding our bikes in front of our house on Fiesta Way.

2. My great aunt Maida pulled into the driveway with her lime green cat in the back window.

3. Lisa and Jon gasped when they saw Puff.

4. Aunt Maida hooked Puff's leash on his collar and led him into the house as if this was just an ordinary day.

5. With Aunt Maida's sense of humor, I never knew what to expect.

3. Have the class get up and share their kernel essays with each other.

Extending or Popping a Kernel Essay Into a Full Essay

4. Once everyone has returned to their seats, write your first sentence on the board (or under the document camera).

5. Ask a student to tell you which word or phrase they would like to know more about. Draw a box around that word or phrase.

Here are the words Tim's students chose from his first sentence: *Jon and Lisa* and *Fiesta Way*.

6. Write a new sentence or two about that word or phrase. If you're stuck, use one of the three voices:

- The jerk: "That's not true. Prove it!"
- The "like what" button: "Like what?"
- The Martian: "What's that?"

Here's what happened to Tim's first sentence after he expanded on those words:

Late in the summer of 1969, just before I was to enter the fifth grade, my family moved back to Ohio and into a small rental house on Fiesta Way. As our family had previously lived in this town, I quickly made new friends, Lisa and Jonathon. The three of us would spend every waking hour of our afterschool and weekend time together playing in Lisa's treehouse, eating grapes from the arbor in Jon's backyard, or racing on our bikes.

7. Repeat Steps 4 and 5 by having a student choose a new word or phrase and writing about it.

For Tim's second sentence, his students chose *my great aunt Maida* and *lime green cat*. Here is what happened after he expanded on those phrases:

Late in the afternoon Aunt Maida swung her sporty Chevy into the driveway with her cat, Puff, lounging in the back window. Puff, named after the cat in the Sally, Dick, and Jane primers, was Aunt Maida's constant companion and must have been at least twenty years old when this visit occurred. I always anticipated the unexpected when my great aunt arrived with her infectious, high-pitched, cackling laughter.

"What kind of cat is that?" Lisa and Jon both gasped when they saw Puff. For this trip, Aunt Maida had dyed him a shockingly bright lime green.

8. The process can be repeated for each sentence until the whole kernel essay has been popped. Every sentence will be based on the one before (just like the kernel essay is connected by the structure). It helps the story to be cohesive, and it will have paragraph-to-paragraph progression.

9. Now that you have modeled it for your students, have them work with a partner to repeat this process for their own kernel essays. If this process is done with a partner, then you will be writing for a reader. The words and phrases your partner chooses can take your story in many different directions, but your kernel essay will help to anchor the narrative.

10. After the students have finished writing, have them share with other writers in the room and then choose a few to share with the whole class. This should be enough for one or two class days.

Revising an Essay

1. On a separate day, once students have finished popping their essays, show them how writers move things around to develop and expand their story. Compare Tim's kernel essay to his final piece.

"Puff the Green Cat"

1. My friends Jon and Lisa and I were riding our bikes in front of our house on Fiesta Way.

2. My great aunt Maida pulled into the driveway with her lime green cat in the back window.

3. Lisa and Jon gasped when they saw Puff.

4. Aunt Maida hooked Puff's leash on his collar and led him into the house as if this was just an ordinary day.

5. With Aunt Maida's sense of humor, I never knew what to expect.

As Aunt Maida would tell the story, she shrieked, "I've killed the cat!" as she frantically tried to rinse bright yellow coloring from Puff's light tan fur. Once as a kitten, Puff had, as kittens do, zoomed around Aunt Maida's house and accidentally jumped into a sink full of Rit dye where some fabric was being treated. A nonplussed Puff sat patiently in the sink as my great aunt dried him. Thus began twenty years of holiday and travel in a rainbow of colors—green or red for the Christmas holidays, bright pastel colors for Easter, Kelly green for Saint Patrick's Day, and always some magical color for travel. Just imagine a dark green and red tabby cat lying in front of a shiny silver aluminum Christmas tree, and you have a glimpse into my great aunt's world.

My extended family, which included my grandparents, great aunts and uncles, and cousins—both first and second—lived primarily in southern Indiana and Illinois. Visits among family happened frequently. Great Aunt Maida, my grandmother's older sister, looked and sounded much like the cartoon character Olive Oyl, girlfriend of Popeye the Sailor. Prior to marrying Uncle Shue, Aunt Maida taught elementary school, and I think this experience gave her a way with children. Even after the death of her husband, I remember my great aunt as a joyful, playful spirit.

Late in the summer of 1969, just before I was to enter the fifth grade, my family moved back to Ohio and into a small rental house on Fiesta Way. As our family had previously lived in this town, I quickly made new friends, Lisa and Jonathon. The three of us would spend every waking hour of our afterschool and weekend time together playing in Lisa's treehouse, eating grapes from the arbor in Jon's backyard, or racing on our bikes.

Soon after our move back to Ohio, my great aunt wrote to let my mother know she would be traveling through our area on her way to visit her daughter in Knoxville. When the day arrived, my mom asked that I stay close to home, so Lisa, Jon, and I spent the afternoon riding our bikes up and down Fiesta Way.

Late in the afternoon Aunt Maida swung her sporty Chevy into the driveway with her cat, Puff, lounging in the back window. Puff, named after the cat in the Sally, Dick, and Jane primers, was Aunt Maida's constant companion and must have been at least twenty years old when this visit occurred. I always anticipated the unexpected when my great aunt arrived with her infectious, high-pitched, cackling laughter.

"What kind of cat is that?" Lisa and Jon both gasped when they saw Puff. For this trip, Aunt Maida had dyed him a shockingly bright lime green.

"Honey, you can pet Puff. He won't bite," cackled Aunt Maida, always the jokester. "You act like you have never seen a green cat. Why, in South Bend where I come from, most of the cats are green or yellow. What kind of cats do you all have around here?"

Lisa and Jon just stood there, still in shock, as Aunt Maida hooked Puff's leash to his collar and led him into the house as if this was an ordinary day. With Aunt Maida's sense of humor, I never knew what to expect.

Strategies for "I Don't Know What to Add!"

For just about any genre, try using one or more of the voices to write more information:

- The jerk: "That's not true. Prove it!"
- The "like what" button: "Like what?"
- The Martian: "What's that?"

Example Voices Questions

The "Like What" Button

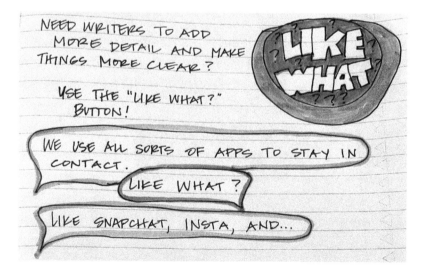

For a nonfiction piece, try using some of the infoshot analogy patterns to write more information about something:

- User/Tool: _____ uses _____.

- Cause and Effect: _____ can cause _____.

- Defining Characteristic: _____ can be described as _____.

- Part/Whole: A _____ is a part of a _____.

- Opposites: _____ is the opposite of _____.

- Synonyms: _____ is almost the same as _____.

- Transformation (Before and After): _____ transforms into _____.

- Item/Category: _____ is a type of _____.

Sample Analogy Patterns
for Infoshots

Source: Infoshots from TrailofBreadcrumbs.net

One of Kayla's sixth-grade students, John Kothmann, tried this technique with the "A Powerful Life" text structure found in *Martin & Anne: The Kindred Spirits of Dr. Martin Luther King, Jr. and Anne Frank* by Nancy Churnin (Lesson 10). He had been reading a lot about the British Empire and had learned about Henry VIII while reading *How They Croaked: The Awful Ends of the Awfully Famous* by Georgia Bragg.

He first wrote his kernel essay about King Henry VIII:

1. King Henry the VIII was born in London, England, in 1491.

2. King Henry became king at 17 years old, and feast after feast he slowly began to resemble more of a swine than a king.

3. Henry had six wives: two of which were executed, one died in childbirth, he divorced two of them, and the last one outlived him.

4. The swine king aspired to have a male heir. The reason he had so many wives is because none of them gave him a male descendant (little did he know that it was his fault he couldn't have a boy). Finally, he got a boy, Edward, but that wasn't the end of his troubles. Henry died at 55 from limited blood circulation.

5. King Henry also made a difference because he put England in a ton of debt and fear, which Elizabeth I, his daughter, would have to fix.

John Kothmann's kernel essay about King Henry VIII

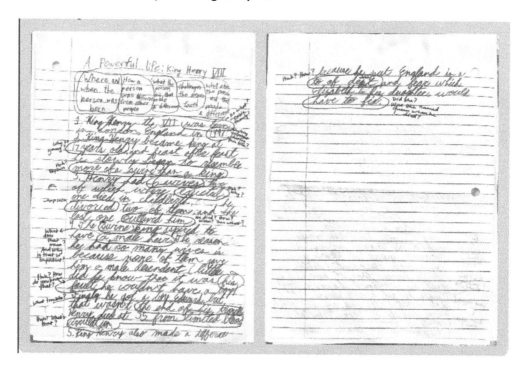

After Kayla sat next to John, reading his kernel essay, circling words and phrases throughout, and including some of the voices questions (see pictures), John voluntarily did a little more research, and this is how he expanded his thinking to pop his kernel essay:

King Henry the VIII was born in London, England, in 1491 to the House of Tudor, also known as the British Royal Family at the time. Henry was born at the time of the beginning of the Ottoman Empire.

King Henry VIII became king at 17 years old because of his father's death due to tuberculosis, and his older brother's death 7 years prior due to a sweating sickness which was an epidemic at that time in England. After his coronation, Henry indulged in feast after feast, and he began to resemble more of a swine than king because of his pig-like body with bloated everything.

Henry had 6 wives (not at the same time), two of which were executed because they spoke out against the way he ruled, one outlived him, two were divorced because they couldn't give him a male heir, and the one that did give him one died in childbirth. Henry wanted a son so badly because (at the time) that was the only way to continue his family's reign as royal family, which Henry's father had fought hard for in the War of Roses, but the rules were broken for the first time after Edward's (Henry's son) death when Lady Jane Grey ascended the throne followed by the infamous Bloody Mary (Henry's daughter).

The thing that the swine king didn't realize at the time was that it was his fault it was so hard for him to have a son or healthy kids at all due to his lifestyle and extreme inbreeding that was going on.

Henry died on January 28, 1547, from a combination of inflammation, chronic pyogenic, suppuration, oedema, and chronic osteomyelitis due to his horrible lifestyle. Henry put England in a ton of debt due to his flamboyant lifestyle and fear due to his short temper, which his second daughter, Elizabeth I, would fix after Bloody Mary's death.

John Kothmann's "popped" kernel essay about King Henry VIII

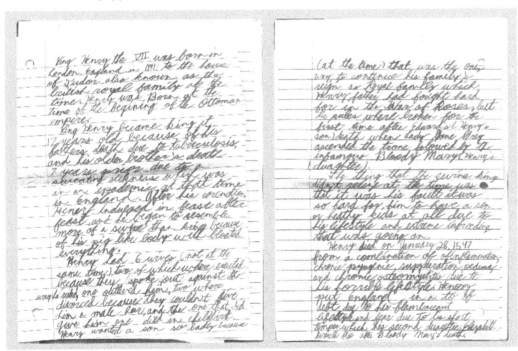

Our colleague and fellow writer Barry Lane[1] says that questions are a gift to the writer. They let the writer know exactly where readers will be curious and want more detail.

Here are some ways to give this gift to students and to help them expand their writing and thinking:

- Partner students together and have them share their kernel essays. Have the partner circle words and/or ask questions about each of the kernel essay sentences. The writer can then take those circled words and the questions and use them to include more detail.

- The teacher can sit next to a student and conduct this process in a small group or one-on-one.

- Have students choose their best kernel essay and turn it in. The teacher can then circle words and/or write questions about each of their kernel essay sentences. Once it is handed back, the student has a clear path for revision and extension.

---

[1]Lane, B. (1993). *After the end: Teaching and learning creative revision.* Heinemann.

Mentor Sentences to Teach Grammar and Make It Stick

What's the Classroom Problem?

As students filter into the classroom, they look at the board to find the same daily oral language exercise or worksheet on the screen. There's a collective groan as they reluctantly (if at all) pull out their notebooks to do the task.

One student complains, "Do we *have* to do this?"

Another whines, "This *again*? I hate this stuff."

Another waits for others to do the thinking by saying, "I don't see anything wrong with the sentence."

The exercise—which usually involves some sort of error correction—is done, begrudgingly, and then put away, never to be thought of again, so the real lesson can begin.

Sound familiar?

Many teachers avoid teaching grammar because they just don't have time, or they can't seem to fit it in. Some believe it isn't worth the time because it doesn't seem to stick. Lots of teachers report that students really hate it because they find it boring, so it doesn't seem worth the hassle. And, if we're honest, after an exercise like the preceding one, we don't really blame them.

So, What's the Solution?

For years, teachers have known we should teach grammar not in isolation but within the context of student writing. Reading, writing, and grammar are not separate subjects. They combine whenever we want to connect with other people. And students constantly want to connect with others as senders or receivers of messages, or both. We have found that teaching grammar in the context of student writing—in their journals—in a way that actually transfers into talking, thinking, and writing is what gets it to stick. But how do we do that?

We believe mentor sentences are a great way to accomplish the goals listed previously, so how can we get the most use out of mentor sentences? Using these high-quality, short pieces of writing, through the combination of discovery, mimicking, and friendly arguments, students can not only internalize grammatical moves but look forward to interacting with them and applying them to their own writing.

Lesson Steps

The Hunt

1. Choose the grammar concept you would like to teach and find a mentor sentence from a written source that uses that concept (picture books, novels, articles—anything will do). It can be helpful to choose things that go with the kind of

writing you are teaching at that time. For example, if you are teaching narrative writing, it would be useful to teach punctuation for dialogue. If you are teaching letter writing, it would be helpful to teach commas in a date or commas in a letter greeting/closing. If you are teaching argumentative writing, why not teach anaphora, epistrophe, or polysyndeton?

- If you're not sure what concept to teach, check out one of the following:

  o Gretchen Bernabei's book *Grammar Keepers*[2] for a whole year's worth of lessons. At the top of each of those lesson pages (in tiny letters), you will find an example of the lesson found in literature.

  o We have also pulled over 200 examples of great writer's craft, many of which appear in the craft challenges of this book and in *Text Structures From Picture Books*.[3]

  o Our friend Matthew Johnson also has some fantastic grammar lessons in his book *Good Grammar: Joyful and Affirming Language Lessons That Work for More Students*.[4]

2. Project the sentence for students to copy into their notebooks or type it up enough times for every student, print and cut the sentences out, and have the students glue them into their notebooks. Choose your hard: students copying or you cutting? We always choose cutting so that students have an accurate copy, and it saves class time.

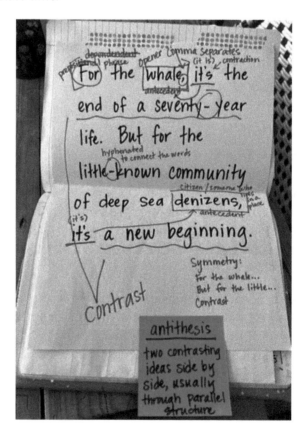

---

[2]Bernabei, G. (2015). *Grammar keepers*. Corwin.

[3]Briseño, S., Briseño, K., & Bernabei, G. (2023). *Text structures from picture books*. Corwin.

[4]Johnson, M. (2024). *Good grammar: Joyful and affirming language lessons that work for more students*. Corwin.

3. Read the sentence out loud.

4. Invite students to silently hunt for anything they notice or find interesting, or maybe even confusing: punctuation, capitalization, word choice, writer's craft, sentence structure, and so on. Have them circle what they find and label it if they can.

5. Once students have had a chance to hunt independently, have them share what they found with a partner and then the whole class. Have a copy of the sentence under the document camera (or on a piece of chart paper) so that you can catch and mark what they say. This is a chance for you to see what students already know, name things they notice (see "Teacher Debrief," page 18), and teach quick lessons about things they find. It is also an easy way to reinforce lessons you have already taught.

The Star Point

6. After you have collected all the things that they found, teach them the lesson you had in your plans for that day, which we call the star point. For example, if you were teaching "too" from *Grammar Keepers* (Lesson 4), show them the notes from that lesson.

7. Once students know the proof (or substitution) for this lesson (for *too*, it is *so* or *also*), have a quick argument with a student. This is what that would sound like:

   Teacher: Luke, would you please read the mentor sentence one more time for us?

   Student: "He has outraged too many wise men and pleased too many fools to hide behind his too-appropriate pseudonym much longer." (Found in *Ender's Game* by Orson Scott Card)[5]

---

[5]Card, O. S. (1994). *Ender's game* (Rev. mass market ed.). Tom Doherty Associates, p. 142.

Teacher:	I noticed the word *too* in there a few times. How is it spelled the first time?
Student:	T-O-O.
Teacher:	Oh, I'm sorry, Luke, but that is wrong.
Student:	Oh really? I spelled it the way it was spelled on the board.
Teacher:	Yeah, but I think it's wrong.
Student:	I think it's right.
Teacher:	Oh yeah? Can you prove it?
Student:	The proof word is *so* or *also*. *Also* wouldn't work, but *so* does. He has outranged *so* many wise men . . .
Teacher:	Ooooh. That does sound right. You're right, and I'm wrong. Sorry about that!

Student smirks because he just shut down the teacher.

The Challenge to Apply

8. Now that students have worked with the mentor sentence and learned the grammar concept, depending on how much time you have, you can have them apply it in two different ways.

Journal Writing

-   Before you begin the daily journal writing, invite students to try out the star point from the day and/or mimic the mentor sentence as they write in their notebooks. If they do decide to use the star point, have them underline it (this means "I *meant* to spell it this way") and put the proof word above it in parentheses (this means "Here's my proof"). This is always an invitation—not a requirement. However, if students use the star point at least five times (with the proof), they will get a star sticker at the top of the page and earn double credit for that day's journal entry.

- Once the invitation has been given, allow students to write for 7 to 10 minutes.

- After the 10 minutes is over, students share with a partner or a group of three and ask, "Did anyone try out today's star point?" If you get any volunteers, have them read just that one sentence with the star point and repeat the argument that was modeled before they wrote. Repeat this step two or three times.

- What about the students who didn't try it? Did they miss out on the learning? Nope. Even if they didn't try it in their writing, they were exposed to it several times through the arguments, and they will have another chance to try it out in tomorrow's journal time.

- If you have room in your classroom, add the star point and/or mentor sentence to your anchor chart or bulletin board for a visual reference.

Mentor Sentence Mimic

- If you are short on time, you might just have students mimic the mentor sentence using the sentence pattern (which already includes the grammar concept).

- Providing them with a sentence pattern like "He has _____ [past tense verb] too many _____ and _____ [past tense verb] too many _____ [plural noun] to _____" can be helpful to accomplish this. We usually just look at the mentor sentence and pull out these patterns on the spot.

- Give students time to write, then have a student share what they tried, and have the argument modeled before with this student volunteer.

- Repeat this step with two or three students.

- Keep a chart of these sentences with student-written examples up in your room so that students can reference it regularly.

Teacher Debrief

What if I don't have time to do these lessons plus 10 minutes of journal writing every day? This can be a daily practice in your classroom or something that you do two to three times a week. You can write anywhere between 7 and 10 minutes. When you regularly expose your students to high-quality writing, encourage them to discover things (instead of looking for mistakes), provide the regular opportunity to write, and celebrate their attempts at applying grammar and craft, students will be equipped with language that they just might want to keep, and build their writing fluency and stamina at the same time.

What if what they notice doesn't have a name?

Occasionally, the craft we notice has a specific name (*simile, metaphor, anaphora, polysyndeton*, etc.). However, sometimes it doesn't, and this is a great opportunity to create a name for it to make it memorable for the students.

Anchor Chart for Mentor Sentences

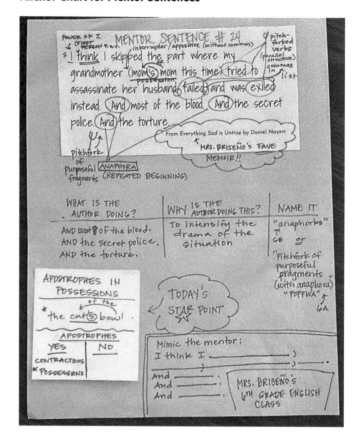

This actually happened by accident in one of Kayla's classes. We were looking at this sentence from *Everything Sad Is Untrue*, a memoir by Daniel Nayeri: "**And** most of the blood. **And** the secret police. **And** the torture."[6] Kayla's students noticed the repeating pattern of sentences starting with *And*, so she told them that it was actually a rhetorical device called anaphora, which is the repeating of a beginning word or phrase in successive phrases. One of the students said, "It's also a pitchfork. No, wait. It's an *anaphork*!" Kayla stopped in her tracks. That was a brilliant name! From that point on (and in all her subsequent books), that is what it was called: an anaphork.

That was the beginning of the naming of many things. Students took hold of writer's craft and named things such as "epistro-versal" when we were looking at this mentor sentence from *Swashby and the Sea* by Beth Ferry: "He didn't need **tea**. He didn't want **tea**. **Tea** was civilized, friendly, neighborly."[7] Kayla's students noticed the repeating pattern at the end of each sentence until the last one. We had learned that the pattern was called epistrophe, which is repeating the end of a sentence or phrase, but when they saw that repeated word used at the beginning of the next sentence, they named it an epistro-versal. They then went on to write their own like this one: *He didn't need **a cure**. He didn't want **a cure**. **A cure** would possibly mean another virus, a weak human body, or the end of the world* (written by then fifth grader Monroe Golden, first published in *Text Structures From Picture Books*).[8]

---

[6]Nayeri, D. (2020). *Everything sad is untrue (a true story)*. Levine Querido, p. 16.

[7]Ferry, B. (2000). *Swashby and the sea*. Houghton Mifflin Harcourt.

[8]Briseño et al. (2023, p. 231).

Infographics

National Park Infographic Created by Kayla Briseño as a Mentor Text for Her Students

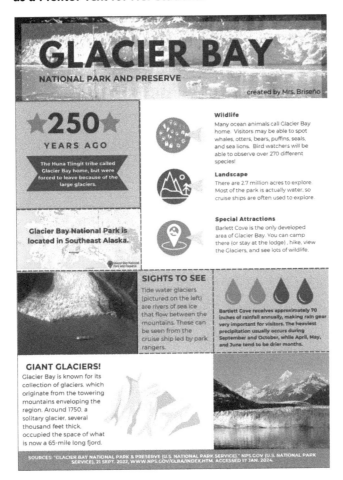

What's the Classroom Problem?

Student: Do we *have* to write a long research report?

Teacher: Do I *have* to grade all these long research reports?

These days, with so much information available, most long research is made available to consumers through information graphics, or infographics. So it makes sense to have students produce research that is consumer-friendly.

So, What's the Solution?

Enter infographics: a combination of information and graphics in a relatively small, visually pleasing package that students can easily create (and actually enjoy creating!).

Lesson Steps

1. **Gallery Walk:** Start with an infographic gallery walk. If you have the space and the resources, print several strong examples of different infographics for students to observe (with a partner or small group). If printing examples is not an option, consider creating a digital gallery walk by sharing a document of links for your students to peruse with a partner. Either way you choose, you may want them to use a sheet like the one pictured to capture their learning and guide your whole-class discussion after the gallery walk.

INFOGRAPHIC GALLERY WALK

Name: _____

TITLE OF INFOGRAPHIC	WHAT DID THIS INFOGRAPHIC WANT YOU TO LEARN?	WHAT IS ONE FACT THAT YOU LEARNED?	WHAT DID YOU NOTICE ABOUT THE COLOR SCHEME, FONT, AND LAYOUT?	WHAT IS SOMETHING THAT GRABBED YOUR ATTENTION?

online resources → Available for download at https://companion.corwin.com/courses/TS-nonfictionpicturebooks.

After the gallery walk, ask your students to share what they discovered, noticed, and wondered about. You may also want to ask/explain these questions:

2. **Mini Lesson:**

    *   What is an infographic?

    An infographic (or information graphic) is a visual representation of information presented in an easy-to-understand format.

    *   How do I create one?

    While creating an infographic from scratch is always an option (Google Docs and Google Slides are useful tools for this method), sites like Canva or Slidesgo take a lot of the design load off students so they can focus on their content rather than spend so much time on their designs. Once you log in to these (usually free) platforms, type "infographic" into the search bar, and several options should become available.

*   **What things do I have to keep in mind as I'm creating?**
    o **Your focus:** What is the information (or research question) I want to present?
    o **Your information/data:** Does my research support my research question? How should I organize the information?
    o **Design:** Do my fonts, colors, and layout reflect the topic I am presenting? For example, if I were choosing a serious topic like cancer, I wouldn't want to choose bright, bubbly letters with cutesy images.
    o **Graphs and charts:** Am I using a graph or chart that represents my research properly? For example, if I were presenting information about cars, I might use car silhouettes in my graph.

- ○ **Your audience:** To whom am I presenting this information? If it is to an older audience, do my language and design choices reflect that? Likewise, if I am presenting to younger students, have I created something that would be understood by and interesting to them?

3. **Make a plan:** Before students dive in, have them make choices first. Here is a helpful list of questions to have them ponder before they get started creating their infographics:
   - What are some topics I am interested in researching?
   - What sites will I use to gather information on my topic?
   - How will I organize my information?
   - What is an attention-grabbing headline/title I can use?
   - What colors, fonts, and graphics should I use?
   - Do I need graphs or charts for my information? If so, what kind?
   - Draw your plan for your infographic.

4. **Research and create:** Once your students have made their plans and discussed them with you, set them loose to do their research and create their infographics. Here are some instructions for using Slidesgo to create an infographic:

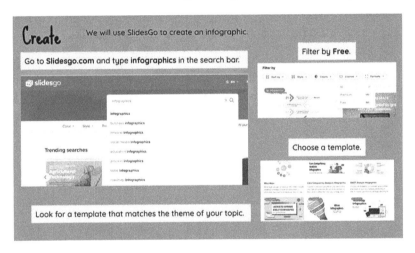

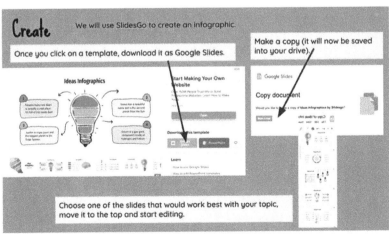

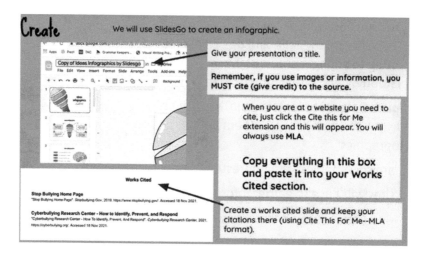

5. **Review with a partner:** Using the infographic rubric, have students review their work with a partner.

6. **Share, assess, and display.**

SHARE: Once students have completed their infographics, have them turn them in and share them in some way.

Infographic Rubric

INFOGRAPHIC RUBRIC

Author's Name:

Reviewer's Name:

BELOW EXPECTATIONS +13	MEETS EXPECTATIONS +16	ABOVE EXPECTATIONS +20
	The Information Your infographic clearly includes the minimum five information choices. The information is easy to understand and shows thoughtful consideration in how the information is laid out.	
	Data and Works Cited The data included in your infographic are accurate data and paraphrased in your own words. You have credited where you found your information somewhere on the infographic by using the correct format for your citation.	
	Design The design of an infographic is thoughtfully based on the content. (For example, if your infographic is about nature, then it should include design elements and colors from nature.)	
	Text Features Your titles, pictures, graphs, and charts display the data in a unique and creative way that ties everything together. You have a gripping headline and clear titles, and you have provided subheadings and/or captions to clearly organize your information and make your infographic clear and appealing to your audience.	

online resources ⇲ Available for download at https://companion.corwin.com/courses/TS-nonfictionpicturebooks.

- **Gallery Walk:** You might have a gallery walk of the finished products using the same Infographic Gallery Walk page from the beginning of the unit.

- **Treasure Hunt:** You might send the students on a treasure hunt with a partner or small group.

INFOGRAPHIC TREASURE HUNT SHEET

AUTHOR'S NAME	TITLE OF INFOGRAPHIC	WHAT IS ONE THING YOU FOUND INTERESTING ABOUT THIS INFOGRAPHIC?	WHAT IS ONE NEW THING YOU LEARNED FROM THIS INFOGRAPHIC?	WHAT IS THE BEST PART OF THIS INFOGRAPHIC, AND WHY?

online resources Available for download at https://companion.corwin.com/courses/TS-nonfictionpicturebooks.

- **Speed Dating Presentations:** You might have students present their work in a speed dating presentation where half the class is presenting their work at the same time while they each have a listener in front of them for two to three minutes. When the time is up, the listener will get up and move to the next presenter, and the presenter (who stays in the same seat) will begin the presentation again for the new listener. Once the listeners have heard each presentation, it will be time to switch roles: The listeners become the presenters, and the presenters become the listeners.

- **ASSESS:** Kayla uses a single-point rubric to assess the students' work. If the students meet all the criteria in the middle ("Meets expectations"), then they will earn a grade of 80 percent. Their grade can then increase or decrease based on the individual criteria.

- **DISPLAY:** Find some way to display the students' hard work, whether it is in a group Google Slides show, on a Padlet, hanging around the room, or displayed on a bulletin board in the hallway. You might even invite other classes or parents to come learn from the work your students have done.

National Park Infographics Made by Kayla's Sixth-Grade Students

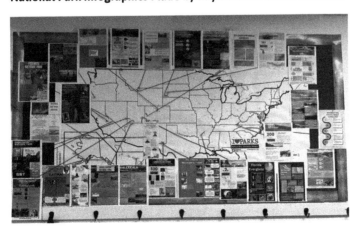

Useful Essay Question Stems for Nonfiction Texts

1. Explain the benefits of _____.

2. Explain the relationship between _____ and _____.

3. What audience is the author addressing in this article/story/book?

4. Explain your opinion about why people should or should not _____.

5. Explain how _____ (character) shows _____ (characteristic) in the article/story/book.

6. Explain how/why _____ changes their feelings/attitude/behavior over the course of the article/story/book.

7. What is the most likely reason the author wrote this article/story/book?

8. Explain how _____ has affected _____.

9. What is most likely the purpose of this article/story/book?

10. Explain how _____ and _____ are beneficial to each other.

11. In the article/story/book, which detail about _____ supports the key idea that _____?

12. What is the best summary of the selection?

13. What is the most likely reason the author uses/includes _____ [chart, diagram, picture, illustration] in this section/article/story?

14. Based on information in _____ [specific place] and _____ [specific place], the reader can conclude that _____.

15. Based on information in this article/story/book, what can the reader conclude about _____?

16. Which detail from _____ [specific place] supports the idea that _____?

17. The details from _____ [specific place] support the key idea that _____?

18. Which phrase/line/sentence/section shows _____?

19. What is the author's main claim in the article/story/book?

20. What sentence best expresses the author's claim about _____?

21. In the section/article/story, what do the events in _____ suggest about _____?

22. Which sentence/events best expresses the theme of _____ in the article/story/book?

23. In _____ [specific place], what is the most likely reason the author uses the phrase "_____"?

24. What is the key/central/controlling idea/thesis of the article/story/book?

25. What does the diagram/chart/image from the article/story/book help the reader understand?

26. What conclusion can be made based on information throughout the article/story/book?

27. In which section of the article/story/book would the reader most likely find information about _____?

28. The author organizes the section "_____" by _____.

29. What is the most likely reason the author includes _____ in the article/story/book?

30. Explain how the author develops the idea in the article/story/book that _____.

31. What is one way the setting in _____ affects _____?

32. Based on the information presented in the article/story/book, the reader can infer that _____.

33. Based on the information in the article/story/book, make an argument that _____ should or should not _____.

34. What is one counterargument the author presents in the article/story/book?

35. What evidence does the author use to rebut the counterargument?

36. The information in _____ [specific place] supports which conclusion?

37. Why does the author include contrasting ideas about _____ in _____ [specific place]?

38. What effect does the shift in tone between paragraphs _____ and _____ have on the author's argument?

39. How does the [organizational pattern] used in _____ (specific place) contribute to the development of the thesis?

Crossover Questions

1. Based on *both* selections, the reader can conclude _____.

2. Based on *both* selections, what is one way _____ and _____ are alike/different?

3. How is the author's purpose for writing [title] *different* from the author's purpose for writing [title]?

4. What ideas are expressed in *both* selections?

5. What theme about _____ is found in *both* selections?

6. The authors of *both* selections suggest that _____.

7. Explain how _____ and _____ are similar to/different from each other.

8. Both the author of _____ and the author of _____ would most likely agree that _____.

9. Explain how the author of _____ and the author of _____ both _____.

Common Extended Constructed Response Prompts and Text Structures

Informational	TWO VOICES, ONE MESSAGE				
How do the two pieces have the same message (or theme, life lesson, purpose, point...)?	The message	How one voice says it	How another voice says it	What does that mean?	Why the message is important to both

Informational	SOMETHING CHANGED				
How does _____ (a character, a situation, a place, an idea) change?	A noticeable change	In the beginning, ...	Later ...	Finally ...	How to explain the change

Informational	WAYS WE ARE ALIKE				
How are _____ and _____ alike (or different)?	We both basically are _____	Another (surprising) similarity	A moment we reacted similarly	How our reactions were similar	Overall, how we are alike

Informational	A SYMBIOTIC RELATIONSHIP				
How do _____ and _____ benefit each other?	Who A and B are	How A helps B	How B helps A	What would happen if A and B didn't have each other	So that's why ...

Argument	THIS IS BETTER THAN THAT				
What's better? _____ or _____ ? (or more important, more beneficial, more valuable, more beautiful, more impactful)	_____ is better than _____	One way I know	Another way I know	Even though some people _____,	... overall, _____ is better

Source: Briseño, S., Briseño, K. & Bernabei, G. (2023).

Questions and Text Structures for Constructed Reading Responses

Questions and Answers About Understanding the Reading

GENERIC QUESTION STEMS	TEXT STRUCTURES TO ANSWER THE QUESTIONS

GENERIC QUESTION STEMS

1. What happens in the story? (Retell the story.)

2. What is the story mostly about right now?

3. How do you think ____feels at the beginning and/or end of the story?

4. What is the conflict or problem of the story so far?

5. Who is more ____(helpful, nicer), ____(a character) or ____(another character)?

6. How does ____ change during the story?

7. Why does ____ do/think/say/believe/ want?

8. What's one word you would use to describe ____(character)?

9. What lesson does ____learn in the story?

10. What is the moral of the story?

11. In sentence ____, what does the word or phrase ____suggest?

12. How are ____and ____alike/different?

13. Why does ____become ____(upset, happy) when ____?

14. What does ____(character) mean when he/she says ____?

15. What can the reader tell (conclude) from the action in sentence(s) ____?

16. What is ____'s reaction when she/he learns ____ show about her/his character?

TEXT STRUCTURES TO ANSWER THE QUESTIONS

QA12345

Question	Answer	How do you know?	What does that mean?	How else do you know?	So . . . your answer is . . . what?

RACE

Restate the question	Answer	Cite evidence from the text	Explain what the evidence means

BA-DA-BINGING THE EVIDENCE

Answer to the question	What the character does, says, and/or thinks that proves my answer	What that shows

FIGURING OUT THE READING

I read the words " ____."	Which told me ____	Then I read " ____."	Which told me ____	And then I knew ____

EXPLAINING A CHANGE

How ____ changes in the story	At the beginning, . . . (with evidence)	At the end, . . . (with evidence)	Another way to describe the change

GENERIC QUESTION STEMS	TEXT STRUCTURES TO ANSWER THE QUESTIONS
17. How do the actions of _____ and/or _____ support the theme or moral?	
18. What causes _____ to realize _____?	
19. Why does _____ agree to _____?	
20. What is _____'s attitude about _____?	
21. What argument does _____ (a character) make to support _____'s (that character's) behavior/opinion?	
22. What challenge(s) does _____ face?	
23. What does _____ represent in the story?	

Source: Briseño, S., Briseño, K. & Bernabei, G. (2023).

Questions About Author's Choices

GENERIC QUESTION STEMS	TEXT STRUCTURES TO ANSWER THE QUESTIONS

GENERIC QUESTION STEMS

1. Why is_____ (an event or character) important?
2. Why does the author_____?
3. How does the author show that _____ (character) is _____ (characteristic)?
4. Why did the author write this story?
5. What does the author show us by including a description of _____?
6. How did the author help visualize _____?
7. What is the main reason the author included the sentence(s)_____?
8. Why does the author choose this setting for the story?
9. In sentence _____, the author uses the word(s)/phrase(s) _____ to suggest what?
10. What does the sensory language in the sentence _____ illustrate?
11. How does the description in the sentence(s) _____ affect the reader's understanding of the setting/character?
12. The author includes the information in the sentence(s) _____ to help the reader do what?
13. What is the author's purpose in writing this story?
14. How does the author's description of _____ help the reader understand _____?
15. What effect does the word/phrase _____ have in the sentence _____?
16. How does _____ contribute to the development of the author's ideas?
17. _____ is important in the story because it shows what?
18. How does the setting influence the plot of the story?
19. What is the effect of the author's use of _____?

TEXT STRUCTURES TO ANSWER THE QUESTIONS

RACE

Restate the question	Answer	Cite evidence from the text	Explain what the evidence means

NOTICING THE AUTHOR'S MOVES

I read the words "_____."	Which told me _____	Then I read "_____."	Which told me _____	And then I knew the author did _____ to create _____

THE EFFECT ON A READER

When I read "_____."	It made me feel/picture/think _____	Which created _____.	If the author had used a different word/phrase, such as _____	It would have had this effect	So I think the author was trying to create _____.

THE EFFECT OF AN AUTHOR'S CHOICE

The author uses (pick one) ☐ Vocabulary ☐ Sensory images ☐ Figurative language ☐ Device: _____ ☐ Something else	An example	Another example	This creates (pick one) ☐ A mood of _____ ☐ A feeling of _____ ☐ A _____ tone ☐ A character who _____ ☐ Interest in _____ ☐ Understanding in _____ ☐ Something else

Source: Bernabei & Hover (2022).

Basic Reading Response Text Structures

STORY OF MY THINKING

I used to think . . .	But this happened	So now I know . . .

CHARACTER FEELINGS

_____ felt _____	I know because they did _____	I also know because they said _____	What this shows

MAKING A CONNECTION

When I read _____	I made a connection to (self, text, world)	Because _____

SUMMARY

Somebody wanted _____	But _____	So _____	Then _____

THE EFFECT OF AN AUTHOR'S CHOICE

The author uses (pick one)	An example	Another example	This creates (pick one)
☐ Vocabulary ☐ Sensory images ☐ Figurative language ☐ Device: _____ ☐ Something else			☐ A mood of _____ ☐ A feeling of _____ ☐ A _____ tone ☐ A character who _____ ☐ Interest in _____ ☐ Understanding of _____ ☐ Something else

Source: Bernabei & Hover (2022).

A Collection of Text Structures Found in Nonfiction Books

| TEXT STRUCTURES FOR WRITING ABOUT PEOPLE | | | | |

| PROBLEM SOLVERS AND WORLD-CHANGERS | | | | |

A PROBLEM SOLVER'S JOURNEY				
The person's background and what brought them to the situation	What they noticed that gave them an idea	How the new idea started to take shape	A new problem that popped up and how they solved it	The result and who all benefitted
Found in *Building an Orchestra of Hope* by Carmen Oliver and illustrated by Luisa Uribe (Lesson 1) and *The Secret Kingdom: Nek Chand, a Changing India, and a Hidden World of Art* by Barb Rosenstock and illustrated by Claire A. Nivola (Lesson 26)				

OUTPOWERING A CHALLENGE				
When/where the person was born	How the person was different from others	Challenge(s) the person faced	How the person dealt with the challenge(s)	What the person did that made a difference
Found in *Emmanuel's Dream: The True Story of Emmanuel Ofosu Yeboah* by Laurie Ann Thompson and illustrated by Sean Qualls (Lesson 2)				

COPING WITH A BAD TIME				
How life was before	Then this happened	How things became painful	One problem this caused	How someone solved that problem
Found in *Fish for Jimmy* by Katie Yamasaki (Lesson 4)				

A HERO'S JOURNEY				
How their journey began	What issues they noticed around them	What they wanted instead	What stood in their way and how they responded	What they became
Found in *Free as a Bird: The Story of Malala* by Lina Maslo (Lesson 5) and *José Feeds the World: How a Famous Chef Feeds Millions of People in Need Around the World* by David Unger and illustrated by Marta Álvarez Miguéns (Lesson 8)				

RISKY SOLUTION				
What the problem was and why it was a problem	How some people were dealing with the problem	How one person helped with the problem	A setback that person faced	How that person kept going and how it turned out

Found in *Hidden Hope: How a Toy and a Hero Saved Lives During the Holocaust* by Elisa Boxer and illustrated by Amy June Bates (Lesson 6)

A POWERFUL LIFE				
Where and when the person was born	How the person was different from other people	What the person did that made a difference then	Challenges the person faced	What else the person did that made a difference (even now)

Found in *Martin & Anne: The Kindred Spirits of Dr. Martin Luther King, Jr. and Anne Frank* by Nancy Churnin and illustrated by Yevgenia Nayberg (Lesson 10)

A GROWING PROBLEM AND A SOLUTION				
Where _____ was when they first noticed the problem	How _____ saw the problem growing bigger	How things got worse	How a solution was born	How the solution changed things (or what they hoped)

Found in *One Plastic Bag: Isatou Ceesay and the Recycling Women of the Gambia* by Miranda Paul and illustrated by Elizabeth Zunon (Lesson 12)

MAKING A CHANGE				
The problem	How things needed to change	Who worked together and how	What stood in their way and how they responded	How change happened

Found in *Sweet Justice: Georgia Gilmore and the Montgomery Bus Boycott* by Mara Rockliff and illustrated by R. Gregory Christie (Lesson 14)

SAVING SOMETHING YOU LOVE				
What someone was interested in	How that interest grew	A problem that the person noticed	What that person figured out	How their idea worked out

Found in *The Brilliant Deep: Rebuilding the World's Coral Reefs* by Kate Messner and illustrated by Matthew Forsythe (Lesson 24)

COOKING UP A NEW IDEA

The inventor: Who the inventor was	The catalyst: What sparked the idea	The vision: What the inventor tried (that didn't work)	The aha moment: What the inventor tried (that *did* work)	The impact: How the invention was received

Found in *Magic Ramen: The Story of Momofuku Ando* by Andrea Wang and illustrated by Kana Urbanowicz (Lesson 9) and *Mr. Crum's Potato Predicament* by Anne Renaud and illustrated by Felicita Sala (Lesson 11)

A CURIOSITY THAT CHANGED THE WORLD

What someone was interested in	What that interest looked like at first	How that interest grew and brought about changes	The larger impact that it had on others

Found in *Joan Procter, Dragon Doctor* by Patricia Valdez and illustrated by Felicita Sala (Lesson 7) and *Swimming With Sharks: The Daring Discoveries of Eugenie Clark* by Heather Lang and illustrated by Jordi Solano (Lesson 15)

DISCOVERING A LIFE PURPOSE

How life was hard for _____	How life got harder for _____	How _____ discovered something they loved	How that changed things

Found in *Queen of Leaves: The Story of Botanist Ynes Mexia* by Stephen Briseño and illustrated by Isabel Muñoz (Lesson 13)

DOING WHAT YOU LOVE

_____ loved _____.	Because they loved _____, they did _____.	They wanted to do/be/create/go . . .	So they did/were/ created/went . . .	This led them to _____.

Found in *Finding My Dance* by Ria Thundercloud and illustrated by Kalila J. Fuller (Lesson 3) and *Whoosh!: Lonnie Johnson's Super-Soaking Stream of Inventions* by Chris Barton and illustrated by Don Tate (Lesson 20)

ACCOMPLISHING A BIG TASK

When _____, this person does this because _____.	First this person does this.	Then this person does this.	When _____, this person does this.	Before _____, this person does this.	When this person finishes, I know this.

Found in *Tamales for Christmas* by Stephen Briseño and illustrated by Sonia Sánchez (Lesson 16)

AN INVENTOR AND THE INVENTION					
Who the person was	What sparked the idea for the invention	The process: What happened first?	The process: What happened next?	The process: What happened last?	How it was received or How it changed things

Found in *The Boo-Boos That Changed the World: A True Story About an Accidental Invention (Really!)* by Barry Wittenstein and illustrated by Chris Hsu (Lesson 17), *The Boy Who Harnessed the Wind* by William Kamkwamba and Bryan Mealer and illustrated by Elizabeth Zunon (Lesson 18), *The Crayon Man: The True Story of the Invention of Crayola Crayons* by Natascha Biebow and illustrated by Steven Salerno (Lesson 19), and *The Floating Field: How a Group of Thai Boys Built Their Own Soccer Field* by Scott Riley and illustrated by Nguyen Quang and Kim Lien (Lesson 25)

TEXT STRUCTURES FOR WRITING ABOUT PLACES

ALL ABOUT A PLACE		
Poetic impression of the place	Factual details about it (Reporter's Formula: *who, what, where, when, how,* and *why*)	One thing that happened there

Found in *Caves* by Nell Cross Beckerman and illustrated by Kalen Chock (Lesson 21)

A PLACE PERSONIFIED			
I [the place] am made of _____.	I [the place] do/have/ am _____.	Infoshot (Facts and information about the place)	Repeat steps as often as necessary.

Found in *I Am Made of Mountains: An Ode to National Parks—the Landscapes of Us* by Alexandra S. D. Hinrichs and illustrated by Vivian Mineker (Lesson 22)

BIRDWALK				
Where we are going	One thing we see (with details)	Another thing we see (with details)	Another thing we see (with details)	How we know when it's time to finish

Found in *Over and Under the Rainforest* by Kate Messner and illustrated by Christopher Silas Neal (Lesson 23)

TEXT STRUCTURES FOR WRITING ABOUT THINGS

ORIGIN STORY

Have you ever wondered where _____ comes from?	Timeline: Ways it was used and/or found in the past	How it is found, made, and/or used now

Found in *Blue A History of Color as Deep as the Sea and as Wide as the Sky* by Nana Ekua Brew-Hammond and illustrated by Daniel Minter (Lesson 28)

THE WHOLE STORY OF SOMETHING

What the thing is	Past: When (and/or how) it started	Past: After that it _____.	Present: Now it is _____ and _____.	Future: It is _____ and will be _____.

Found in *Fire Shapes the World* by Joanna Cooke and illustrated by Cornelia Li and Diāna Renžina (Lesson 30)

ALL ABOUT SOMETHING (WITH INFOSHOTS)

Why aren't things this way?	Because _____.	_____ is _____ and does _____.	It causes _____.	It is made of _____, and it comes from _____.	It gives you _____.

Found in *The Secret Code Inside You: All About Your DNA* by Rajani LaRocca, MD, and illustrated by Steven Salerno (Lesson 34)

EXTENDED METAPHORS

_____ is _____.	_____ is _____.	_____ is _____.	_____ is _____.
(Plus a pitchforked explanation)	(Plus a pitchforked explanation)	(Plus a pitchforked explanation)	(Plus a pitchforked explanation)

Found in *Fry Bread: A Native American Family Story* by Kevin Noble Maillard and illustrated by Juana Martinez-Neal (Lesson 31)

EXTENDED ADJECTIVES

_____ is _____.	_____ is _____.	_____ is _____.	_____ is _____.	Recap (everything that was said before)
(And why)	(And why)	(And why)	(And why)	

Found in *Your One and Only Heart* by Rajani LaRocca, MD, and illustrated by Lauren Paige Conrad (Lesson 35)

STEPS FOR DOING SOMETHING: A HOW-TO STRUCTURE				
You know it's time to do something when _____.	First, do this.	Then, do this.	Then, do this.	When you're done, do this.
Found in *Bee Dance* by Rick Chrustowski (Lesson 37)				

STEPS FOR DOING SOMETHING: A HOW-TO STRUCTURE (PLUS A TRUISM)					
When you _____, you need _____.	First, do this.	Then, do this.	Then, do this.	When you're done, do this.	Truism
Found in *The Only Way to Make Bread* by Cristina Quintero and illustrated by Sarah Gonzales (Lesson 33)					

SOLVING A MYSTERY				
The question	How _____ helped find the answer	How _____ helped find the answer	The answer they found	A new question
Found in *Winged Wonders: Solving the Monarch Migration Mystery* by Meeg Pincus and illustrated by Yas Imamura (Lesson 41)				

TEXT STRUCTURES FOR WRITING ABOUT NATURE, WEATHER, CYCLES, AND SYSTEMS

HOW SOMETHING GROWS			
The first stage: How it begins	The next stage: How it develops	The last stage: How it finishes	Some interesting facts about it
Found in *Fungi Grow* by Maria Gianferrari and illustrated by Diana Sudyka (Lesson 32)			

A WEATHER EVENT			
What things are like before the event	What happens first (during the event)	What happens next (during the event)	What it feels like when the event is over
Found in *Zap! Clap! Boom! The Story of a Thunderstorm* by Laura Purdie Salas and illustrated by Elly MacKay (Lesson 36)			

AN ENDING THAT CAUSES A CYCLE				
When _____ ends	This cycle begins	First this happens	Then this happens	Then this happens
Found in *Whale Fall: Exploring an Ocean-Floor Ecosystem* by Melissa Stewart and illustrated by Rob Dunlavey (Lesson 40)				

ZOOMING IN ON A SYSTEM					
In _____ [place] is _____ [a system].	How that system was built	Parts of the system and what each part does (This part does this . . .)	If this happens, this problem occurs	If this happens, this good thing occurs	That's why . . .
Found in *A Garden in Your Belly: Meet the Microbes in Your Gut* by Masha D'yans (Lesson 27)					

TEXT STRUCTURES FOR WRITING ABOUT STORIES AND MEMORIES

A MEMORY				
Where were you, and what were you doing?	What happened first?	What happened next?	What happened next?	What happened last?
Found in *Branches of Hope: The 9/11 Survivor Tree* by Ann Magee and illustrated by Nicole Wong (Lesson 29)				

A MEMORY (PLUS A TRUISM)				
Where were you, and what were you doing?	What happened first?	What happened next?	What happened last?	Truism
Found in *Sergeant Reckless: The True Story of the Little Horse Who Became a Hero* by Patricia McCormick and illustrated by Iacopo Bruno (Lesson 39)				

A MEMORY REFLECTION				
Where were you, and what were you doing?	What happened first?	What happened next?	What happened last?	How did you feel?
Found in *Ivan: The Remarkable True Story of the Shopping Mall Gorilla* by Katherine Applegate and illustrated by Brian Karas (Lesson 38)				

Index

At Corwin Literacy we have put together a collection of just-in-time, classroom-tested, practical resources from trusted experts that allow you to quickly find the information you need when you need it.

DOUGLAS FISHER, NANCY FREY, DIANE LAPP

Like an animated encyclopedia, this book delivers the latest evidence-based practices in 13 interactive modules that will transform your instruction and reenergize your career.

JUSTIN M. STYGLES

Learn how to build relationships so shame-bound readers trust enough to risk enough to grow.

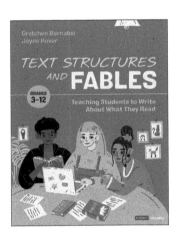

GRETCHEN BERNABEI, JAYNE HOVER

Use these lessons and concrete text structures designed to help students write self-generated commentary in response to reading.

CHRISTINA NOSEK, MELANIE MEEHAN, MATTHEW JOHNSON, MATTHEW R. KAY, DAVE STUART JR.

This series offers actionable answers to your most pressing questions about teaching reading, writing, and ELA.

CORWIN

A Sage Company

CORWIN HAS ONE MISSION: to enhance education through intentional professional learning.

We build long-term relationships with our authors, educators, clients, and associations who partner with us to develop and continuously improve the best evidence-based practices that establish and support lifelong learning.